Praise for Positive Discipline A–Z

"In the most user-friendly format possible, *Positive Discipline A–Z* offers hundreds of specific suggestions for our parenting tool boxes, suggestions that are oriented not toward making our kids 'pay' for their mistakes but toward learning life skills and developing healthy self-esteem for the future. A winner!"

—Michael L. Brock, educator and author of *School-Smart Parenting* and coauthor of *7 Strategies for Developing Capable Students*

"Knowing these authors is synonymous with understanding that things can always get better, and they have proven that again with their revised and expanded edition of *Positive Discipline A–Z.* Parents looking for insight into troubling childhood and teen behaviors will discover within these pages sound, practical information and advice. Applying these principles will truly improve the quality of life for each member of any family!"

—Suzanne J. Smitha, M.S., school psychologist

"More than any other book, I recommend *Positive Discipline A–Z* to my clients for the immediate help they need with everyday parenting problems. It is entirely consistent with the principles of healthy, respectful family relationships I am teaching them to create."

—Barbara Mendenhall, marriage, family, and child counselor

"*Positive Discipline A–Z* is particularly advantageous because it consists of those strategies that are based upon changing behavior in a positive, nurturing, and respectful manner, rather than punishment and power."

—Jim Bird, Ph.D., chairman, Department of Child and Family Studies, Weber State University

"Positive Discipline is a proven program for parenting in this challenging world. *Positive Discipline A–Z* provides a ready reference in seeking solutions. We have found Positive Discipline to be an outstanding approach in developing citizenship in public schools. Discipline problems have been reduced 90 percent by this program."

—Dr. M. Kent Larsen, principal, Heber Valley Elementary, Heber City, Utah

ALSO IN THE POSITIVE DISCIPLINE SERIES

Positive Discipline: The First Three Years
Jane Nelsen, Cheryl Erwin, and Roslyn Duffy

Positive Discipline for Preschoolers, Revised 2nd Edition
Jane Nelsen, Cheryl Erwin, and Roslyn Duffy

Positive Discipline for Teenagers, Revised 2nd Edition
Jane Nelsen and Lynn Lott

Positive Discipline in the Classroom, Revised 3rd Edition
Jane Nelsen, Lynn Lott, and H. Stephen Glenn

Positive Discipline: A Teacher's A–Z Guide, Revised 2nd Edition
Jane Nelsen, Roslyn Duffy, Linda Escobar, Kate Ortolano, and Debbie Owen-Sohocki

Positive Discipline for Single Parents, Revised and Updated 2nd Edition
Jane Nelsen, Cheryl Erwin, and Carol Delzer

Positive Discipline for Your Stepfamily
Jane Nelsen, Cheryl Erwin, and H. Stephen Glenn

Positive Discipline in the Christian Home
Jane Nelsen, Cheryl Erwin, Michael L. Brock, and Mary L. Hughes

Positive Discipline for Childcare Providers
Jane Nelsen and Cheryl Erwin

Jane Nelsen, Ed. D., Lynn Lott, M.A., M.F.C.C., and H. Stephen Glenn, Ph.D.

Positive Discipline A–Z

REVISED AND EXPANDED 2ND EDITION

From Toddlers to Teens—
1001 Solutions to Everyday
Parenting Problems

THREE RIVERS PRESS
NEW YORK

Published by Three Rivers Press, New York, New York.
Member of the Crown Publishing Group, a division of Random House, Inc.
www.randomhouse.com

Originally published by Prima Publishing in 1999.

Printed in the United States of America

Illustrations by Paula Gray

Library of Congress Cataloging-in-Publication Data
Nelsen, Jane.
Positive discipline A–Z : from toddlers to teens—1001 solutions to everyday parenting problems / Jane Nelsen, Lynn Lott, H. Stephen Glenn.—2nd ed.
p. cm.
Includes bibliographical references and index.
1. Discipline of children. I. Lott, Lynn. II. Glenn, H. Stephen. III. Title.
HQ770.4.N435 1999
649'.64—dc21 98-51638

ISBN 0-7615-1470-8

10 9 8

Second Edition

To our loved ones
and
to parents everywhere
who want to show their love
by empowering their children.

CONTENTS

PART TWO Positive Discipline Solutions from A to Z · 31

HOW TO USE THIS BOOK

You will benefit by reading every subject. Even if the topic does not concern you now, you will be gaining knowledge about your child and yourself. Each subject contains suggestions that would fit many other concerns. The feelings of dignity and respect that you will absorb will stimulate your wisdom and creativity to deal with any situation. Perfection is not the goal; the goal is to gain understanding, compassion, and wisdom that will help you enjoy your child, yourself, and parenting.

Many of the suggestions for a specific subject will give you ideas for everyday parenting that help your children gain courage, confidence, and life skills. As you read, keep the following guidelines in mind.

1. Remember the long-range purpose of parenting: to help your children develop healthy self-esteem and the life skills they need to be effective, happy, contributing, and respectful members of the family and society.

2. Choose the suggestion, or combination of suggestions, that feels right to you.

3. Put what you say in your own words so you don't sound like an insincere parrot. The words we use are meant to demonstrate the feelings of empathy, dignity, and respect that are necessary for effective adult-child interactions.

4. Tap into your wisdom and imagination for ideas of your own. This will get easier as you use this book as a catalyst.

5. When you are unable to calm down and be objective, this book can serve as an objective friend. Sometimes just reaching for the book gives you time

to cool off a bit. When you calm down, you become less hooked into the problem and can approach it objectively.

6. To create the feelings and actions that will be most effective with your child:

- Maintain dignity and respect for yourself and your child.
- Keep long-range goals in mind. (See item 1 above.)
- Focus on solutions for the future instead of punishment for what has already happened.
- Whenever possible, involve your child in working on solutions. Involvement invites cooperation and the development of life skills.
- Work with the principles and techniques in this book thoughtfully and flexibly, since no two children are the same and relationships change constantly. Ask yourself: "What am I trying to accomplish? How can I tell when I'm moving toward it? What seems to be effective in moving toward this goal with this child at this time?"

INTRODUCTION

What should I do when my child has a temper tantrum in the grocery store? What should I do when she won't eat her dinner? What should I do when he bites another child? What should I do when my children won't go to bed at night, won't get up in the morning, won't do their chores, and so on, and so forth?

Wouldn't it be nice if you had a book that addressed just about every parenting problem you could imagine, in alphabetical order so your particular concern could be found easily? Wouldn't it be wonderful if the book offered not just one but several short, simple, "what to do" solutions to each problem, on one or two pages? Wouldn't it be fantastic if this book included suggestions that would help prevent the problem in the future? Would it be too much to ask that this fantasy book help you understand more about child development, offer parenting pointers that could be generalized to solve other problems, and help you understand what your children are learning in response to your actions? We're on a roll now. Why not go for the ultimate bonus and ask that the suggested solutions not only solve the behavior problem but also help your children feel good about themselves and gain self-confidence, self-discipline, a sense of responsibility, problem-solving skills, and healthy self-esteem?

Sound too good to be true? Well, here it is, in your hands. You may want to hang it around your neck as a quick, easy reference while you learn to stop reacting and become a proactive parent.

Once you get a few Positive Discipline principles under your belt, you too can gain the kind of self-confidence, problem-solving skills, and healthy self-esteem that will allow you to tap into your heart and deepest wisdom to find personal answers.

Positive Discipline A–Z begins with some basic Positive Discipline parenting tools and concepts in Part 1. The "what to do" suggestions under the A to Z subjects in Part 2 will refer back to these basic principles.

Think of this book as a kettle of alphabet soup that can be nourishing to the physical and mental health of your family. Keep it simmering at all times. Let the aroma permeate your home. Enjoy!

PART 1

Basic Positive Discipline Parenting Tools

We refer to Positive Discipline parenting tools and concepts throughout the book. To give you a basic understanding of them, each is explained here briefly.

Family Meetings

If we had to choose only one parenting tool to use, it would be family meetings.[1] The fact that many problems can be solved through family meetings is only a fringe benefit. The main benefits are all the life skills children learn, such as problem-solving skills, communication skills, co-operation, mutual respect, creativity, brainstorming skills, responsibility, expression of feelings, and how to have fun as a family. They experience the value of using mistakes as wonderful opportunities to learn. The last (or is it the first?) important benefit is family closeness.

Parents can solve many hassles with their children (over four years old) by suggesting that problems be put on the agenda for discussion and/or solutions during the weekly family meeting. Following are the important components for successful family meetings:

1. Set a regularly scheduled meeting time, once a week, that everyone can count on.
2. Post an agenda (usually on the refrigerator) that everyone can see and write on.
3. Start with compliments and appreciations so everyone gets an opportunity to give and receive validation.

---

1. Detailed information on family meetings can be found in Chapter 8 of Jane Nelsen, *Positive Discipline* (New York: Ballantine, 1996).

4. Rotate the chairperson and recorder. The chairperson calls the meeting to order, reads the item to be discussed, calls on people who want to speak, and generally keeps the meeting on track. The recorder writes down suggestions and circles the one agreed upon.

5. When solutions are brainstormed, take a vote on all the suggestions. Everyone in the family must agree before a suggestion is implemented. Sometimes a subject needs to be discussed for several weeks or months (allowing for cooling off and information gathering in between) before a family can achieve an agreement.

6. If the problem does not concern the whole family, the person (or people) who asked for problem-solving help can choose the suggestions she (or they) thinks will be most helpful. A concensus is required only when the problem involves everyone in the family.

7. It is important to note that discussion or just hearing people's feelings is often enough to inspire people to make changes.

8. Go over the family calendar to coordinate schedules, plan for rides, and ensure attendance at important events. Be sure to plan a family fun time and put it on the calendar.

9. Some families like to end with a game or dessert. Family meetings should be fun as well as productive.

It often takes time for family meetings to be successful (they are never perfect). Parents have to learn to give up lectures and control, and children must realize that they will be listened to and taken seriously. Some families give up on family meetings because they think solutions should last forever. That is unrealistic. Choose an idea and try it for a week to see how it works. If it doesn't work, put the problem back on the agenda and try again—and again, and again. Remember the long-range benefits are more important than short-term frustrations and failures. Failures are simply an important part of the growth and learning process.

Kindness and Firmness

Being kind is easy for some parents, but they have difficulty being firm. This formula usually leads to excessive permissiveness. Other parents find it easy to be firm and forget about kindness. This formula usually results in excessive strictness. Neither formula is healthy for children. Strictness and permissiveness do not help children develop the life skills they need to be happy, contributing, capable, young people.

The formula that develops capable young people is a balance of firmness with kindness. Firmness means using appropriate parenting principles with confidence. Kindness means maintaining dignity and respect for yourself and your child while using those parenting principles.

Wishy-washy kindness invites children to manipulate and avoid responsibilities. Dictatorial power (firmness without kindness) invites children to defy and rebel. Firmness with kindness guides children to cooperate and learn boundaries while feeling secure.

Less Is More

Have you heard the term "less is more"? If we would talk less, we would help our children so much more because they would feel validated for their thoughts and ideas. Often, they work through problems themselves just because they have had a sounding board. Other times, they feel better because they feel supported even when they can't think of a solution. The next six tools show ways to stop lecturing or trying to solve your child's problems, because less is more.

"What" and "How" Questions

Too many parents tell children what happened, what caused it to happen, how they should feel about it, and what they should do about it. Telling discourages children from developing their wisdom and judgment, figuring out solutions, and seeing mistakes as opportunities to learn. Telling them what, how, and why teaches them *what* to think, not *how* to think. This is very dangerous in a society filled with peer pressure, cults, and gangs.

We help children develop thinking and judgment skills by asking them these kinds of questions: "What happened? What do you think caused it to happen? How do you feel about it? How could you use this understanding next time? What ideas do you have to solve the problem now?"

It is important to remember that "what" and "how" questions are appropriate only when you have a genuine interest in wanting to know what the child thinks and feels. Don't ask until you are ready and willing to listen.

Be aware that "why" questions are often inappropriate when exploring personal motives or feelings. Asking "Why did you do that?" or "Why do you feel that way?" or "Why are you angry?" sounds judgmental and threatening. It is difficult for people to respond to these questions, because they invoke defensiveness and feelings of inadequacy.

Consider the following example, which shows a parent asking questions instead of lecturing when her eight-year-old's bicycle is stolen:

Juanita came into the house crying, and her mother comforted her.

Juanita: I can't find my bicycle. Someone must have stolen it.

Mom: I'm so sorry. I can see how upset you are. Tell me what happened.

Juanita: I left my bike on Sally's front lawn, and now it is gone. I hate people who steal bikes. That is so mean.

Mom: Yes, it is. It is too bad we can't control everyone in the world and make them nice.

Juanita: Yeah!

Mom: Since we can't control others, what could you do in the future to protect your possessions?

Juanita: Well, I'd better not leave my things out.

Mom: Sounds like you learned a lot from this painful experience. Maybe later you would like to talk about what you will need to do to get another bike and how you will take care of it so this doesn't happen again.

Juanita: Can't we talk about that now?

Mom: I think we are both too upset now. How long do you think it will take for us to feel good enough to talk about it?

Juanita: How about tomorrow?

Mom: Sounds good to me.

Curiosity Questions

When children tell us something, we are often tempted to defend ourselves, explain ourselves, give a lecture about how they should feel differently, or solve their problem. You can help your child explore deeper feelings by asking, "Can you tell me more about that? Could you give me an example? Is there anything else you want to say about that? Anything else?" You may ask, "Anything else?" several times before your child can't think of anything else. Trust your instincts about where to go from there. It could be that your child feels satisfied to have a sounding board. You could ask, "Would you like my help to brainstorm possibilities?" Avoid the temptation to help if your child doesn't ask for your help.

Reflective Listening

Reflective listening means that you reflect back to your child what you hear. It is best to use words that are a little different so you don't sound like a parrot. However, you stick closely to what the child is saying.

Child: I hate Karen.

Parent: You hate your best friend.

Child: Yes, she talked about me behind my back.

Parent: She said something to others that she wouldn't say to you?

Child: Yes.

Parent: I'm glad you told me how you feel. Want a hug?

Child: Yes.

The next day the girls were best friends again. Mom was wise enough to avoid reminding her daughter of her old feelings.

Active Listening

You can help your children achieve emotional security when you use active listening. The sooner you listen to your children's feelings without trying to explain them away or fix them, the healthier your children become. They learn that it is okay and normal to have feelings.

Active listening goes beyond reflective listening. Through active listening you listen for the feelings between the words. This means making guesses that help your child feel deeply understood and validated.

Make sure you use feeling words when using active listening. Feelings can usually be described with one word: happy, hurt, comfortable, scared, hungry, sleepy, angry, sad, helpless, hopeless, irritated, embarrassed, ashamed, joyful. When you find yourself using more than one word to describe a feeling, search for the one word that best describes what your child is experiencing. This will help him pay attention to the feeling, give it a name, and tell others how he feels. Often, once your child feels understood, there is no need to do anything more about a situation.

You can also share *your* feelings by using "I" statements. When you are having feelings, tell your children about them. Use this formula until you are practiced in sharing feelings: "I feel _____ because _____ and I wish _____." For instance, "I feel *angry* because *you are dawdling* and I wish *you would be ready on time*." Children respond better to your honesty than to constant nagging and coaxing because they really do care about your feelings.

Child: I hate Karen.

Parent: You're really mad at Karen.

Child: Yes, she talked about me behind my back.

Parent: You don't like it when she says mean things about you.

Child, in tears: How could she do that?

Parent: Your feelings are really hurt.

Child begins to sob.

This is the time to stop active listening and just hold her for a while. You don't have to fix the problem, but you could ask your child if she wants help figuring out how to tell her friend that her feelings are hurt.

Listening with Your Lips Closed

Because it is so difficult for many parents to avoid lecturing or talking to much, it may be helpful to listen with your lips closed. You can let your child know you are listening closely by saying, "Hmm. Uh-huh." You may be surprised how much your children will talk more when you talk less.

"I Notice" Statements

Don't ask setup questions. A setup question is one to which you already know the answer and still ask for the purpose of trapping your child: "Did you do your homework?" "Did you brush your teeth?" "Did you clean your room?" You may not know for sure that she didn't do her homework or that she didn't brush her teeth, but you know for sure that she didn't clean her room—you can smell it.

Instead of asking setup questions, use "I notice" statements. "I notice you didn't brush your teeth. Let's do that now." "I notice you didn't do your homework. What is your plan for getting it done?" "I notice you didn't clean your room. Shall we call in the fire department for a big hose or hire a maid with your allowance?"

If your child says, "Yes, I did," you can say, "My mistake" or "Great, I'd like to see it." This will not be effective if you are still trying to trap your child. If your child is deceiving you, work on the power struggle or revenge cycle (read about the four mistaken goals of misbehavior below).

Choices and Consequences

Whenever appropriate, give children a choice between at least two acceptable options. The key words here are "appropriate" and "acceptable." There are many times when a choice is not appropriate, especially for younger children. It is not appropriate to let them choose whether or not they should go to school, hurt someone else, or be in a dangerous situation such as climbing on the roof. Acceptable means that you are willing to accept either option the child chooses: "You may save your money or do without." "Either practice the piano or give up lessons." "You can go to bed at 8:15 or 8:30." "Put your dirty clothes in the hamper or wear them dirty." If you are not willing to let your children do without money or wear dirty clothes, don't offer those choices.

Young children need limited choices. As children get older, the choices need to be much broader, or you invite power struggles. For instance, with a teen you might ask, "Would you like me to set a curfew for you or would you like to be involved in that decision?"

Reveal Choices in Advance

If kids aren't involved in the planning, they can at least have advance notice—the choices can be revealed. It can be revealed to kids that people who use the living room disrespectfully will be asked to leave the room until they are ready to use it respectfully. To increase responsibility, accountability, and shared power, it is effective to add, "You decide how much time you think you need to cool off and calm down. If you are having a problem and need help solving it, you can put the problem on the family-meeting agenda."

Natural Consequences

Natural consequences are simple and very effective in the learning process. Natural consequences happen naturally. When you stand in the rain, you get wet. When you forget to eat, you get hungry. When you don't wash your clothes, they stay dirty. Children learn naturally if parents can resist the urge to rescue or punish them.

Logical Consequences

Logical consequences have been grossly misunderstood by many parents, who try to disguise punishment by calling it logical consequences. The point of logical consequences is to help kids learn for the future instead of pay for the past. Let's remember the long-range goals of parenting—to give our kids the courage, confidence, and life skills to live successfully now and when we are no longer around. It is important for children to learn that experiencing the consequences of their choices can help them learn valuable life lessons. They can learn it's okay to make mistakes, learn from their mistakes, and try again. They can learn that it is okay to be accountable for their choices, because they will be treated with dignity and respect. These goals can be achieved when logical consequences are used in the following eight ways:

1. Focus on the future instead of the past. Do not use logical consequences as a way to make kids pay for what they have done in the past. Instead, help them learn for the future. One way to do this is by asking "what" and "how" questions as discussed previously.

2. Opportunity = Responsibility = Consequence. This formula can help define when logical consequences might be appropriate. For every opportunity children have, there is a related responsibility. The obvious consequence for not accepting the responsibility is to lose the opportunity. A teenager who has the opportunity to use the family car may accept the responsibility of leaving the tank at least half full. When the tank is not half full, the consequence is to lose the use of the car for a previously agreed-upon time. This formula is effective only if the consequence is enforced respectfully and children can regain the opportunity as soon as they show they are ready for the responsibility.

3. Focus on solutions instead of consequences. It is a mistake to think there must be a logical consequence for every behavior. Try putting less emphasis on consequences and more emphasis on problem solving.

4. Get kids involved in solutions. Kids are our greatest untapped resource. They have a wealth of wisdom and talent for solving problems. The benefits are numerous when kids are involved in solving problems. They have the opportunity to use and strengthen their skills. They are more likely to keep agreements in which they have ownership. They develop self-confidence and healthy self-esteem when they are listened to, taken seriously, and valued for their contribution. When we value their contribution, they experience belonging and significance. When they feel belonging

and significance, they feel less need to misbehave and are more willing to learn from their mistakes and work on solutions to problems.

The following example shows how a parent involved his kids in setting up a consequence. He began by asking questions about playing ball in the house.

Dad: What problems do you think we might have if you continue to play ball in the living room?

Kids (speaking at once): We might break things. You might get mad at us. We might get the dog too excited. We might be too noisy.

Dad: What suggestions do you have for solving these problems?

Kids: Well, we could play ball outside unless we're playing with a Nerf ball. Even then, it would be a good idea to stay out of the living room.

Dad: What do you think would be a related, respectful, and reasonable consequence if you guys don't keep your agreement about playing outside with the ball?

Kids: It would be okay to send us outside to finish playing. Or we could put the ball away until the next day.

5. Plan ahead. Kids won't feel punished if they help decide on solutions in advance. During a family meeting or a problem-solving session, ask kids for solutions that would help them learn. "What do you think would be logical to help you remember to use the telephone respectfully?" "What do you think a logical consequence would be when you bring the car home with an empty gas tank?"

6. Avoid piggybacking. It is easy for parents to turn consequences into punishment by piggybacking. Piggybacking is adding shame and humiliation to the consequence, which is unnecessary and hurtful: "Maybe this will teach you!" "You can just sit there and think about what you did!" Piggybacking punishes for the past instead of solving for the future. It is based on the belief that we have to make children feel worse in order to make them do better.

7. Show empathy. When a child is experiencing a painful consequence because of a poor choice, show empathy. Your child is much more likely to learn from his mistake when he feels your empathy than from lectures or punishment that invite him to feel defensive.

Eight-year-old Brent was angry and pouty because he had to sit on the grass instead of continue to play in the pool. Even though he had agreed in advance that this is what would happen to anyone who was running and pushing others into the water at the

pool, he was not happy. His dad sat next to him and said, "I know it's tough to have to wait, but you'll be able to try again in no time. Can I bring you a glass of lemonade while you wait?" Brent said, "No thanks" with a sullen expression, but then he asked, "Hey, Dad, how about bringing me an orange instead?"

8. Be aware of other tools that incorporate logical consequences in a respectful way. Many of the tools discussed in this book incorporate logical consequences, although they are not recognized as such because they do not "make" the child do anything (for example, see the "Decide What You Will Do" and "Act, Don't Talk" sections). Logical consequences can be nonverbal. If a toddler treats the family pet badly, quietly remove the child or the pet. If a child doesn't put his dirty clothes in the hamper, don't say anything and don't wash the clothes. He will catch on in due time.

Decide What You Will Do

Will we ever learn that the only behavior we can control is our own? You may be able to make your children act respectfully, but you can't make them feel respectful. The best way to encourage them to feel respectful is to control your own behavior and show respect for yourself and others.

Deciding what you will do instead of trying to control others may be a new thought for some parents. Many parents have been so busy trying to control their children that they haven't considered dealing with problems by controlling their own behavior. We hope the following examples will start your creative juices flowing on deciding what you will do.

One mother got tired of repeating herself all the time. She told her children that she would make sure she had their full attention and then say things only once. If they had questions, she'd be happy to answer them, but she was no longer going to repeat herself. She soon noticed how much better her children listened when she said something. If they weren't paying attention, they would ask one of their siblings what Mom had said.

Try making an agreement with a child based on what you are willing to do. You might tell a child, "I will be available for helping with homework every night from seven o'clock until nine o'clock. If you want my help, I'll be there." If the child then wants help at a time that is inconvenient for you, say, "I'll be available again at seven o'clock tomorrow evening." Other examples include refusing to drive when it's too noisy; instead, stop the car and wait in silence for the unruly children to settle down. You might decide not to advance money from your children's allowances when they ask for a loan. Or you might decide to ignore children who continually come out of their rooms at nap time and disrupt your work.

Act, Don't Talk

Try acting instead of talking. Listen to yourself for one day. You'll be amazed how many useless words you say. If you act more and talk less, your children will begin to notice the difference. Instead of asking your children to be quiet over and over, try waiting quietly for them to give you their attention. If children are fighting over a toy, quietly remove it and put it where they can't reach it. You don't need to say a word for them to get the idea that they can have the toy back when they stop fighting over it.

Stop saying things you don't mean. If you mean something, be prepared to follow through with action instead of words. Since that means giving a matter your full attention from start to finish, you'll soon begin to ignore minor interruptions and deal with the ones that are really important to you.

For example, most dawdling disappears as if by magic when parents say what they mean and mean what they say and follow through with actions instead of reminders and nagging. Using the clock and a mutually agreed-upon schedule, follow through by moving yourself instead of trying to move your child with words. For young children, simply act without talking by taking them gently but firmly by the hand and moving on to the next activity. Dawdling may also be a way to avoid becoming overstressed. Are you pushing your kids too much? Is dawdling a way for a hurried child to survive?

Children tune parents out because parents talk too much. Have you ever listened to parents at the mall or in the supermarket? You would think the parents would notice that their attempts to control their children through words are only met with more defiance. It is perfectly okay to take children by the hand and start walking, or lift them up and carry them to bed, or set them in the bathtub when they are having a fit about taking a bath. It is disrespectful to yell, nag, lecture, beg, order, and threaten. Give up counting to three; zip your lips and act. You'll be amazed at the results.

Another act-don't-talk tip is to make sure you are in the same room before you make requests of children. If you can see the whites of their eyes and establish eye contact with them, you have a better chance of getting through.

You have to get their attention before children can hear what you have to say. Action is a great tool for this. Notice how much quicker you get results if you stand up or move toward your children while you are talking instead of sitting in an armchair yelling instructions across the room.

Follow-Through

Follow-through can greatly reduce frustration and conflict with children while teaching them many positive life skills.

Follow-through means parents decide what they are going to do and then follow through with kind and firm action instead of lectures and punishment.

When you use words, keep the message short—ten words or less—and stick to the issue. One word can be very effective. For example, when a child under six years of age is refusing to go to bed, get up without saying a word, go to the child, take her by the hand, and kindly and firmly lead her to the bedroom, saying, "Bedtime." If the child resists, give a limited choice, "Do you want to pick out your bedtime story or do you want me to? We have until eight o'clock to read your story." If the child still resists, you are in a power struggle and need to back off and deal with the power struggle (read about the four mistaken goals of misbehavior below).

What does the child learn? She learns that you mean what you say and will follow through with firm and kind action. The child is learning about responsibility. She has a choice to get ready for bed quickly and have time for a longer story or get ready slowly and have less time for a story. One of the greatest benefits for a child is the opportunity to learn about treating oneself and others with dignity and respect, which you can demonstrate.

When children are younger (toddler to age eight), follow-through is relatively simple. When you say something, mean it. When you mean it, follow through with kindness and firmness. Or, as psychologist Rudolf Dreikurs said, "Shut your mouth and act."

As children get older, follow-through is more effective and teaches more skills when children are involved in the process of solving problems and making agreements. The following four steps describe this process.

Four Steps for Effective Follow-Through

1. Have a friendly discussion in which everyone gets to voice his or her feelings and thoughts around the issue. The greatest incentive for cooperation is getting children involved in solutions.

2. Brainstorm for possible solutions and choose one that both you and your child agree to.

3. Agree on a specific time deadline (to the minute).

4. Understand children well enough to know that the deadline probably won't be met and simply follow through with your part of the agreement by holding them accountable, as in the following example.

Seventeen-year-old Larry had accepted the job of mowing the lawn. He hardly ever did it until his father scolded and threatened to ground him for a week if it wasn't done. His dad decided to try follow-through. He asked Larry if he would be willing to work together on a solution so they could end their power struggle over the lawn mowing. Larry agreed reluctantly because he was expecting a lecture and punishment.

Dad: Larry, I would really like to hear what is going on with you regarding the lawn. Do you think it is too big a job for you, or unfair, or are you too busy?

Larry: No, Dad. I know I should do it. I always intend to. I just get busy and forget.

Dad: I have a hunch that something else might be involved too. I have been pretty bossy about telling you what to do and very insulting to you when you don't jump to my commands on schedule. Could it be that you are showing me that I can't make you do it if you don't want to?

Larry shows a sheepish grin.

Dad: I thought so. I don't blame you. In fact, when I think about it, I have to admire your spunk for refusing to be treated that way. I really want to stop being bossy and insulting. Are you willing to work with me on ways to treat each other respectfully?

Larry (suspiciously): Yeah, I guess.

Dad: How about brainstorming with me on some solutions to the lawn-mowing problem? I have one suggestion. We could both get extra jobs so we could earn enough money to hire a gardener.

Larry (laughing): We could just let it grow and call it a jungle.

Dad: We could try to con your mother into doing it.

Larry: Or I could just do it. I know it isn't much for me to do.

Dad: Well, that's the solution I would prefer, if you are really willing and don't feel coerced by a bossy dad. Would you be willing to agree to a specific deadline by which it will be done? Then I won't say a word unless it is not done by the deadline.

Larry: How about Sunday night?

Dad: I could enjoy the weekend a lot more if it was done before Saturday.

Larry: Okay, I'll do it by Friday.

Dad: What time on Friday?

Larry: Let's not get picky, Dad. I'll do it by Friday.

Dad: It will be easier for me to keep my agreement to keep my mouth shut until the deadline if the deadline is very specific.

Larry: Okay, okay. How about Friday by 6 P.M.?

Dad: Sounds good to me, Son.

At 6 P.M. the next Friday, the lawn is not mowed and Larry is plopped in front of the television. His father is not surprised. He expected this and is ready to follow through.

Dad: Larry, it is six o'clock and the lawn is not mowed.

Larry: Aw, Dad, I'm interested in this program. I'll do it later.

Dad: What was our agreement?

Larry: Come on, Dad. Don't be uptight. I'll do it right after this program.

His dad smiles, gives Larry a knowing grin, and points to his watch.

Larry: Okay, okay. I'm going. Talk about uptight!

Dad (ignoring the insult): Thanks, Larry. I really appreciate your willingness to keep our agreement.

Some parents will say, "My son (or daughter) wouldn't give in that easily." We disagree. When you follow the four steps for effective follow-through and avoid the following four traps, kids do cooperate, even when they don't especially want to.

Four Traps That Defeat Effective Follow-Through

1. Wanting kids to have the same priorities as adults.

2. Getting into judgments and criticisms instead of sticking to the issue.

3. Not getting agreements in advance that include a specific time deadline.

4. Not maintaining dignity and respect for your child and yourself.

If you reread the example, you will see that his father did not expect Larry to be excited about mowing the lawn. When his dad thought about it, he could name many things that were a greater priority for Larry: having friends; paying for a car, insurance, and gas; doing homework without being called a nerd; wondering about drugs, sex, and college; and worrying about rejection from girls. Mowing the lawn is not in the top hundred. However, it is still important for Larry to contribute to the family in meaningful ways.

Notice that Larry's dad avoided judgments and criticism and stuck to the issue of the agreement. The more Larry talked, the less his father said. He simply gave Larry a knowing grin and pointed to his watch. This was effective because Larry knew he had agreed to the deadline. Larry's dad maintained dignity and respect for Larry and himself throughout the follow-through process. He avoided the four traps that defeat effective follow-through and used the following four hints.

Four Hints for Effective Follow-Through

1. Keep comments simple and concise. ("I notice you didn't mow the lawn. Please do that now.")

2. In response to objections, ask, "What was our agreement?"

3. In response to further objections, shut your mouth and use nonverbal communication (point to your watch, smile knowingly, give a hug, and point to your watch again).

4. When the child concedes to keep the agreement (sometimes obviously annoyed), say, "Thank you for keeping our agreement."

Part of sticking to the issue is ignoring other concerns that arise. These concerns (such as resistance or hurt feelings when the child makes a snide remark) can be put on the agenda and discussed at a later time.

Some people object to follow-through. They say, "We don't want to have to remind our kids to keep their agreements. We expect them to be responsible without any reminders from us." We have three questions for these people: When you don't remind them with dignity and respect, do you spend time scolding, lecturing, and punishing them for not keeping their agreements? Have you noticed how responsible your kids are about keeping agreements that are important to them? Do you really think household chores are important to them? Even though chores are not important to them, it is important to have kids do them anyway. Follow-through takes less energy and is much more fun and productive than scolding, lecturing, and punishing.

Adults are not using common sense when they expect kids to use their free will to follow adult priorities. They are very good at using their free will to follow their own priorities. Follow-through is a respectful way of helping kids live up to appropriate adult expectations and priorities.

Once we understand that kids have their own priorities but still need to follow some of ours, follow-through can make parenting pleasurable, magical, and fun. We can see the things kids do as cute and normal instead of lazy, inconsiderate, or irresponsible.

Follow-through helps parents be proactive and thoughtful instead of reactive and inconsiderate. Follow-through empowers kids by respecting who they are while teaching them the importance of making a contribution to the family. It is an excellent alternative to authoritarian methods or permissiveness. With follow-through, we can meet the needs of the situation while maintaining dignity and respect for all concerned. Children learn the life skills they need to feel good about themselves and to be contributing members of society.

Routines

Children need routines.[2] Some parents think routines destroy spontaneity. In fact, when a family has routines, the members usually have a lot more spontaneity and creativity. Without routines, most families experience chaos instead of spontaneity. Once routines are firmly in place, there is time for the family members to enjoy their freedom within them. If you think of routines as the railing at the edge of a cliff or the guardrails on a bridge, you can see how

---

2. For more detailed information on establishing routines, see Lynn Lott and Riki Intner, *Chores Without Wars* (Rocklin, CA: Prima Publishing, 1998).

without them there is insecurity and with them there is freedom of movement.

Children enjoy routines and respond favorably to them. The younger the child, the more comfortable they are with routine. Picture the preschooler who is used to crackers and milk before story time trying to adjust when a substitute teacher changes the order. Once routines are in place, the routine is the boss and the parent doesn't have to give orders continually.

To set up routines, pick a time when everyone is relaxed or discuss the issue at a family meeting. It is important for all family members to be involved in developing the routines. Focus on one problem at a time. Ask for everyone's ideas. Use limited choices when an idea is not appropriate. For example, if your child says, "I don't want to do it at all," give a limited choice, such as, "You may do it before breakfast or before dinner or decide on another time. Not doing it at all isn't one of the choices."

Make visual aids to help the family remember the routines you have created together, such as charts and lists. It can be fun to use a kitchen timer and play "Beat the Clock" in completing the routine. When everyone agrees on the new routine, practice it through role playing. Finally, follow through to implement the routine with action in a firm and kind manner. Refer to the chart or list, or ask, "What was our agreement?" Resist rescuing and lecturing.

Another tip for setting up routines is to have a deadline. When planning the routine, work backward from the deadline to figure out how much time is needed to accomplish the task. For instance, if you want to have housecleaning done by 2 P.M. on Sunday so the family can have time for an outing, think through what the tasks are, how long they will take, and when everyone needs to start.

Notice that most routines involve the whole family. Children cooperate better when everyone works together instead of parents handing kids lists of chores to complete. Establishing routines is key to eliminating all those hassles about bedtime, mornings, mealtime, homework, shopping, and chores (all of these are covered in Part 2).

Following are some typical routines and how family members can participate in them together.

Housecleaning

Pick a time each week to clean the house together. Each family member can choose one or two rooms to clean or one or two activities, such as dusting, vacuuming, or cleaning sinks. If everyone works together, you'll be amazed at how little time it takes to clean the house.

Meal Planning and Preparation

List the jobs—perhaps one person cooks, another assists, another sets the table, and another cleans up. During a family meeting, each person chooses at least one night for each of the jobs. Make a meal chart, where the cook lists what he or she wants to prepare for each meal. Use this chart to make a grocery list to make sure the needed ingredients are purchased in advance.

Grocery Shopping

Use the grocery list you've prepared together. Before leaving for the store, let each family member choose from the master list the items they want to find. Go to the store and let each person find the items on their lists. Meet at the checkout counter. When you return home, carry in the items and put them away together.

Morning and Bedtime Routines

These routines are covered in Part 2.

Laundry

All family members have a laundry basket in their room and their own day of the week for doing laundry. Teach all children six years of age and older how to run the washer and dryer. Let older children help younger children carry clothes back to their rooms and put them away. Stay out of your children's drawers—if they choose to stuff their clothes in without folding, that is their choice. Give yourself a break and stop doing for children what they can do for themselves.

Bath Time

Let reticent bathers know that it is not a choice to bathe, but that they can choose the days and time. When it is time for their bath, firmly but kindly remind them of their agreement and give them a choice: would they like you to turn off all distractions, such as television, video games, and computers, or do they want to do it? It may help to give them an egg timer to set ten minutes before bath time—again, so they can share the power and control. Let children who never want to get out of the tub decide, using limited choices, if the bath should be fifteen or twenty minutes long, and if they will open the drain or if you will. Make bath time fun. Let the kids have special toys they can only use in the tub. Anything that squirts or pours water is usually a lot of fun. Plan enough time for children to play in the tub while you supervise.

Brushing Teeth

When children are young, they need your help to brush their teeth. Do it with them and help them floss. As they get older, add toothbrushing to the list of activities they do before school (see *Morning Hassles* in

Part 2) and before bed. You may also use reminders, like "I want you to brush your teeth," since children may not see or share your concern. Some families establish a routine of everyone brushing together just before bedtime.

If your children resist brushing teeth, instead of nagging have the dentist use a fluoride treatment regularly to help prevent decay. It is better to treat tooth decay than live with power struggles. Using bribery or punishment is disrespectful. Many dentists and hygienists will take time to talk to your children about dental hygiene to help you out. Trust that brushing teeth will become more important to your children as they mature.

Quiet Time

You have a right to quiet time, and it is okay to expect your children to entertain themselves for a while. You could schedule a one-hour rest after lunch as an opportunity for you to have time to yourself and for your kids to play quietly in their rooms. Do not insist that children sleep during quiet times, but ask that they respect other people's need for space. Encourage your children to have some quiet time without television, music, or video games, to develop an inner life of reflection.

* * *

These are just a few examples of how some families have set up routines. Be realistic—routines may not work perfectly at first. Children who are used to behaving in certain ways need time before they believe their parents mean what they say. Remember, it is human nature to resist change, even when we want it or know it is good for us. When we understand this, we can keep following the planned routine until the resistance ends.

Once in place, a routine may work automatically for years. With younger children, the earlier you start, the more they think a routine is just the way things are. Routines help eliminate power struggles and give all family members ways to belong and contribute to the family.

The long-range benefits of routines are security, a calmer atmosphere, trust, and life skills for children. Children learn to focus on doing what needs to be done. They learn to be responsible for their own behavior, to take pride in being capable, and to cooperate in the family.

Know Who—Not Where—They Are

"Do you know where your child is?" What do you feel when you see that question glaring at you from a poster or a bumper sticker? Guilty because you don't know? Smug because you think you do know? Do you feel that you are a bad parent if you don't know? Does that phrase shame you into thinking you should do a better job of policing your child? Do you think you should join the parents who try to control their children's behavior with punishment (grounding, taking away privileges, lecturing, shaming, searching their bedrooms)? Do you think you should be in charge of your children's lives (their choice of friends, their schoolwork, their report card results, their career choices)? How will we ever teach our children to take charge of their own lives with confidence and responsibility when we take all the responsibility for their lives, chip away at their confidence, and rob them of the opportunity to learn life skills?

We would like to see a new bumper sticker: "Do you know your child?" What does your child think? How does your child feel? What does your child want in life? What are your child's values, hopes, and dreams? Not yours, but your child's. Do you ever get into your child's world and try to understand and respect his or her point of view? Are you curious about who your child is, or are you too busy trying to mold your child to fit your values, hopes, and dreams?

Other questions need to be asked: Do you have faith in your child? Do you believe your child is a magnificent human being who has the potential to learn and grow from life's challenges? When you have faith in your children, it is easier to stop trying to control and punish them and to start supporting them with respectful methods that teach the life skills they need when adults aren't around.

Have Faith

Having faith in children does not mean having faith that they will always do the right thing. It means having faith in children to be who they are. This means they will act appropriately for their age most of the time—which means they will not always do the dishes or mow the lawn as promised. Instead of getting upset about this and acting disrespectfully, we can expect it and use respectful methods to motivate them. With faith in our children and in ourselves, we can help each other learn from mistakes.

Having faith in your children does not mean they are ready to be on their own. They still need your love, support, and help in learning life skills. When we have faith, we don't need to control and punish. Faith gives us the patience to teach with empowering methods such as joint problem solving, follow-through, family meetings, and asking "what," "how," and "why" questions to help kids learn from their mistakes. Having faith includes keeping an eye on the long-range picture and knowing that who your kids are now is not who they are going to be forever.

Remember all the mistakes you made as a kid—including the things you didn't want your parents to know about? And didn't you turn out okay? Aren't you now a responsible, caring person? Having faith in your children means having faith that with your love, support, and the life skills you are teaching, they will also grow up to be responsible, caring people.

Mistakes

At our workshops, we often ask parents: "What were you taught about mistakes during your childhood?" Your answers may be similar to the ones we get:

- Mistakes are bad.
- You shouldn't make mistakes.
- You are stupid, bad, inadequate, or a failure if you make mistakes.
- If you make a mistake, don't let people find out. If they do, make up an excuse even if it isn't true.

We call these "crazy notions about mistakes," which not only damage self-esteem but also invite depression and discouragement. It is difficult to learn and grow when you feel discouraged. We all know people who have made a mistake and then dug themselves into a hole by trying to cover it up. They don't understand that people are often very forgiving when others admit their mistakes, apologize, and try to solve the problems they have created. (Wouldn't it be wonderful if politicians understood this concept?)

Hiding mistakes keeps you isolated, because you can't fix mistakes that are hidden, nor can you learn from them. Trying to prevent mistakes keeps you rigid and fearful. Remember, "Good judgment comes from experience and experience comes from poor judgment."[3]

Parents can be sure their children don't share these crazy notions about mistakes. Tell your children that every person in the world will make mistakes as long as he or she lives. Since this is true, it is healthier to see mistakes as opportunities to learn instead of statements of inadequacy. Teach kids to see making a mistake as an opportunity to get valuable help from others. This will encourage them to take responsibility for what they have done, even if it was a mistake, because they know it doesn't mean they are bad or will get in trouble. They are, however, accountable, which is necessary in using mistakes as opportunities to learn.

Sometimes mistakes require that you make amends where possible and at least apologize when amends are not possible.

3. We found this scribbled on a rest room wall at the Squeeze Inn Restaurant in Truckee, California.

The Three Rs of Recovery is a tool that takes the guilt, shame, and blame out of mistakes.

The Three Rs of Recovery

Tell your children that making mistakes isn't as important as what they do about them. Anyone can make mistakes, but it takes a secure person to say, "I'm sorry." If a child would like to make amends for a mistake, the Three Rs of Recovery can help them do so.

1. *Recognize* the mistake with a feeling of responsibility instead of blame.

2. *Reconcile* by apologizing to the people you have offended or hurt.

3. *Resolve* the problem, when possible, by working together on a solution.

If you make a mistake, the Three Rs of Recovery can help you make amends with your children. Don't hesitate to let them know when you make mistakes. Your children will be very forgiving and can learn from your modeling.

Positive Time-Out

One of the most popular discipline methods used by parents today is some kind of isolation or time-out. Time-out can be an encouraging and empowering experience for children instead of punitive and humiliating. Time-out is encouraging when the purpose is to give children an opportunity to take a break for a short time and then to try again as soon as they are ready to change their behavior. We all have our times when, for one reason or another, we don't feel like doing what is required and may act out instead. Positive time-out provides a cooling-off period.

Time-out is encouraging when parents are more concerned with long-range benefits to children than short-term control at the expense of children. Punitive time-out may stop misbehavior for the moment. The benefits, however, are short-term if the child decides to get even or to give up. The key to using time-out respectfully is in the attitude of the parent and the explanation given to children.

To set up a positive time-out area that is encouraging, offer the following explanation to your children: "Everyone needs a time-out once in a while, because we get so upset at times that we lose our perspective and behave irrationally. It helps to have a place to sort out our feelings, calm down, and then make a decision about what to do. Your feelings are different from your actions. What you feel is never inappropriate. What you do sometimes is. If your behavior is inappropriate, I may ask you if you think it would help you to go to your positive time-out area. This is not meant for punishment but for a time to calm down until you feel better. As soon as you feel better—and you can decide when that is—you can come out." Some parents provide a timer for children to set according to how much time they think they will need to feel better.

This is quite different from the way many parents send their children to their rooms. With a punitive attitude, they say, "Go to your room and think about what you have done." We have to laugh at this statement. It is so ludicrous to think we can control what our children will think about. We speculate that most kids are not thinking about what they have done but are thinking about their anger at what their parents have done. These parents believe guilt, shame, and suffering will motivate their children to do better. They do not. Kids do better when they feel better. We don't motivate kids to do better by making them feel worse through punitive time-out. It does not help to tell children, "Go to your room and think about what you have done." It is helpful to tell children, "When you are in your room, do something to help you feel better. You may want to read a book, take a short nap, listen to music, or play with your toys until you feel better and are ready to change your behavior." Some parents object to the idea of telling children to go to their rooms and do something that is fun. They are afraid this is rewarding the misbehavior. These parents don't listen to the last part of the instructions: "Come out when you feel better and are ready to change your behavior."

The point of positive time-out (and all other nonpunitive methods) is to teach children that mistakes are opportunities to learn, to teach them life skills that will serve them when adults are not around, and to help them feel that they belong and are significant so they don't feel a need to engage in nonproductive behavior.

Put Kids in the Same Boat

Quite often, adults get in the habit of picking on one child; instead, they should start using the term "kids" and putting everyone in the same boat. If you have more than one child, one of the handiest words for preventing sibling rivalry, good kid–bad kid labels, and hurt feelings is the word "kids." Instead of trying to figure out who starts a fight, try, "Kids, if you want to continue fighting, please take the fight outside or into another room." If the children are fighting over who sits in the front seat of the car, try, "Kids, no one can sit in the front seat until you have figured out a plan for sharing the seat. Please work out the details on your own time."

If you want help after dinner, try, "Kids, please come up with a system for sharing the dishwashing." If children are fighting over a toy, say, "Kids, toys aren't for fighting over; they're for playing. I'll put the toy away, and when you kids decide you want to try again, come get me and I'll get the toy for you."

Even when there is a wide age span, you would be surprised at how many problems you can avoid when you say to your baby and the two-year-old who is hugging too hard, "Kids, I see you are having a hard time getting along right now. One of you can stay in the playpen for a while and the other can play in the toy area. You both can try again in a few minutes." You are training yourself along with your children. When you choose sides, you train victims and bullies. Even young children will soon catch on that it doesn't pay to cause problems so they can manipulate adults to rescue them.

Putting kids in the same boat is great for dealing with a tattler. When children come to you to tattle, simply say, "I'm sure you kids can work it out." If your children respond with, "That's not fair. I wasn't doing anything wrong" or "Mom, it was Tom, not me," simply say, "I'm not interested in finding fault or pointing fingers but in getting the problem remedied. Let's talk about it at the family meeting."

Let Kids Figure It Out

When adults try to settle conflicts between children, they often escalate the situation. Kids have ways of working things out that are both efficient and effective. Kids may not always use the same methods grown-ups would, but many grown-ups have less skill in conflict resolution than their children. Think of the times when parents in the neighborhood were at war while the kids had already forgotten whatever they were arguing about and were off playing happily together. Give the kids a chance.

Many parents think it is their job to fix everything and that they are the only ones with good ideas. Try asking the kids to figure out what to do, and watch their creativity at work.

In one family, the kids were fighting over who got to use the Nintendo game. Dad said, "I'm putting the game away until you kids figure out a system for sharing without fighting. Let me know when you've worked it out, and you can try again."

At first the kids grumbled, but later one of them said, "We worked it out. John can use the game on Mondays and Wednesdays, and I get it on Tuesdays and Thursdays. We can both use it on Fridays. We agreed."

If the kids start squabbling again, Dad can simply say, "Back to the drawing board. The game-sharing plan seems to be falling apart. Let me know when you are ready to try again."

Two Tongues

If you want to understand people, pay more attention to what they do than to what they say. Watch their tongues. The tongues in their mouths (words) may say one thing, while the tongues in their shoes (actions) give a different message. People may convey good intentions with their words, but their actions tell us the truth about what they are doing.

This works two ways. It is important for parents to be consistent with their children, making sure that their words and actions match. It is also helpful to trust kids to be who they are by paying more attention to what they do than to what they say. Many parents say, "I just can't trust my child," but if they altered their definition of trust, it would be easy. Alfred Adler said repeatedly, "Watch the movement, not the words." Actions do speak louder than words.

You move toward healthy communication when your words and actions are congruent. When the tongues in your mouth and in your shoes match, you are respectful and encouraging to yourself and others. When they go in different directions, you're giving a double message, and people don't know which one to believe.

Promises

Don't make promises unless you intend to keep them. Instead of saying, "Tomorrow I'll take you shopping," wait until you are ready to go, and then tell the children, "It's time to go shopping. Would you like to go with me?"

Promising children you'll think about something and then forgetting to get back to it is very discouraging. Instead, tell the children that you aren't ready to commit just yet. They can put the item on the family-meeting agenda, or they can come and talk to you at an agreed-upon time. Making promises without checking out the details of what you have promised or checking with your partner backs you into a corner and builds resentment with the kids.

If your children make a lot of promises to you, say to them, "I don't take promises. Show me when you are ready instead, and I'll celebrate with you."

Beliefs Behind Behavior

There is a belief behind every behavior, but we usually only deal with the behavior. Dealing with the belief behind the behavior does not mean you don't deal with the behavior. You are most effective when you are aware of both the behavior and the belief behind it.

The following is a classic example of the belief behind a behavior. Consider a four-year-old boy whose mother goes off to the hospital and brings home a brand-new baby. What does the four-year-old see going on between Mom and the baby? Time and attention. What does the boy interpret that to mean? "Mom loves the baby more than me." What does the four-year-old do in an attempt to get the love back? He acts like a baby himself, cries, wants a bottle, and soils his pants.

Mrs. Jacobs had a four-year-old daughter who was feeling dethroned by the birth of a baby brother. One evening, when the baby was asleep, Mrs. Jacobs sat down at the kitchen table with her daughter and said, "Honey, I would like to tell you a story about our family. These candles represent our family." She picked up one long candle and said, "This is the mommy candle. This one is for me." She lit the candle as she said, "This flame represents my love." She picked up another long candle and said, "This candle is the daddy candle." She used the flame from the mommy candle to light the daddy candle and said, "When I married your daddy, I gave him all my love and I still have all my love left." Mrs. Jacobs put the daddy candle in a candle holder, picked up a smaller candle and said, "This candle is for you." She lit the smaller candle with the flame from her candle and said, "When you were born, I gave you all my love. And look. Daddy still has all my love, and I still have all my love left." Mrs. Jacobs put that candle in a candle holder next to the daddy candle, then picked up the smallest candle and, while lighting it with the mommy candle, said, "This is a candle for your baby brother. When he was born, I gave him all my love. And look—you still have all my love. Daddy has all my love. And I still have all my love left, because that is the way love is. You can give it to everyone you love and still have all your love. Now look at all the light we have in our family with all this love."

What happens to us is never as important as the beliefs we create about what happens to us. Our behavior is based on those beliefs, and the behavior and beliefs are directly related to the primary goal of all people—to feel that we belong and are important.

The Primary Goal of All People

We all want to belong and feel significant. We are active participants (not victims) in the process of deciding things about ourselves, others, and life, and our behavior is based on our decisions. Understanding the decision-making process and how your children create their beliefs is the first step to understanding their behavior. With this understanding, you can be encouraging to your kids and provide opportunities for them to change their unhealthy beliefs and behaviors.

All of us seek ways to belong and be important. Sometimes they work and sometimes they don't. If we think we aren't loved or don't belong, we usually try something to gain the love, or we hurt others to get even. Sometimes we even feel like giving up because we think it is impossible to do things right and to belong. We try to find belonging and importance in unhealthy ways, such as those described by the four mistaken goals of misbehavior.[4]

The Four Mistaken Goals of Misbehavior

1. Undue attention
2. Misguided power
3. Revenge
4. Assumed inadequacy (giving up)

We call these hidden reasons for doing what we do, because we are not consciously aware of them. It is important for you to understand the hidden beliefs behind what your children do. Then you might be able to think of ways to encourage them when they are feeling discouraged. When you understand your children's beliefs about themselves, others, and life, you are in a better position to influence them in positive ways. You are effectively dealing with the belief behind the behavior instead of with only the behavior.

How to Encourage Discouraged Children

Instead of reacting to the misbehavior, react to the motivation behind the misbehavior.

Undue Attention

Give lots of spontaneous hugs throughout the day. Schedule regular special time. Ignore bids for attention that make you feel irritated. (Let your child know in advance that you will do this.) Brainstorm with your child on ways to get attention that are good for everyone. Whenever you look at a child whose behavior is demanding undue attention, picture that child really saying, "Notice me. Involve me." This will help you automatically find a way to encourage your child without promoting the negative behavior.

Misguided Power

Take responsibility for how you create power struggles, and share this with your child, such as by saying, "I can see that I have been too controlling. No wonder you rebel." Ask for help in working together on solutions after you have both calmed down. When you feel defeated or angry, picture your child as really saying, "Let me help. Give me choices." This will help you create

4. More information on the four mistaken goals of misbehavior can be found in Jane Nelsen, *Positive Discipline* (New York: Ballantine, 1996) and Jane Nelsen and Lynn Lott, *Positive Discipline for Teenagers* (Rocklin, CA: Prima Publishing, 1994).

a win/win situation instead of escalating a power struggle or turning it into revenge.

Revenge

Understand that the child who is hurting you or others feels hurt. Deal with the hurt by checking with the child about how he feels hurt. Be accountable for anything you might have done (even though unintentionally) or listen empathetically if someone else is involved in the hurt. Help your child decide what he can do to feel better. Realize that your child's behavior is really a code for an underlying request that says, "Help me. I'm hurting." Then, instead of hurting back or rejecting the child, you can behave in a way that helps the child to feel belonging and significance in a positive way.

Assumed Inadequacy (Giving Up)

Don't give in to your own discouragement. Keep encouraging your child by making tasks easy enough to ensure success. Take time for training. Keep telling your child that you have faith in his ability to learn and improve. When your child acts in a way that invites you to give up, picture your child as really saying, "Don't give up on me. Show me a small step." Doing this will help you automatically come up with a positive and encouraging action on your part that can help your child move forward with confidence and hope.

Make Sure the Message of Love Gets Through

Making sure the message of love gets through is the greatest gift you can give your children. They form their opinions of themselves through their perception of how you feel about them. When they feel loved and that they belong and are important, they have a strong foundation to develop their full potential. Your positive influence gets through when the message of love gets through.

Special Time Together

Children need time alone with each parent. When they are young, it is important to spend a little time each day one-on-one with your children. As they get older, special time could become a weekly routine. Plan activities that you both enjoy for your special time. If other children interrupt, explain and ask them to leave.

Play spontaneously with your kids, too. Roughhouse on the floor, go to the park, cook together, or play games—whatever you get a kick out of. The important thing is to make time for fun. Build some pleasant memories of fun times instead of staying too serious. Family fun doesn't have to take a lot of time or cost a lot of money.

All it takes is a commitment and a playful spirit. Many problems disappear when children experience plenty of special time.

Encouragement vs. Praise and Rewards

Rudolf Dreikurs, an Adlerian psychologist and author of *Children: The Challenge,* said, "Children need encouragement like a plant needs water."[5] Encouragement shows the kind of love that conveys to children that they are good enough the way they are. Encouragement teaches children that what they do is separate from who they are. Encouragement lets children know they are valued for their uniqueness without judgment. Through encouragement, we teach children that mistakes are simply opportunities to learn and grow instead of something to be ashamed of.

There is a difference between praise and encouragement. It's easy to praise or reward children who are behaving well, but what can we say to children who are misbehaving and not feeling good about themselves? And yet that's when they need encouragement the most.

Praise and rewards teach children to depend on the judgments of others instead of trusting their own wisdom and self-evaluation. A steady diet of praise and rewards inspires children to believe "I'm okay only if others say I'm okay." It also teaches them to avoid making mistakes instead of learning from their mistakes.

Following are some examples of giving encouragement:

- "How do you feel about _____?"
- "Would you like some help with ____?"
- "Hey, anyone can have a bad day. We still like you a lot."
- "You put a lot of effort into that."

Family members can write notes of encouragement to each other. In some families, people take turns watching for encouraging things to say and do it for each other. It can also be that person's job to have a compliment ready for other family members once or twice a week. Encouragement goes a long way toward creating a positive family climate.

5. Rudolf Dreikurs with Vicki Soltz, *Children: The Challenge* (New York: Plume Books, 1990).

Teach your children how to give compliments. Ask them to think of a time when someone said something that made them feel good about themselves. Have them think about something they would like to thank others for or something they wish someone would compliment them on. Don't be afraid to compliment your children or to ask them to give you a compliment. At first, the kids may feel uncomfortable or think giving compliments is silly. Have faith and stick with it until giving compliments becomes a habit. In too many families the only things they say to each other are criticisms, orders, putdowns, or "pass the salt." The good feelings will grow in your family as you practice encouragement and compliments.

Say No

It's okay to say no. If all you ever say is no, that's a problem, but some parents don't think they can say no without lengthy explanations. Suppose a child knows that snack time is a time for healthy treats but he asks for ice cream.

Mom: No.

Child: Why not? That's not fair. Mrs. Smith lets her kids have ice cream for a snack.

Mom: Watch my lips: no.

Child: Aw, come on, be a sport. You're so uptight.

Mom: What part of no don't you understand?

Child: Okay. You're no fun. I guess we can't have ice cream today.

Most children have figured out when their parents really mean no—there's that certain tone of voice or look on the face, or the parent starts counting to three. Children wouldn't be children if they didn't try to get parents to change their minds, but it is perfectly appropriate to handle their manipulations with a clean, clear no.

Use Your Sense of Humor

Parenting can get too serious, especially as the children get older. With babies and toddlers, it seems like everything they do is cute and adorable. See if you can get to the point with your children, whatever their ages, where you can truly say, "Aren't they cute?"

Developing an "aren't they cute?" attitude can help you put your children's behavior into perspective. When you recognize their behavior as appropriate for their age, it helps you see otherwise annoying behavior as cute. Babies with food all over their faces and under their high chairs are adorable, so how about looking at a teenager's room—which looks like a whirlwind blew through—as another kind of "cute"?

Think of the ways your children dress as their uniforms and expressions of their personalities instead of statements about you and reflections on your parenting. When kids are three years old, they may want to dress like a superhero; at age seven, a baseball player; and at age fifteen, the uniform of the day may be baggy clothes from the Salvation Army. Some parents forget to use their sense of humor or to see the humor in situations with children. It's okay not to be serious all the time. Try telling the kid reluctant to do chores that there is an article about him in the newspaper. Then pretend to read the interview, which says how much your child loves to wash the dishes and that he's happy to have his parents remind him when he forgets. You can pretend that you are reading his horoscope: "Remember to hug your parents five times today."

Nicknames can be a fun way to express your sense of humor, as long as they aren't used as a put-down. For example, on a ski trip, one of the kids shot down the hill before everyone else got to the top. His nickname became "Slow-mo Beau." His brother, who refused to ski at all, loved being called "I-don't-want-to-you-can't-make-me-no-I-won't-not-ever Don."

For those kids who have a hard time finishing what they start, try introducing them to the beginning-middle-end concept. Let them know they are great at beginnings and fair on middles, but you haven't seen an end in years. Later, you can ask, "How are those ends coming?" Children like being joked with when parents accept their idiosyncrasies and use a sense of humor.

Get a Life

Too many parents try to live through their children. They want their children to accomplish the things they didn't accomplish in life—or they think their children should accomplish the exact same things they did. They don't honor the feelings and desires of their children as unique people. Kahlil Gibran says it so beautifully in his book, *The Prophet:*[6]

Your children are not your children.
They are the sons and daughters of Life's longing for itself.
They come through you but not from you,
And though they are with you yet they belong not to you.

You may give them your love but not your thoughts,
For they have their own thoughts.
You may house their bodies but not their souls,
For their souls dwell in the house of tomorrow, which you cannot visit, not even in your dreams.

6. Kahlil Gibran, *The Prophet* (New York: Alfred A. Knopf, 1963), 18–19.

You may strive to be like them, but seek not to make them like you.

For life goes not backward nor tarries with yesterday.

Getting a life means actively following your dreams while supporting your children in following their dreams. It does not mean neglecting your children or being permissive. When you have a full life of your own, you will have room to enjoy your children because you will not be depending on them for your fulfillment.

Take Small Steps

The road to success is one step at a time. If you set your sights too high, you may never start or you may feel discouraged if everything doesn't happen overnight. If you take small steps, you will move forward, and you and your children will all benefit.

PART 2

Positive Discipline Solutions from A to Z

Addictions

"How do I know if my child is addicted to drugs? What are the signs and what should I do if I suspect a problem? My children are in middle school, and I hear so much about drugs that I want to be prepared to help my children deal with the problems they may encounter."

Understanding Your Child, Yourself, and the Situation

An addiction is different from experimentation, occasional use, and perhaps even regular use of a substance. Children (or adults, for that matter) can become addicted to any number of substances—alcohol and drugs being only two. Your children may become addicted to sugar, television, reading, video games, or collecting baseball cards. These habits can become the substance of abuse. People are addicted when they plan their life around a substance and their relationship with that substance becomes more important than anything else. Young people may experiment or go through periods of time when they seem preoccupied with a substance, but this does not mean they are addicted. When adults allow fear to motivate their behavior (which seems pretty natural when drugs are involved), they tend to react instead of to be proactive, and they do things that inadvertently invite their children to have bigger problems. Learning to be proactive instead of reactive is the best approach to the problem of addiction.

Suggestions

1. Don't overreact. Don't lecture or punish. Don't search rooms. Don't become an enabler. The first step may be for you to simply sit down with your child and share your concerns and then ask your child what is going on.

2. If you suspect your child has a drug problem, seek professional help, whether from a treatment program, an Alcoholics Anonymous or Narcotics Anonymous group, a counselor, or a drug education specialist. Find a good Al-Anon[1] group for help with your own behavior. It's too hard to deal with drug problems alone, and there is no shame in asking for help for both you and your child.

3. Once the addiction has developed, treatment is usually required before you can begin to work effectively with an addict. You can love, care for, negotiate with, and extract all kinds of agreements from an addict; but as long as the substance is in charge, it has only one goal—to go on feeding itself. Starving the substance out is essential and should be done with professional guidance and help.

Planning Ahead to Prevent Future Problems

1. Use nonmedical solutions for physical ailments whenever possible. Many adults get hooked on tranquilizers, diet pills, and headache remedies. This is not providing a good model for children.

2. Pay attention to your own drug use. What kind of example are you setting? Do you pop a pill for everything or drink in front of your children? What messages are you giving your children about drugs?

3. Let your children feel their feelings instead of trying to fix everything for them. Are you giving your children a lot of drugs to take care of minor aches and pains? They may get the idea that drugs are a way to solve problems.

4. Talk to your children about the difference between doing things in moderation and going overboard. Get them involved in setting limits around the amount of television they watch, video games they play, sugar they eat, and sodas they drink. During a family meeting, plan together which TV programs to watch, and then stick to the plan instead of getting into the habit of having the TV on all the time. This will teach them the importance of having a well-thought-out plan that includes limits

---

1. You can reach Al-Anon by calling 800-344-2666.

so they will have this skill when they are presented with drug temptations.

5. When your children are young, do not use the television set as a baby-sitter, which teaches them to become passively dependent on external entertainment.

6. Give your children information about drugs. Giving information is very different from lecturing It is best to get them involved by taking them to the library to find information or reading together information that might be available from their school. Be sure this includes information about tobacco and nicotine. Most children do not understand how addictive nicotine is. Find people who are addicted who will share with your children how certain they were that they wouldn't get addicted when they started using a substance.

7. Talk regularly with your children, for example at the dinner table, asking them if anyone has offered them drugs or if they have thought about whether they would ever use drugs. Let them fill you in on what they are learning at school about drugs. Avoid lecturing and ordering. Be curious and do tell your kids what you think about drug use. Let them know that people often use drugs so they don't feel their feelings and it is important that we learn to listen to what our feelings are trying to tell us. Remember, though, that your children hear what you do more than what you say.

8. Ask your children what they would do if someone approached them with drugs. With younger children, it is especially important to role-play saying no. It helps if they have practiced this skill before they need to use it. Remind them that there are people who want to hurt children by getting them hooked on drugs. Let them know they can tell you or another grown-up if someone is trying to get them to do something they don't want to do.

9. Help your children explore the consequences of drug use through "what" and "how" questions. This invites them to use their own thinking abilities instead of resisting lectures. Ask questions such as: "What kind of life do you think people live when they are addicted to drugs?" "How do you think people become addicted?" "What reasons do you think people have for starting drugs in the first place?" "What do you want your life to be like?" Remember that these questions are not effective if children think you already have specific answers in mind. "What" and "how" questions are effective only when

you are truly curious about what your child thinks and are helping him explore his own thinking.

10. If you have a family history of drug dependency, tell your children about the possible dangers to them, as their risk of becoming addicted is increased with every family member who has had a problem.

11. Create the kind of relationship with your children in which they know they will not be punished when they talk to you about troubling issues. One way to do this is by validating their feelings and/or helping them explore their own solutions instead of getting them to dread your lectures.

12. Spend quality time with your children on a regular basis.

Life Skills Children Can Learn

Children can discover that they have a safe place to talk about their feelings, behaviors, and attitudes without being judged. Children can learn that it is okay to feel feelings instead of trying to make them go away with the use of external substances. Children can learn that it is possible to be-

Booster Thoughts

Mary announced to her mother that she had decided to get drunk at the eighth-grade graduation barbecue. Her mom took a big gulp to keep from overreacting. Then she proceeded to ask questions that invited Mary to explore her feelings and the consequences of her choice.

"Why did you decide that?" Mom asked in a truly curious manner.

Mary said, "The other kids do it, and it looks fun."

"What do people usually say about the kids who get drunk?"

Mary remembered, "They are usually called losers."

"How do you feel about your reputation for not drinking?"

It was obvious that Mary was already changing her own mind. "I kind of like it. Actually, my friends really respect me. I know they would be disappointed if I got drunk. I guess I won't after all."

Mom said, "I really admire the way you think things through and decide what is right for you."

come addicted if they don't practice moderation and that they can enjoy something without letting it run their lives.

Parenting Pointers

1. Know your family history, since it is the best predictor of potential for addiction. Share this history openly with your children, allowing for their level of maturity, and discuss their understanding of what this means to them. Advocate abstinence as a goal whenever possible and work on refusal and assertiveness skills and strategies.

2. Children who have accurate information and good feelings about themselves are less likely to become addicted to drugs, even though they may experiment. Make sure your children know your love for them is unconditional and that you are there to help if they have drug problems.

3. Watch for signs of abuse, including dramatic changes in behavior, drug paraphernalia around the house (do not search their rooms), loss of appetite, decline in school performance, frequent mood changes, and a desire to spend long hours alone and away from the family, as well as acting drunk or stoned.

Adoption

"At what age should I tell my child she is adopted, and is there any way to prevent being part of the latest craze of adopted children wanting to find their birth parents to find out who they really are?"

Understanding Your Child, Yourself, and the Situation

Your attitude about adoption has a great influence on your child. If you truly believe adoption is special, your child may also. Create closeness and trust through open communication and joint problem-solving so you can be aware of your child's beliefs. What happens in a child's life is not as important as the decisions he or she makes about it. For instance, some children think they are more loved because their adoptive parents picked them, while other children decide that parents are just saying that to make them feel better because they aren't good enough. Have faith that your relationship with your child will provide love and strength to surpass any mistaken beliefs he or she may create about being adopted.

Suggestions

1. Tell your child that he is adopted before he can comprehend its meaning. "We are so lucky that we could adopt you. We wanted you so much." By the time he understands

Booster Thoughts

"I hate you, Mummy. I wish you were dead. You aren't my real mother anyway. You're only my adopted mother." Six-year-old Patty clenches her fists, stamps her foot, and, through her tears, shouts these defiant words at her mother, who is hustling her off to bed.

Once Patty is stormily in bed, her mother talks things over tearfully with Patty's daddy. "I knew it," she complains. "I knew that the day would come when she would throw it up to us that she was adopted."

Fortunately Patty's father had a good memory about their birth son. "Don't you recall Nat when he was that age? He used to say he was going to get a different mother. And I even remember one spell he had when he thought he was adopted. I don't think you should take it too seriously, dear," he concluded. "I don't think it's just because Patty is adopted that she talks this way. I suspect that it's just the way children around this age talk when they get mad."[2]

---

2. From Frances L. Ilg and Louise Bates Ames, *The Gesell Institute's Child Behavior from Birth to Ten* (New York: Harper & Row, 1955), 330.

what adoption means, it will be old hat and may invoke a feeling of joy.

2. Don't take it too seriously when your child says, "I hate you. I wish I could find my real mother." Children who aren't adopted go through similar phases. They might say, "I hate you. I wish I had a different mother" (see *Angry Child*).

3. When a neighbor or school friend teases your child about being adopted, listen empathetically before using "what" and "how" questions to help your child process the experience: "What happened? How did that make you feel? What do you think about that? What do other kids get teased about?"

Planning Ahead to Prevent Future Problems

1. During a close moment, discuss possible problems before they become impor-

tant. "I've noticed there is a lot of publicity about adopted children wanting to find their birth parents. What do you think about that? Why do you think they would want to do that? What are your plans about that?" Just listen. Don't try to talk your child into or out of her thoughts, feelings, or plans.

2. Let your child know that you will support her if she ever wants to find her birth parents—that you will understand and not feel jealous or unappreciated. Keep albums, school papers, videos, and other memorabilia so that your child can share these with her birth parents if the situation arises.

3. Your child needs to know that her birth parents gave her up for adoption because of their personal situation, not because there is anything wrong with her. Tell her that you have a lot of compassion for her birth parents and that you are glad you have the opportunity to give her all the love she deserves.

Life Skills Children Can Learn

Adopted children can experience the love that lets them explore their feelings, thoughts, and conclusions about their origins. They can learn that upsetting events pass with time and the joy of life goes on.

Parenting Pointers

1. Wondering about birth parents is similar to fantasizing about having different parents (who are rich, or famous, or not so mean). This phase can pass when not taken too seriously.

2. If your child does take it seriously, remember that it is easier for a child to love two mothers or fathers than to feel he has to choose between them. Let your child know this. Also let him know you will be a sounding board if what he finds is disappointing.

3. Don't use adoption as an excuse or explanation if your child starts misbehaving.

Aggression

(See also *Angry Child*)

"My child loses his temper too quickly, picks on younger children and animals, refuses to cooperate at home or at school, and argues with me constantly. Everyone tells me he is an aggressive child, as if he has some kind of disease. Why does he act this way, and what can I do?"

Understanding Your Child, Yourself, and the Situation

Children aren't born aggressive, but they can become this way when no one asks their opinion or considers their needs.

When parents assume they know what is best for their children, they inadvertently may be inviting a lot of pent-up anger that comes out as aggressive behavior. If parents are aggressive, punitive, or controlling, children may decide unconsciously that this is the way to behave to accomplish things. Aggressive children may not have been taught how to ask for what they want or to have acceptable outlets for their feelings.

Suggestions

1. Instead of focusing on the behavior, try to understand the belief behind the behavior. Use your intuition to see if any of the following questions apply to your child: Does your child believe the only way he can get his needs met is by acting aggressively? Is he trying to punish someone he is angry with? Is he rebelling against parents who are too controlling? Does he believe acting aggressively is the way a person is supposed to act? Is he frustrated because he lacks skills for getting his needs met, and is he reacting with anger and violence? Does he feel dethroned by the birth of a new baby (see *Birth Order*)? Simply trying to modify the behavior will not solve problems of beliefs or other causes of aggression. The belief or the cause must be addressed.

2. Whenever possible, put all children in the same boat by using the expression "kids." Many aggressive children are just plain angry because they perceive an injustice being done to them when another sibling seems to get special treatment or consistently gets off the hook for trouble (see *Fighting, Siblings*).

3. If your child is hurting others with his aggressive behavior, let him know you realize he may be feeling hurt and upset about something but you're not sure what it is and wonder if he could let you know, as you aren't a mind reader. He may not be consciously aware of his troubling belief, so you might need to make some guesses. When you find out what is bothering your child, tell him it is okay to be upset and help him find another way to share his hurt feelings because it is not okay to hurt others.

4. Avoid reacting to aggression with aggression, which creates a power struggle and models the opposite of what you hope to achieve. Also avoid reinforcing aggression by giving in to it. Instead, acknowledge the need and then invite change by saying, "That sounds like it is important to you. When you are willing to approach me in a respectful way, I will consider it."

Booster Thoughts

A society's values are reflected in its heroes and pop culture idols. America, through its media, has elevated aggression to a high level of respectability. We pay an aggressive athlete millions of dollars a year, while we won't pay a decent salary to a teacher quietly trying to pass on civilization to the next generation.

The Teenage Mutant Ninja Turtles model aggression and dominance to small children. *The Simpsons* and *Married with Children* are classic models of dysfunctional families filled with aggression and disrespect. Through our modeling and attitudes, we can counteract these influences and show our children that mutual respect is preferable to aggression.

Planning Ahead to Prevent Future Problems

1. If you are using too much control or any kind of punishment, stop immediately. This does not mean you should act permissively. Find ways to help your child learn self-control and problem-solving skills.

2. Set up family meetings, limited choices, and joint problem-solving sessions so your children learn that their opinions matter and that they can solve problems. Teach your children to put their problems on the family-meeting agenda—both for a cooling-off period and to get help from the whole family.

3. Learn how to listen to feelings, and don't tell your children they shouldn't feel the way they do. Let children know that however they feel is just fine, and help them find behaviors that express their feelings in ways that don't hurt themselves or others. Have a punching bag; hammer, nails, and a board to pound into; or other nonhuman objects that are okay to hit. Redirect children to these objects when they are acting aggressively. After a cooling-off period, work on the first two items above.

4. Help your children design a cooling-off area and teach them that it helps sometimes to take time to calm down before trying to solve a problem (see "Positive Time-Out" in Part 1).

5. Take time for training your children to use words to express feelings and to ask for what they want.

6. If your children are allowed to play video games or to watch television programs that feature aggression, spend time discussing your feelings about aggression and listening to your child's ideas about what he or she is doing. With your child's input, limit the amount of time spent watching TV or playing video games (see *Television and Video Games*).

Life Skills Children Can Learn

Children can learn that what people believe influences how they feel and that how they feel is separate from what they do. Children can learn that their feelings are real and legitimate but that the behaviors that follow don't have to hurt themselves or others. They can learn appropriate methods for getting what they want and for solving problems. Children can learn they have choices as to how they behave and that there are people who care how they feel and care about what they want. They can learn that what they say is valued.

Parenting Pointers

1. There is a difference between aggression and assertion, and it is important to help children learn this difference. Teach children to ask for what they want; listen to their opinions. Show children how to get their needs met without putting someone else down.

2. Watch out for a double standard for girls and boys. Sometimes boys are excused for rude and hurtful behavior, or girls are discouraged from being outspoken and expressing their needs. It is equally important for boys and girls to know their feelings are okay and that behavior is separate from feelings.

Allowances

"Should I give my children allowances for doing their chores?"

Understanding Your Child, Yourself, and the Situation

Allowances give children an opportunity to learn many valuable lessons about money. The amount given depends on your budget and their needs. If the money is used for punishment or reward, the lessons will be negative. This creates an arena for power struggles, revenge, and manipulation. The lessons are positive when children are given allowances so that they can learn life skills. Chores are a separate issue and should not be connected to an allowance (see *Chores, Age-Appropriate* and *Chores, Getting Cooperation*).

Suggestions

1. Do not rescue your children when they run out of money. Learn to say no with dignity and respect when they try to con you into rescuing them after they make mistakes with their money.

2. Be empathetic without trying to fix things. You might say, "I'm sure you feel disappointed that you don't have enough money left to go to the game."

3. Offer your services as a budgeting consultant, but do not give advice unless asked.

4. Help them explore what happened, what caused it to happen, what they learned from it, and how they will use this information in the future. This is effective only if they agree to explore and only if you are truly curious about the perceptions of your children. It is not effective to try disguising a lecture in the name of exploration.

5. It is okay to be reasonable and flexible. When children run out of money, you can offer them a loan and discuss the terms of how they will pay it back. (This is not the same as rescuing.) Show them how to set up a payment plan and agree together on an amount you can deduct from their allowance. Do not make the amount so high your child won't be able to manage during the week. Another possibility is to make a list of special jobs to earn money for extra items or to help pay back their loan. Don't make new loans until the first loan is repaid.

Planning Ahead to Prevent Future Problems

1. During family meetings, have periodic discussions about money in which you share some of your mistakes with money and what you learned (without lecturing or moralizing). Allow others to do the same. Create a sense of fun so everyone can laugh while they learn.

2. For children aged two to four, give your children ten pennies, a nickel, a dime, and a piggy bank. Each year, add a few more pennies, nickels, dimes, and even quarters. They like putting money in the piggy bank and are starting a saving habit before they know it.

3. For children aged four to six, take your child and the piggy bank to a big bank and open a savings account. Every one to three months, take your child to the bank to make a deposit. It can be fun to watch the balance grow in the bank book. Parents might even get excited about developing the saving habit themselves, if they haven't already done so.

4. At ages four to six, you might want to suggest two piggy banks: one for the savings account and one to save for items on a wish list.

5. Help your children start a wish list of things they would like to save money for.

Booster Thoughts

One father says, "When my daughter rushes up to me and says, 'Dad, I need some designer jeans,' I have learned to say, 'Listen, honey, I got into this business to cover your body, not decorate it, and I can do that for $25 to $30 at many department stores. What you *need* is modesty and what you *want* is style. The difference will require some contribution on your part because I have a lot of other pressures and issues concerning finances to deal with.'"

There was a time in America when children wore jeans because parents were poor—now parents are poor because children wear jeans.[3]

The father of a six-year-old noticed that money was missing from his wallet and dresser top. His six-year-old brought in a container filled with money and said she found it. The father was very upset and wondered why his daughter would be "stealing" from him.

Upon further discussion, it was discovered that the parents told their daughter she could get a new bicycle when she earned $30 toward the purchase. Her weekly allowance was fifty cents, and it didn't take her long to figure out that she would have to wait forever for the bike. Using her ingenuity, she figured out a way to get the bike quicker.

Not wanting to start their six-year-old on a life of crime, the parents decided to raise her allowance to $2 a week. They told her that if she put half of her allowance away each week for the bike, they would match it. Then they sat down with a calendar and showed her how long it would take to save $30. They said that if she didn't want to wait that long, she could do special jobs for pay, which they posted on a list in the kitchen. Within a month, their industrious child had saved the $30 and the "stealing" never occurred again.

3. From H. Stephen Glenn and Jane Nelsen, *Raising Self-Reliant Children in a Self-Indulgent World* (Rocklin: CA, Prima Publishing, 1989), 133.

Whenever you are shopping and they say, "Can I have this?" you can say, "Would you like to add this to your wish list and save your money for it?" (They seldom want the item enough to save their money for it, but they want it enough for you to spend *your* money right now.) You can even offer to pay half if they will save half. It is amazing how many shopping hassles this stops when you are kind and firm in your offer.

6. For children aged six to fourteen, schedule a planning session with your child to decide together how much money he needs and how it should be allocated for savings, weekly needs (such as lunches), and fun. You might also encourage your child to save money to give to community organizations and those in need.

7. Set up guidelines, such as, "Allowances will be given only once a week during family-meeting time. If you run out before then, you have an opportunity to learn what that feels like and what to do about it, such as go without or find a job to earn extra money."

8. Set up periodic times (once a year or every six months) when an allowance can be raised based on a child's thoughtful presentation of greater need. Some families raise the allowance of all the children on every child's birthday.

9. For teens aged fourteen to eighteen, add a clothing allowance so teenagers can learn how to plan. (Children who learn to handle money from an early age can handle a clothing allowance much sooner. In the beginning, instead of giving them money, tell them the total amount they can spend on clothing, and then deduct their purchases from a running total that you keep.) They quickly find out that if they spend too much on a few items of clothing, they won't have enough left for an adequate wardrobe. The clothing allowance can be given monthly, quarterly, or twice a year.

Life Skills Children Can Learn

Children can learn that they can develop their judgment skills by making good or poor decisions about money and learning from the consequences of their choices without punishment or humiliation. They can learn to budget, a skill they'll use all their lives.

Parenting Pointers

1. Using money for punishment or reward is a short-term solution. Giving allowances

as an opportunity to teach children about money is long-range parenting that leaves children with life skills.

2. Keeping long-range parenting goals in mind, it is best to be kind and firm at the same time.

Angry Child

"My child seems so angry all the time. She hits her sister, argues with me, kicks and throws her toys around, and is generally in a bad mood. Even her teacher complains about her attitude. What can you do with an angry child?"

Understanding Your Child, Yourself, and the Situation

There is a difference between experiencing a feeling and displaying emotions, such as a temper tantrum. Anger usually follows the belief that we can't get what we want or that we are powerless in a situation. It can also be a cover-up for hurt feelings. Children who seem angry may be frustrated with their parents, other children, themselves, life, or other people who are angry with them. Children usually have good reasons for feeling angry, even if they don't know what those reasons are. When children are bossed and controlled and have no choices, they will probably feel angry. Children who are overprotected often feel angry. If adults abuse children either physically or verbally, children will feel angry. Parents often respond to anger with more control and intimidation, making the situation worse. If you or your child feels angry, there may be a power struggle going on, and it is important to disengage from the power contest and work for cooperation.

Suggestions

1. Say to your child, "You're really angry. It's okay to feel angry, but can you tell me in words instead of actions who or what you are angry with?" Wait for the child's response and listen with interest instead of saying, "You shouldn't be angry."

2. Sometimes children can't identify their feelings when they are upset. Let your child know it is okay to wait a while and to talk with you as soon as he is ready.

3. You can help your child defuse her anger by finding out (perhaps through guessing) what she wants and helping her obtain it, such as, "You're angry because your sister gets to stay up later and you wish you could, too. When you are her age, you'll be able to stay up as late as she does."

4. Don't choose sides when your children fight. Tell them, "Kids, I see you are having a hard time working this out. You can take

Booster Thoughts

Often, we are unaware of how we are upsetting our children and are treating them disrespectfully. They get angry when that happens. Usually, if we ask our children what they are angry about and are willing to listen, they'll tell us.

A young man of fifteen came to a counseling appointment with his mother. She was concerned about his anger problem. He would soon be driving, and his mother was afraid that if he didn't get some help, he might take it out on other drivers once behind the wheel.

The counselor asked him what he was angry about. He said that when he agrees to do a job for his mother, she takes it back and does it herself. His mother explained that she does this because it doesn't look like he is going to do it.

Her son exploded, pounding his fists on the table and screaming, "You never trust me! I told you I would do the job! Why can't you believe me?"

His mother was amazed at the intensity of her son's rage over what to her was an insignificant problem. When she realized how upset he was, she asked, "How can we work this out so we both feel good? I'm not willing to let the job go undone, and you don't want me to nag."

The counselor suggested they have a nonverbal signal between them if the mother was wondering if the son was going to remember his chore. The son said it would be okay if his mother asked him if he was still planning to do what he agreed to—just not to do the chore for him.

some time to cool off and try again later, or you can both finish this fight somewhere else, or you can work it out here, but I'm not taking sides" (see *Fighting, Siblings*).

5. If you have children who argue, try letting them have the last word or hugging them instead of arguing back. Ask your children for their opinions instead of telling them what to do. When you recognize a power struggle, stop and say, "I don't want to control you, but I would appreciate your help. Let's see what we can work out after we calm down."

Planning Ahead to Prevent Future Problems

1. Set up family meetings so your children know there is a place and time each week where they can talk about the things that bother them, be listened to, and solve problems if needed.

2. Use limited choices with younger children instead of telling them what to do.

3. Set up a routine so that the routine is the boss and not you. Children respond better to "It's time for dinner" than "I want you to come to the table now." Children feel even more empowered when you ask them, "What is next on our dinnertime (bedtime, morning) routine chart?"

4. When your child is in a good mood, mention that you notice she is often angry and ask for her help to think of a way she could show her anger that won't hurt anyone. Suggest a pillow she can punch or listening to a tape of her favorite music or finding a special cooling-off place. For older children, suggest they write down what they are angry about or draw a picture of their anger.

5. If you are a single parent, avoid any derogatory comments about your children's other parent. Do not expect your children to take the place of another adult (see *Divorce* and *Single Parent*).

6. Don't be afraid of your own anger. Anger is an important feeling that warns you of possible abuse—physical and emotional. Learn to say, "I'm angry." You provide a good model for your children when you express those feelings in words instead of with displays of temper.

7. Model respectful ways for dealing with your own anger. Use emotional honesty: "I feel _____ about _____ because _____ and I would like _____." Model taking time out until you can calm down and handle your anger in respectful ways.

8. Model using your anger as a motivator to solve a problem in respectful ways.

Life Skills Children Can Learn

Children can learn that what they feel is different from what they do—that it is okay to feel angry, but it is not okay to hurt others or to act disrespectfully. Children can learn that they can have power and control over themselves and their lives. No one enjoys feeling powerless, and children prefer to know how they can contribute and succeed without having to fight for their needs.

Parenting Pointers

1. Anger may be a sign that your children see themselves as powerless and out of control. They may think you are trying to run their lives instead of empowering them to be capable and successful. Instead of trying to stop children from expressing their anger, talk with them about ways they are

feeling frustrated and how they might respond differently.

2. Look for places you may be inviting anger. Are you sticking your nose in your children's business, such as lecturing about schoolwork, friends, clothing, and so on? Do you nag your children instead of setting up routines and using follow-through?

Attention Deficit Hyperactivity Disorder[4]

"Someone at the school has suggested my child might have attention deficit hyperactivity disorder. They are complaining that he gets up and down from his seat and won't pay attention. I notice the same problem at home. He has trouble concentrating and finishing things he starts. How can I tell if this is due to AD/HD or if he simply has a more active temperament than some children?"

Understanding Your Child, Yourself, and the Situation

Most parents want their child to be a good child (see *The "Good Child"*). However, children have their own developmental needs, abilities, and temperaments.[5] When there is a big gap between adult expectations and a child's abilities, parents and teachers often become frustrated, discouraged, and stressed and resort to more authoritarian or permissive approaches. This is much more likely if the adults do not understand that the child is struggling with a difference and is not intentionally causing trouble or making a "choice." For the most effective results with children of all abilities and temperaments, it is critical to use nonpunitive Positive Discipline tools. When children rebel against authoritarian methods or become manipulative in response to permissive methods, their behavior may be similar to some AD/HD symptoms.

Attention deficit hyperactivity disorder (AD/HD or ADD) refers to a neurological disability characterized by a developmentally inappropriate lack of control in three

---

4. Many thanks to Pamela LeBlanc, M.A., parent educator, AD/HD consultant in private practice in Santa Rosa, California, and mother of two AD/HD children, for her insights and help with this section.

5. For information on temperament, see Jane Nelsen, Cheryl Erwin, and Roslyn Duffy, *Positive Discipline: The First Three Years* (Rocklin, CA: Prima Publishing, 1998) and Jane Nelsen, Cheryl Erwin, and Roslyn Duffy, *Positive Discipline for Preschoolers* (Rocklin, CA: Prima Publishing, 1998).

areas: attention, impulsivity, and activity level. AD/HD is basically a protein metabolism problem, and when it is treated as such, many problems quickly fall into place. The severity varies from mild and manageable to severe and disabling. These children tend to share the following characteristics: usually boys, with blond or red hair and blue eyes; may have had birth problems; hyper as a baby; feeding, crying, and sleeping problems in the first four months; excessive rocking, head banging, and climbing out of cribs; three or more ear infections before age two; and reckless, aggressive, destructive, incorrigible, and overactive behavior as a toddler. These children are picky eaters and crave sugar, cheese, and salty foods, all having to do with the fact that their brains are craving trace minerals, amino acids, and more fuel. There are bedtime hassles and sleep disturbances, including bed-wetting, sleep talking, night terrors, teeth grinding, and excessive thirst, with preoccupied and careless behavior in the morning. Because of their tendency to speak constantly without thinking, to fidget and wiggle and bounce around, and to make strange noises, they are often very unpopular children both at home and at school.[6]

To help a child with attention deficit hyperactivity disorder to succeed, parents need to have well-developed Positive Discipline skills. They also need accurate information and effective tools for the specific challenges presented by their unique child.[7]

Suggestions

1. Avoid labeling your child because the label can become a self-fulfilling prophecy and you may be missing something else that is really going on with your child. If you believe your child is having difficulties, get a complete evaluation by a professional who is familiar with AD/HD and related concerns to identify the areas of difficulty and the most appropriate solutions.

2. Give as much positive input as possible to help compensate for the constant stream of frustration and discouragement. Based on his research, AD/HD expert John Taylor recommends that you tell your child the following: "There is nothing wrong with you except your body doesn't make enough of certain chemicals. If it did, you would be calm, your IQ would go up,

6. The list of characteristics was given by John Taylor, Ph.D., at a workshop called "Mega-Answers to AD/HD" in Santa Rosa, California, in June 1998. Out of twenty parents who volunteered to be polled about their children with this diagnosis, more than 85 percent of them strongly agreed that the characteristics were present in their children diagnosed with AD/HD. Their agreement confirmed the research that Dr. Taylor has conducted for over two decades.

7. More information on attention deficit disorder can be found in John F. Taylor, *Helping Your Hyperactive or Attention Deficit Child* (Rocklin, CA: Prima Publishing, 1990).

you'd understand things better, and you'd stop and think before you do things."

Make special time a priority and find ways to truly enjoy your child during this time. Be sure to notice and celebrate successes of any size, and encourage your child's areas of interest.

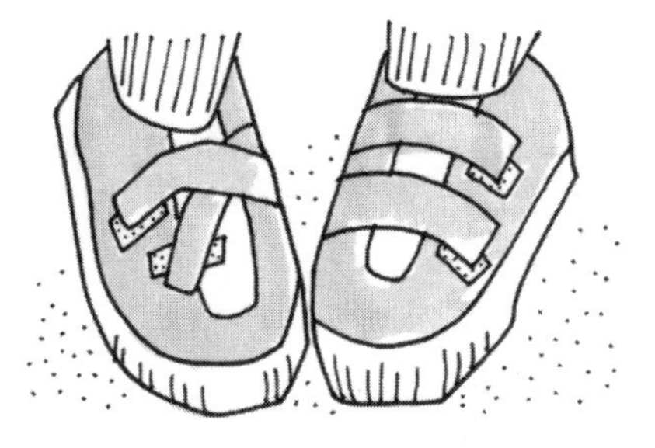

3. Be willing to help your child according to his needs, based on what your child actually does as opposed to what may be expected for his age group or intelligence level. If your child can't learn to tie a shoe in kindergarten, use Velcro until his fingers are ready, even if it takes longer than everyone else.

4. Use computers so your child can learn at her own pace and bypass the writing difficulties that are common.

5. Give instructions one at a time and limit the number of words you use. For a child who is easily distracted, anything more than five to ten words at a time is too many. Make sure you have the child's complete attention and say things only once. When the child is distracted, use simple and respectful cues like a tap on a table, a hand on a shoulder, or a one-word reminder to regain focus. Touch is especially helpful with children who are diagnosed with AD/HD to help gain their attention.

6. Observe your children at play to see how they prefer learning. Are they physically active? Do they prefer touch? Do they learn in short attention bursts? Use that information to create activities that emphasize your children's strengths or preferences.

7. Sometimes drug therapy may be beneficial, but too often drugs are prescribed too quickly without trying other alternatives first. Pay attention to ways that you may be invalidating the uniqueness of your child or putting pressure on him to perform according to your standards instead of his ability. If the other suggestions in this section are not working, you may wish to proceed with solutions that affect the biochemistry of the brain. The Feingold diet is effective for 65 percent of children diagnosed with AD/HD. The most effective biochemical intervention, according to recent research by Dr. John Taylor and others, is the use of blue-green algae.

8. While some children do better as they get into their teens, many have great difficulty in junior and senior high school. Help your child learn strategies to keep herself on track. Encourage her to use resources at school and in the community, like tutors and study hall. Listen to her concerns about problem teachers and subjects and encourage her to research alternatives for those classes, including independent study. Be an

Booster Thoughts

One of our authors, Stephen Glenn, generally sleeps four hours a night and has done so since he was born. His mother assumed that he should sleep ten hours a night during his childhood. Lying in a dark room for five hours nightly, waiting for sleep to come, was excruciating. An article in *Reader's Digest* came to the rescue. Steve's mother read that many people didn't need that much sleep and that some people, such as Thomas Edison and Albert Einstein, in didn't sleep or hold still for days when their minds were excited about a discovery or project. From that point on, Steve's parents said, "We need you to go to your room now so we can rest." They filled Steve's room with projects and didn't worry about whether or not Steve got in bed. Steve learned that his most creative time was while other people were asleep.

advocate for your child. Your child's self-esteem and your relationship with her is more important than any grade.

Planning Ahead to Prevent Future Problems

1. To help children control their attention and behavior, provide extra structure for time and space. Use simple and consistent routines you create with your child. Help your child learn how to organize a place for everything, close to where items are needed. Have an area near the door for items such as shoes, coats, backpacks, and lunches. Help children use binders, lists, and notes to keep information organized. Teach about time management with calendars, clocks, and timers. Provide special equipment like short, fat, bottom-heavy cups filled halfway to minimize spills.

2. Build your children's ability to concentrate by getting them into some kind of physical training that requires concentration, remembering sequences of moves, and physical and mental discipline (it may be even better to do these activities with them). Activities include aerobics, dance, martial arts, and sports. Help your child find activities he enjoys and can do well.

3. Explore alternative learning opportunities at the school. Keep track of the teach-

ers that your children do well with and be prepared to discuss this with the school. The most helpful teachers are caring and flexible while being well organized. Smaller classes and schools will also improve success. If you find that the teacher or school is not willing or able to meet your child's needs, be prepared to do whatever is necessary to protect your child from being punished for her difference.

4. Get your children involved in deciding what they should do at school when problems occur. Call a parent-teacher-child meeting to work together on nonpunitive solutions. Some children decide it is best if they can walk around the room a few times and then return to their seats without getting in trouble. Others may need a quiet corner where they can go to spend more time on a task. Another method that works well is to ask the child to turn down his "energy dial" from ten to three. Some children will make a deal to squirm with their hand and give the teacher the rest of their attention or to use a large plastic comb to comb out the squirmies.

5. Prioritize your time and energy. An activity schedule that is too full or that doesn't allow for reasonable routines will soon lead to disaster.

Life Skills Children Can Learn

Children can learn that they have adults who will consider their individual needs and will help them help themselves so they have some sense of control over their lives. Instead of feeling like a victim of their behavior, they have a plan for controlling it. It's okay to be a unique individual.

Parenting Pointers

1. Make sure you don't ignore yourself or other children by focusing all your time and energy on one child. Take time for yourself and spend special time with the other members of your family.

2. Get support. If you have a child with AD/HD, the job can easily become overwhelming. Ask for help and share the load with others who may be available. Get in touch with other parents and share ideas, resources, and understanding. Prepare yourself for controversy and misunderstanding and don't let it discourage you. C.H.A.D.D. is a great resource.[8]

3. By adulthood, most children with AD/HD will experience a significant reduction of symptoms. When the hormones change at puberty, it may alter the way the brain works, so take the long view, give your child a chance, and wait for puberty.

---

8. You can contact C.H.A.D.D. at 499 Northwest 70th Avenue, Suite 109, Plantation, FL 33317, 954-587-3700.

Baby-Sitters and Child Care

"My child is five years old and has never been to a baby-sitter. My friends are putting pressure on me to use a sitter. They say that I'm doing him a disservice by not giving him the opportunity to get used to being with people other than his parents. I think my child will feel more secure if he gets to spend his early childhood years with me."

Understanding Your Child, Yourself, and the Situation

We believe it is beneficial for you to be away from your children periodically and it is beneficial for your children to be away from you occasionally. Even though it is natural at some ages for children to experience separation anxiety at leaving their parents, this anxiety goes away when they practice separation for short periods of time. Children develop courage and self-reliance when they learn that they can handle the separation. Overprotection may prevent valuable learning. Parenting a child, especially an infant, can be extremely draining. One way to "fill your cup back up" is to take time for yourself away from your child and to take time as a couple without any children around.

Suggestions

1. Begin with small steps with a newborn. The first step is for the child to be home with the other parent or a relative while you take a few hours off.

2. By the time your child is a month old, set up two-hour visits with a friend or relative at his or her place one or two afternoons a week. Your child will be fine. Bring his favorite blanket and stuffed animal and give yourself a break. Inform the person about your child's habits and needs in detail, and bring any special equipment that is needed for your child to be safe and content. Make sure the home is babyproofed or childproofed instead of assuming that your friend or relative remembers what is needed for a child in this age group.

3. Find neighbors or friends who are willing to swap child care.

4. Some working parents start their children in infant child care by the time they are three months old. Choose a place where the ratio of children to adults is low. Also, look for a place where there are toddlers as well as infants. Babies love to watch older children, and toddlers like to fuss over babies. Insist on visiting the place in person and spend time watching to see how things are done. You have every right

Booster Thoughts

Mrs. Tremonton wanted to find child care for her three-year-old only child. She had a list of qualities for a good child care center, such as one adult per ten children, developmentally appropriate activities, loving staff people, and no punishment. She found three centers that met her requirements according to their written philosophy. She visited each center with her child for a few hours. One of the centers required children to sit still during story time for a longer time than was developmentally appropriate for some children—namely, hers. Her son was not happy when that staff acted as though he, and not the center's inappropriate expectation, was the problem.

Another center was teaching math and reading to three- and four-year-olds—a policy that did not fit her requirements. Her son had a wonderful time at the third center. The staff was cheery and loving. Mrs. Tremonton observed that the staff kindly and firmly helped children solve problems—sometimes redirecting them to another activity if they were having trouble in one area. They did not require tasks that were developmentally inappropriate, yet they had many activities that kept her son enthralled for the three hours they were there.

Mrs. Tremonton was glad she had spent time in the centers with her son. She had taken the time to experience what her son would experience. She felt confident that her child would thrive in this environment.

to expect the care provider to follow standards that meet your approval. Give yourself plenty of time to find a place that will be to your liking, as it may take several weeks to make the right match for you and your child. Even if a place is recommended by someone you know, it might not be the best place for your unique circumstances and needs.[9]

5. Our experience has been that thirteen- and fourteen-year-old teenagers can be

---

9. Jane Nelsen, Cheryl Erwin, and Roslyn Duffy, *Positive Discipline for Preschoolers* (Rocklin, CA: Prima Publishing, 1998).

excellent baby-sitters. They are usually more interested in the children than in the opposite sex. Many of them have taken Red Cross child care courses and have a certificate of completion. Take the time to get several references regarding anyone you hire to take care of your children—even teenagers. Let the person watch your child while you are home doing other things so that you can be available for questions as well as giving feedback about how you like things handled. Put your wishes in writing before you leave for the first time so your child care provider can refer to a list if something is forgotten.

6. Set guidelines for teenage baby-sitters: no phone calls from friends until the kids are sleeping; spend time playing and reading with the children; and clean up any messes. You should be clear about where you can be reached and what time you will be home. Leave numbers for the sitter in case of emergencies or ask if the sitter's parents are home and are willing to come over to help out or be available by phone if needed for consultation to the teen.

7. Have a bag of special games and toys that you bring out only when the baby-sitter arrives. Ask baby-sitters if they have any games, toys, or books that would be a change for your children.

8. When children cling or cry, have faith in them that they can handle this "crisis." Children are usually fine soon after parents leave—especially when the parent gently detaches and leaves with confidence.

Planning Ahead to Prevent Future Problems

1. Ask your friends, neighbors, church members, and school staff who they use for baby-sitters. Try prospective baby-sitters while you are home. They can play with the baby or child while you take a bath, do a chore, or read a book. This way, you can observe the interaction between your children and the sitter.

2. Many young families get together in the neighborhood or at church or preschool and form baby-sitting co-ops, taking turns watching each other's children.

3. Get kids aged four and older involved in planning what they will do with the baby-sitter: what games they want to play, what books they want to read, perhaps to have a popcorn party or bake cookies. Agree on a bedtime and let them discuss or role-play how they will handle bedtime.

Life Skills Children Can Learn

Children can learn that their parents like to spend some time away from them and that it doesn't mean the parents don't love them. They can learn to enjoy themselves even when separated from their parents and that manipulation doesn't cut it at home.

Parenting Pointers

1. If your children complain about the baby-sitter or act afraid to go to child care, do some investigating or switch sitters to see how they react. There are some people and places that aren't a good match for your kids, and it's okay to change. Make sure your sitters know that it is *never* okay to use physical violence to discipline your child. This means no spanking, hitting, slapping, arm squeezing, or any other form of physical disrespect to your child. If your children complain about the sitter hitting them, get a new sitter.

2. If you are a working parent and need extended child care, make sure you find a place where the kids are fed, have activities to do, are rested, and aren't just plunked in front of a television. Perhaps your workplace has child care, which would be preferable for nursing mothers or parents who would like to be able to visit their child during the workday.

3. While driving to or from child care, use the time in the car to visit with your kids, ask about their day, and enjoy them. When you get home, take time to be with the kids instead of immediately beginning chores.

4. The rule of thumb for choosing a babysitter is your reaction to the person and your kids' feelings about the person, not whether the person is male or female. People of either sex can be good child care providers if they are respectful of themselves and the child. Use local agencies that license child care providers if you are unsure who to hire. Ask for references and check them.

5. The child care provider's main job is to be with the children, not clean your home or do the dishes. If your kids are happy, don't make a fuss over a few messes.

Bedtime Hassles

"Our kids drive us crazy every night. They know it's time for bed, but they want another drink of water, one more story, the light on, the shades down, then the shades up. They keep us busy for an hour, making extra trips to the bathroom, and then scream like crazy when we finally refuse to come to their room one more time. The last straw happened the other night, when our eight-year-old cried because he couldn't stay up as late as our ten-year-old."

Understanding Your Child, Yourself, and the Situation

There isn't a kid who doesn't try to extend bedtime at least once in a while. Wanting to belong and be part of the action is a human need. Serious bedtime problems, however, are most often created by parents. The more families establish routines, the more they experience organization and order. Kids function best when they have a routine and a sense of order. It's important for them to have input but not to run the family. Parents who let kids work them like trained circus animals at night are clearly letting the kids call the shots.

Suggestions

1. Be available during the bedtime routine (see "Planning Ahead to Prevent Future Problems," item 1 below) instead of trying to do ten other things. One reason children seek more attention is that they haven't received a good dose of your full attention.

2. Once you have given your undivided attention for at least twenty to thirty minutes of bedtime routine, stick to the allotted time for the routine to end with confidence. Your children know when you say what you mean and when you mean what you say. They know when there is room for argument and when there is not.

3. After your child is in bed, refuse to play the game. If she leaves her room, gently take her by the hand and kindly and firmly return her to her room. Use no words. Actions speak louder than words and don't leave room for argument. You may need to repeat this action several times before children learn that you mean what you say and will follow through with kind and firm action. If they come to your bed in the middle of the night, take them gently and quietly back to their bed, give them a kiss, and walk back to your room. Do this as many times as you need to until your children know that your bed is for you (see "Parenting Pointers," item 3).

4. If your children have developed the habit of manipulation, it may take three to five nights of kindness and firmness (returning them to their beds, without words) before they learn they can trust you to mean what you say. Children feel more secure with parents who are kind and firm than with parents who can be manipulated.

5. Sit down with your children and admit your mistake. Tell them that you have allowed them to form some bedtime habits that aren't good for them or for you. This is a good time to start teaching them that mistakes are wonderful opportunities to learn, so now you can learn together how to solve the problem.

6. Some parents put locks on the outside of their children's doors to keep them in their rooms. This is dangerous and disrespectful. Keep taking your child back to her room. If you remain kind and firm, it probably won't require more than ten to twenty trips the first night. Remember that weaning has never been easy for the "weaner" or the "weanee" but is necessary for both to reach interdependence.

Planning Ahead to Prevent Future Problems

1. Set up the bedtime routine during the day. Let the kids help you make a list of all the things that need to be done before they go to bed (pajamas on, teeth brushed, items picked up off the floor, bathroom cleaned, homework done, clothes chosen for the next day). Working backward from bedtime, figure out how much time is needed and what time the kids need to start to complete all tasks on time. Help them make charts of the things to be done. Small kids enjoy finding pictures in magazines to represent the things they need to do. The charts can be posted on the doors of their rooms.

2. When it is time to begin the routine, tell the kids, "It's time for bed" instead of "You have to go to bed." Encourage involvement by asking questions that involve the children, such as, "What is the first thing we need to do to get ready for bed?" Or offer limited choices, such as, "Do you want to choose a story or do you want me to?"

3. Some kids find it helpful to play "Beat the Clock" at bedtime. Set a timer for the agreed-upon time, and let the kids scamper around getting everything done before the timer goes off.

4. Let the kids know that you will be available for story time ten minutes before bedtime. If they have completed their tasks, there will be time for a story; if they haven't, there is time for a tickle and a kiss, but the story has to wait until the next day.

5. For kids who think it's unfair that an older sibling stays up later, let them know it's okay to be upset but it's not okay to stay up later.

6. As the kids get a little older, involve them in discussing bedtime and give them a limited choice, such as, "You can decide if you would like to go to bed at 7:15 or 7:30."

7. As they get even older, let them pick any bedtime they like, as long as the adults have "quiet, no-kid time" from 9 P.M. on. Offer kids a chance to stay up a little later on Fridays and Saturdays.

8. Let kids know that bedtime means time to go to their rooms, not necessarily time to go to sleep. Kids are different, and some may like to play or read before they fall asleep. If they aren't bothering anyone else, let them fall asleep when they're ready. Usually, if kids can fall asleep when they like, they won't fight parents as much about what time they go to bed.

9. Many parents struggle over bedtime because they are afraid their children will be tired and crabby the next day if they don't get enough sleep. Treat bedtime as a separate issue. If your children are tired and crabby, you can ask them to be tired and crabby in their rooms. They may even take a nap. Earlier bedtimes are not the solution to irritable kids, unless they decide that

Booster Thoughts

One parent relates: "Our three-year-old continually came out of her room. We walked her back, and she kicked and screamed for an hour the first night until she fell asleep exhausted in her doorway. The second night she cried for half an hour. The next three nights this routine lasted ten minutes. After that, bedtime became a fun time for us all with a pleasant routine filled with hugs, tickles, stories, and cooperation."

Another father found bedtime hassles ceased when he asked two questions while tucking his children in bed at night: "What is the saddest thing that happened today?" "What is the happiest thing that happened today?" After each question, he would listen carefully and then would share his own saddest and happiest moments of the day. This seldom took longer than two or three minutes with each child, although sometimes more time would be required. He said, "I was amazed at how much my children told me when I took the time to ask and to listen. The closeness we felt during these times seemed to help them settle down and be ready for sleep."

would help. You might ask, "What do you think would solve the problem when you get tired and crabby?"

Life Skills Children Can Learn

Children can learn self-reliance instead of manipulation skills or dependence on someone else to help them perform a natural bodily function. They learn to respect their parents' need for time alone or time together without children around. They learn that their parents will treat them with respect but will not become involved in their manipulation efforts. Children can learn that they don't always get what they want, that it is okay to feel upset about it, and that they can still survive.

Parenting Pointers

1. It is better to teach children to listen to their inner voices about when they are tired than to insist that you know when they are ready to go to sleep. It is also respectful to yourself to insist on a time the

kids go to their rooms even if they don't go to sleep so you can have some time to yourself.

2. Some parents believe they are doing the loving thing by capitulating to the unreasonable demands of children. They are not thinking about the long-range effects of what this teaches children. None of us always gets what we want. Adults complain. Babies and toddlers cry. We all learn that we can still survive and even be happy. It is not respectful to children to give them the impression that they can always have what they want. Since you are giving your children lots of love during the bedtime routine and at other times during the day, they will not be traumatized by learning that they can go to sleep by themselves. The opposite is true: They will learn the skills of capability and self-reliance.

3. It's fun to let your children snuggle in bed with you on weekend mornings, and we would encourage having a special time each week that your kids can hop in your bed for wholesome family fun time. Many parents allow their children to sleep in bed with them as a regular occurrence. There are some organizations that support the "family bed." Others believe this is disrespectful to children because it may convey the message that children are the center of the universe and that they are not capable of falling asleep on their own. Instead of teaching self-reliance, it may teach children manipulation skills and dependency.

Extensive research by Richard Ferber, M.D.,[10] concluded that children need a place of their own to sleep, whether it is their own bed or a room that is separate from the parents. In this way, the child learns self-soothing and other valuable lessons: "I can handle being in my own space and I am not the center of the universe. I am an important member of my family, but my parents are also important and need time for rest and rejuvenation."

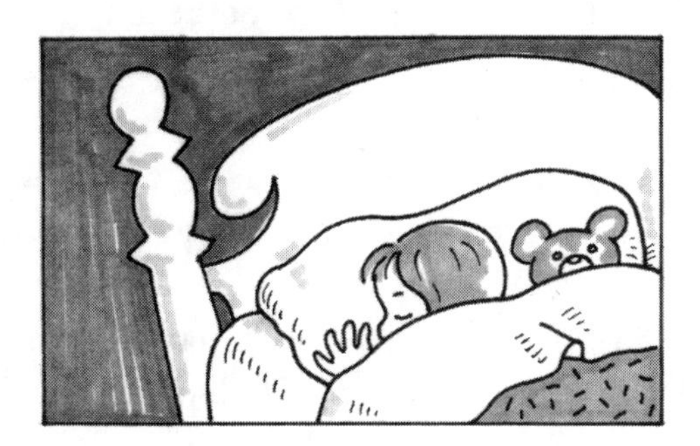

Parents need courage and skills to follow a plan of their choice instead of feeling manipulated by children into a predicament that is not their choice.

10. Richard Ferber, M.D., *Solve Your Child's Sleep Problems* (New York: Simon and Schuster, 1986).

Bed-Wetting

(See also *Toilet Training*)

"My eight-year-old boy still wets the bed. I've heard of all kinds of remedies, from waking him up several times a night to getting a sheet that sounds an alarm. They all sound like a hassle for me or a frightening and intimidating experience for him. Any suggestions?"

Understanding Your Child, Yourself, and the Situation

There are many reasons for bed-wetting. Bed-wetting can be the result of a developmental issue, a physical condition, a sign the child is being sexually or physically abused, or it can be for any of the four mistaken goals of misbehavior (see Part 1). A child may unconsciously choose a mistaken goal when she experiences some kind of stress, such as a new baby in the house or moving to a new location. The first thing to do is have a medical checkup to see if the problem is physical or developmental. If you suspect abuse, read the *Sexual Abuse* entry for more information.

Suggestions

1. Take a look at what you might be doing to create the need for undue attention, power struggles, revenge cycles, or helplessness. Many parents of bed wetters create this problem by nagging, reminding, coaxing, and trying to control the child's bladder. Stop! Instead, spend special time with your child. Get him involved in family meetings to solve problems, share feelings, and deal with hurt feelings. Give him meaningful jobs to enhance his sense of belonging and contribution.

2. If your family is going through a change that might create stress, such as the birth of a baby, moving, or a new job, spend extra time with your child to increase her sense of belonging and significance. The bed-wetting will stop when she feels secure.

3. Decide what you will do instead of trying to control what your child does. You might want to cover the mattress with a plastic sheet. You might want to make sleeping bags out of old sheets that are easy to throw in the washing machine. You may choose to stay out of his room because you can't stand the smell. Whatever you do, do it with dignity and respect.

4. Instead of compounding the problem by using humiliation, get into the child's world. Ask the child how she feels about the problem and how it is for her to have this happening. Ask if your child needs help or if she can handle it by herself. Listen respectfully to what she says.

Planning Ahead to Prevent Future Problems

1. Do not attempt toilet training too early. This invites behavior problems. We suggest waiting until the summer after your child

Booster Thoughts

Here's the experience of one family:

"We became familiar with our children's bladder control capabilities on family camping trips. If Josh announced that he needed to go to the bathroom, we knew we had about twenty minutes to find a suitable stopping place. If Katey said she needed to go, we knew we had about ten minutes. If Brian announced a need, we pulled over to the side of the road immediately.

"Brian was also a bed wetter into his early teen years. We knew it was physical and very embarrassing for him. At the age of fourteen, he was invited to an overnight camp-out with his friends. He stayed up all night because he was afraid he would wet the bed and be ridiculed. We were grateful that we knew his problem was physical so we didn't add to his problems by hassling him. We simply gave him empathetic understanding and worked with him on many possible solutions. The funniest was our agreement that he would tie a string around his toe. Since I have to get up several times in the night to go to the bathroom, he asked me if I would pull on the string around his toe to wake him up.

"Eventually we became so unconcerned about the problem, and Brian became so good about taking care of his own sheets, that we don't know for sure when he stopped wetting the bed. I think he stopped. I'll ask his wife."

reaches two and a half years of age before you even start. Of course, there are exceptions to this. Some children start the toilet training process on their own. Our point is to not get anxious about it too early.

2. To avoid behavior problems, take time for toilet training and then stay out of the way. Teach your child how to use the washing machine. Even a three-year-old can handle this job. Also, you could teach him how to change his clothes and sheets in the middle of the night if he is uncomfortable. Once you have taken time for training, keep your nose out of his business and let him take care of himself however he chooses. He may choose to sleep in wet and smelly sheets and experience ridicule from his friends.

3. Share respectful stories about bed wetters so your children know it can be a

common problem. Michael Landon wrote a television movie about bed-wetting based on his childhood experience. We have a friend who said that in the U.S. Marines there was a special tent for bed wetters. The sergeant in charge woke the residents up every two hours.

Life Skills Children Can Learn

Children can learn that their parents respectfully and lovingly help them learn to deal with problems that are physical or developmental. Both parents and children can learn effective ways to interact with each other.

Parenting Pointers

1. One clue that the problem is developmental is if your child has difficulty with bladder control during the day. (See the "Booster Thoughts" on the previous page.)

2. Another clue that bed-wetting is developmental is if the child is a heavy sleeper and has difficulty waking up in the night. Don't wake the child up, try to monitor his fluid intake before bed, or ask him if he has gone to the bathroom before bedtime. Instead, let him know that some people take longer to develop bladder control and that you are sure he will be able to handle it on his own schedule.

Birthdays

"My children get jealous when one of their siblings is having a birthday party. They cry when their brother or sister gets a present and they don't. It's embarrassing, because they are even rude at their friends' parties, complaining because their friend is getting presents and they aren't."

Understanding Your Child, Yourself, and the Situation

It is natural for children to feel left out when another child is in the limelight, but they can learn to handle these situations better if parents allow them to have their feelings and don't try to fix things or make everything equal.

Suggestions

1. Let children have a say in planning their birthday parties. Give limited choices when they are younger and more freedom as they get older in planning the festivities. Stress that their birthday is their special day and you want to work with them to make it that way.

2. Before a party for a sibling or friend, discuss with your child how he feels about someone else getting so much special attention. Ask if he can think of ways to make the party special for the sibling or

friend. Help him find a special job if the party is at your home, such as greeting people, handing out the presents, or serving the cake.

3. Don't ignore the children who aren't having a party. Let them sit by you or hold your hand while the birthday person is opening her gifts.

Planning Ahead to Prevent Future Problems

1. Sometimes children misbehave because they are unconscious of being rude. Let them know before the party, either through discussion or role playing, which behaviors enhance the celebration and which ones detract from it.

2. Involve your children in gift shopping for their friends and siblings. Tell them your budget and let them help pick out and wrap the gift.

3. Remind children who aren't having a birthday that theirs will be soon. Invite them to brainstorm how they want to be treated so they will have ideas about how to treat the birthday child.

Life Skills Children Can Learn

Children can learn that it is fun to be special and that it feels good to help others

Booster Thoughts

Rob's mother was in the habit of planning giant extravaganzas for his birthdays. By the time Rob was ten, his mother was tired of spending so much time and money planning activities that she spent half the year paying for. She was worried that Rob would be disappointed, but she just couldn't bring herself to do one more spectacle. She sat down with Rob and told him that this year she would like to work out the party plans with him.

Rob, to his mother's surprise, asked if he could have a party like his friends, where everyone went to the roller skating rink and then out for pizza. Rob's mother said, "I don't know how to roller skate."

"That's okay, Mom," said Rob. "When the other mothers go, they bring a friend and sit and talk while the kids have fun."

Rob's mother said, "Thanks, son, for the great idea. I'm awfully glad we planned this party together."

enjoy the limelight. Children can also learn how to plan an occasion and make their dreams come true.

Parenting Pointers

1. Planning extravagant parties for children without their input robs them of the opportunity to see that wishes can become realities and that they have the ability to help make that happen.

2. Make sure that birthdays aren't the only special days of the year. Plan special time with each child on a regular basis where he has you all to himself for activities that you both enjoy. This is especially true in divorced and blended families, where the temptation is to do activities with all the children together.

Birth Order

(See also *Sibling Rivalry*)

"Is there anything to this birth order stuff? Everyone says it's important, but I can't see the significance myself."

Understanding Your Child, Yourself, and the Situation

Our personalities are influenced as much by our birth order and the decisions we make about how we fit into the family as they are by genetics, parenting style, cultural background, and economic status. The first place we make decisions about how we are different is in the family of origin. Oldest children in different families have more in common than with their own siblings, and so forth down the birth order. Children are not consciously aware of the process, but they look around in their family and make comparisons with their siblings. We call these comparisons *competition.* They try to figure out how they can belong and be significant in areas different from those already taken by their siblings. If one child is already good in academics, another child might try to be popular, another the good child, another the rebel, another the charming manipulator.

The firstborn in a family is the first child faced with finding his or her place of belonging. Often oldest children decide they belong by being the first and the best. (Remember, this is not a conscious process.) They might decide they can be significant by being responsible, helpful, smart, perfectionists—and the boss, when another child arrives on the scene.

The second child usually finds the first place taken and is faced with the challenge of choosing a different way to be special. The exceptions are those who decide to challenge the firstborn for the spot of being first and best and become "Avis" kids who "try harder." Second-born children might be easygoing, socially popular, noisier, or less responsible and adequate because of their perceived inability to keep up with their older siblings. If a third child is born, the second child becomes a middle child and might feel squeezed, seeing life as unfair with neither the privileges of the oldest nor the advantages of the youngest.

Youngest children might decide to be cute and entertaining. Some decide they need to be taken care of and learn skills of charm and manipulation. They often think they are entitled to special treatment. Others become competitive and try to catch up with and surpass the rest.

Only children often share the characteristics of the oldest or the youngest. It depends on what they decide. Some find belonging and importance in being the one and only.

Suggestions

1. Use your knowledge of birth order to encourage your children. Oldest children need appreciation for being leaders and helpers but encouragement to avoid being caretakers who do for younger siblings what they can do for themselves. They also need encouragement to express what they need and want. They can learn that they are okay when they make mistakes and don't have to be perfect.

2. Second children need outlets that are different from those of their older siblings. If second children think life is unfair, listen to their feelings and hear their anger and hurt. Let them know it is normal for them to feel that way.

3. Middle children need contact on a one-to-one basis. It's important to build a relationship with these children, who may hide their needs as a way of feeling safe. Small steps such as holding hands, a kiss on the cheek, and spontaneous hugs are important ways to make a connection. We need to point out and encourage their strengths, talents, and creativity. Middle children often think they have to be the peacekeepers in the family. Family meetings can take some of the pressure off the middle child because everyone is involved in solving problems.

4. It's critical to take youngest children seriously so they know they can develop skills other than being cute and entertaining. We can ask for their ideas and encourage them to share their feelings. Give them the opportunity to grow up and to be responsible by having them share in the chores, get themselves up in the morning with an alarm clock, choose their own clothes,

Booster Thoughts

Kyle, like many firstborn children, was reading long before he began kindergarten. He and his mother spent hours poring over library books from the time he was only six months old. When his younger sister, Sandy, tried reading, Kyle would say the word before she had a chance to figure it out and then make some comment about how dumb Sandy was. Sandy would act silly and say she hated reading and books.

Because their mother had learned about birth order in her parenting classes, she realized that both children were feeling discouraged. Kyle wanted to maintain his special place of superiority by being the smartest and the only reader. Sandy was beginning to fit into the family by being a clown and stubborn. Mom decided that she would spend special time with Sandy when Kyle was at child care or preschool to help Sandy catch up. She also spent a lot of time with Kyle, helping him see how unique he was and that a family could have two children who read. Both children grew up to be excellent students and avid readers, yet completely different from the other in many ways.

make their lunch, and manage their allowance. They also need lots of affection. Families tend to keep the youngest children babies instead of helping them learn the skills the other siblings already know.

Planning Ahead to Prevent Future Problems

1. Hold regular family meetings so that all members of the family have a place where they can be heard and their unique differences can be used to help the family.

2. Don't compare your children. Each has a different perspective and needs to find ways to be unique in the family. See each child for the unique and special person he or she is.

3. Don't expect older children to raise the younger children. All of the kids need your encouragement and help to grow up.

4. If you blend families, be sensitive to the loss of position that a child feels and her need to redefine her special place in the family. This takes time, so practice patience.

Life Skills Children Can Learn

Children can learn that they are unique individuals, and that is just fine. Their special personalities and talents can help their family. They don't have to compare themselves to others, because they are good enough the way they are.

Parenting Pointers

1. Information about family position helps us understand the beliefs behind our children's behavior. This information will give us many clues about what children need in order to change some of the beliefs that are not helpful to them. We are much more effective when we deal with the belief behind the behavior instead of with only the behavior.

2. Generalizations about birth order are based on research that shows typical decisions made by people of the same birth order. There are many exceptions, and each individual also makes many unique decisions. The point is to help us be aware that our children are making decisions that affect their behavior. Understanding this process can help us become more aware of separate realities and the possibility for change.

Biting

"How can I make my child stop biting her little friends? She probably won't have any before long. Whenever she is frustrated, she just bites."

Understanding Your Child, Yourself, and the Situation

We hope it helps you to know that biting is a temporary behavior in some children from the time of teething until around age three. Even though biting is embarrassing for parents of the biter and upsetting to the parents of the child who gets bitten, biting is not a misbehavior in most cases but is due to a lack of skills. Children who bite often do so when they become frustrated in social situations and do not know how to express themselves in acceptable ways. Some toddlers may bite because that is their way of exploring ("I wonder what Suzie will taste like or feel like").

Children also may bite their parents and think it's a game. It is important to deal with biting in ways that do not leave residual problems, such as children feeling they are bad or deciding it is okay to hurt others smaller than they are because adults punish by hurting them.

Suggestions

1. Do not bite the child back or wash the child's mouth out with soap. Hurting a

child does not help her learn to stop hurting others.

2. If your child has a history of biting, supervise closely. Intervene calmly and quickly when disputes begin (see *Fighting, Friends*).

3. Watch the child closely for a few days during play with other children. Every time she looks like she is ready to bite, cup your hand over her mouth and say, "It is not okay to bite people. Tell the other child what you want." If the child is preverbal, after cupping your hand over her mouth and saying it is not okay to bite, offer a distracting choice: "Do you want to play on the swings or with the blocks?"

4. When your child bites before you are able to intervene, quickly remove the child, give her a hug, and say, "It is not okay to bite people." You may need to do this several times while you are teaching the child other skills or waiting for her to outgrow biting.

5. Comfort the child who has been bitten and apologize to the parent. Be honest with your feelings. "I feel very embarrassed about this, and I will do everything I can to help my child stop biting. However, I do not believe punishment solves anything." Comforting the child who has been bitten, after hugging the biter, models loving ways to deal with people.

6. If you are dealing with another parent who thinks you should punish your child, stand your ground. "I can see we have different philosophies and that it would not be respectful for either of us to try to change the other." Then walk away with dignity and respect for yourself and the other person. Your child is more important than what others think of you.

7. If your child is at the teething stage and continues to want to bite, offer her a stuffed animal or cloth to bite. Help her find relief for sore gums by offering a frozen juice bar.

Booster Thoughts

If you really pay attention, you can tell when your child is about to bite you. She gets a little gleam in her eye, throws her head back, and charges with an open mouth. So that your child knows this is not a game you wish to play, hold her away from you and say, "It is not okay to bite people. If you want to bite, Mom will get you a rubber toy to bite." If you say this and mean it, your child may stop biting in a few days.

Planning Ahead to Prevent Future Problems

1. Play "Let's Pretend" with your child. Pretend the two of you are fighting over a toy and that you are going to bite him. Stop and ask, "How would you feel if I bit you? What would you like me to do instead?" Then pretend you are fighting over a toy and let your child try whatever he suggested to do instead of biting.

2. Brainstorm other ways to handle problems. If your child doesn't have any ideas of what to do instead of biting, teach him to use words. You can make suggestions, such as suggesting that he tell the other child, "I'm mad at you" or "Let me have a turn" or "I'll go get another toy and we'll trade," or that he ask an adult to help settle the problem. Then play "Let's Pretend" so he can practice these ideas.

3. Use emotional honesty: "I feel bad when you bite other people because I don't like to see people get hurt. I wish you would find something else to do besides bite people."

4. If your child is preverbal, it is important to accept the fact that he needs close supervision and kind and firm distraction until he learns socially acceptable ways to handle frustration. Take comfort in knowing that he will not be biting by the time he goes to kindergarten—if not much sooner.

5. When you are supervising closely, you will be able to understand what your child is trying to accomplish. Verbalize his intention before showing him another way: "I can see that you want the ball. It is not okay to bite to get the ball. Let's find another ball."

Life Skills Children Can Learn

Children can learn that it is not acceptable to hurt other people. They can learn that their parents love them no matter what they do and that adults will help them find acceptable ways to solve problems. Children can learn that they are capable of solving problems in ways that don't hurt other people and that their parents will remain lovingly kind and firm while they learn.

Parenting Pointers

1. Some people think hugging a child who has just bitten another child is rewarding the misbehavior. It is not. Hugging gives the child reassurance of your love while not accepting the child's behavior. Hugging helps the child feel belonging and helps reduce the need to misbehave. It also shows the child an acceptable way to behave—to love the other person and tell him or her what you don't like.

2. Some parents believe you should bite children back to teach them how it feels. By biting them back, you could accidentally be teaching them that biting is an acceptable way to behave—even if it hurts.

Boredom

"My child complains about being bored and expects me to drop everything to entertain him."

Understanding Your Child, Yourself, and the Situation

We live in a society where children are used to being entertained. Television and electronic games are major contributors to this dilemma. Children can passively sit and watch *Sesame Street* or play with a video game and be highly entertained. (It is true that *Sesame Street* is educational and that electronic games teach eye-hand coordination; however, they limit creativity and resourcefulness.) Another contributor is the belief of many parents that they must fix every problem their children have. Children do need our help to become involved in sports, outside interests, hobbies, and other activities, but they do not need to be entertained or have their time controlled by parents every minute of the day.

Booster Thoughts

Iku and Harry were going crazy because their daughter was pestering them and demanding constant attention, especially at times when they wanted to be otherwise engaged, like at the end of a long day. Iku and Harry thought Kirsten, age six, was bored and didn't know how to entertain herself. They felt it was their job to fill all her time with interesting and educational activities, but they also believed they had a right to take a break at the end of the day. What really confused them was when Kirsten finally went to bed, she would continually turn her light on and read, play with the computer, draw pictures, and engage in numerous activities. The next morning, Kirsten would crawl out of bed with dark circles under her eyes.

One day, the three of them sat down to talk about the problem. Kirsten said she needed to stay up later because she had so many things to do that were important to her, like making a card for her friend's birthday or rereading her favorite book, and there wasn't any time during the day to get these things done. Iku and Harry looked at each other in shock as Kirsten explained her thinking to them. Kirsten told them that in school her teacher had something called personal activity time, or PAT.

Suggestions

1. Ask, "What ideas do you have to solve your problem?" If your child says, "I don't know," do not get hooked into giving him answers. You might say, "I have faith in you to work it out."

2. Listen in an empathetic way and acknowledge without trying to fix the problem: "I can understand that. I feel bored myself sometimes." If your child keeps badgering you, keep listening and acknowledge him with noncommittal sounds ("Umm, uh-huh"). Eventually, your child will get so bored with his unsuccessful efforts to get you to handle his problem that he will find something else to do.

3. Another possibility is to say, "That is good. Perhaps your mind and body need some quiet time. Would you like to learn how to meditate?" She will probably run the other way. However, meditation could be a good practice to model for your children and to teach when they are ready.

4. Limit time for television and electronic games so children are used to being creative and resourceful instead of being passive or

Once all their schoolwork was done, the children could do things of interest to them as long as they didn't disturb the others. Kirsten said the time in her room at night was her PAT time.

Iku and Harry realized that they needed to help Kirsten with her scheduling, as her problem wasn't really one of boredom but one of scheduling. They suggested that they change bedtime to fifteen minutes later and then told Kirsten that she could have PAT time as soon as her dinner chores were done and she was ready for bed. Currently it was taking Kirsten over an hour to get ready for bed. Kirsten agreed to the plan with a big smile on her face.

The first night of the new plan, Kirsten completed her evening chore and bedtime routine in nine minutes and then ran into her room, turned on her computer, and started to listen to her favorite CD story. Iku and Harry looked at each other in amazement. Every night after that, Kirsten efficiently completed her chores so she could have time to do the things that were important to her. Iku and Harry realized their assessment that Kirsten was bored was wrong and that she had simply been frustrated by an inability to figure out how to structure her time to fit everything in.

depending on electronic gadgets (see *Television and Video Games*).

Planning Ahead to Prevent Future Problems

1. During a family meeting or a problem-solving session, brainstorm with your children to see how many ideas you can all come up with for things to do when they feel bored. Have each child choose his or her favorite things from the big list and make a "Things to Do When I'm Bored" list.

2. The next time a child complains, say, "You might want to check your list."

3. Once a child has a plan for what to do when bored, you can give a choice: "You may either continue to be bored, or you can find something to do. I have faith that you will do what is best for you."

Life Skills Children Can Learn

Children can learn that it is up to them to take care of how they structure their free time. They can go to others for understanding, emotional support, and inspiration, but ultimately they are capable of taking care of themselves.

Parenting Pointers

1. Children have a sense about when they can hook you into feeling sorry for them and trying to fix things. You may have noticed that when you try to fix things for them, nothing you do is good enough.

2. Have faith in your children. It is contagious. Your children will follow your lead and develop faith in themselves. Don't be afraid to involve your children in tasks around the house or in a routine that fills in some of their time. This will also help with boredom.

3. Your children may be bored because they need some adult help to set up programs, activities, and outside interests that they can be engaged in. There are cases where children are bored because they are being neglected by their parents and need adult help to learn about resources that are available and how to access them.

4. Avoid the temptation to believe it is your job to overprotect your child from experiencing every frustration life has to offer. However, don't see this as an excuse to go to the other extreme and justify neglect.

Borrowing

"My daughter takes my clothes out of my drawers and closet and wears them without my permission. Later, I find them thrown in a heap with her dirty clothes. I've asked her to stop, but she won't."

Understanding Your Child, Yourself, and the Situation

The family is one of the first places children learn about limits and boundaries. Each family member is entitled to a space where he or she can be safe, know his or her possessions won't be disturbed, and that no one will enter that space without permission. Boundaries and limits must be taught, as children aren't born with this information. It is up to parents to help children establish respectful boundaries within a home.

Suggestions

1. At a family meeting, discuss how each person's room is his or hers and that others shouldn't enter without asking permission first. If children share a room, establish a part of the room that is each child's safe territory. If young children are getting into their older sibling's possessions, help the older child find a safe space to keep things away from little fingers.

2. Don't expect your children to share their toys unless they want to. Watch out for a double standard in which you expect a child to let other siblings play with her things but they don't have to share with her. Make sure family members know that it is okay to say no (see *Sharing*).

3. Get agreements ahead of time about borrowing toys, clothing, or other items. Be clear on how long the person will keep the item and what condition it should be in when it's returned. Emphasize that borrowing means giving back.

4. Sometimes it is necessary to hide or lock up certain items to keep them from being "borrowed." Some things are too tempting to leave alone, such as your favorite sewing scissors or your new screwdriver.

5. When a child complains about borrowing, suggest he put it on the family-meeting agenda so you can keep working together on solutions.

Planning Ahead to Prevent Future Problems

1. Establish collateral for borrowing. If a child wants to wear your sweater to school, have her give you something she values to hold until your sweater is returned. Do not return the collateral until your sweater has been returned in the agreed-upon condition.

2. If your children are repeatedly borrowing certain items, such as staplers, scissors, tape, and tools, perhaps it's time for them to have their own supply.

3. Children often trade clothing with their friends. Stay out of their business and let

Booster Thoughts

Fifteen-year-old Sean was forever taking his mother's hair gel, shampoo, tennis balls, and scissors and his father's white socks. Instead of writing what he needed on the grocery list, he found it was easier to borrow the item when he ran out. Instead of washing his socks, it was easier to borrow his father's. Sean didn't respect boundaries and limits, and no matter how many discussions and agreements the family members had, Sean continued his behavior. With Sean, the only thing that worked was to hide the items that he most frequently borrowed. If the item wasn't immediately available, Sean would give up and figure out some other way to meet his needs. Some people may think this is a great inconvenience and resent having to hide their possessions, but there are times when the best approach is to take care of oneself instead of trying to change someone else. Eventually Sean got the idea that these items weren't available to him, and he began to write them on the grocery list.

them work it out. Your children's clothing is theirs. If you think someone is taking advantage of another, share your opinions and feelings. Ask your children if they would like to hear some ideas you have about handling the situation.

4. If your child loses or damages something he borrowed, help him figure out how to fix or replace the item. If it is expensive, take an agreed-upon sum out of his allowance each week until he has paid for the repair.

Life Skills Children Can Learn

Children can learn that they have the right to privacy and control over their possessions. They also learn to respect others' boundaries and that others should respect their boundaries. Children learn that there are limits and responsibilities that go with owning property.

Parenting Pointers

1. For some parents, allowing children to borrow their clothing may be a real stretch. If you are willing to stretch yourself, begin slowly and try it out before making it a habit. Sharing can create a feeling of closeness and cooperation when done respectfully.

2. Never tell children they are selfish if they don't wish to share or loan out their

toys. Labeling them is cruel and unhelpful and tells them that the way they think and feel is not okay. You can always tell your children what you feel and wish. For instance, "I feel sad that you won't let your brother play with your train set when you aren't playing with it. I wish you would let him play for fifteen minutes and see if he can be responsible about how he cares for your things." Other than telling them how you feel, keep your nose out of business that is essentially between the children.

Candy

"My kids want to go to the store every day and fill up on candy. They use their own allowance money, but I don't think it's good for them to eat so much candy."

Understanding Your Child, Yourself, and the Situation

When parents become fanatical about an issue, they often end up with a result opposite to what they intended. Instead of teaching moderation and making good choices, they end up trying to control their children's behavior at all times. Candy is one of those issues where parents become fanatical and kids end up craving something they otherwise might enjoy just on special occasions. Candy is also frequently used to bribe or reward children or to modify their behavior. This is disrespectful, as children prefer to do what is in their best interest and cooperate until they sense they are being manipulated.

Suggestions

1. When children are young, one way to limit the amount of candy they can eat is to have a special candy day. Let the kids decide which day that will be so they participate in setting limits.

2. Teach children how to balance what they eat and make wise choices. If they make their own lunches, tell them they can have a sugar treat if they also include healthy choices.

3. Don't use candy as a bribe or reward.

4. Don't forbid your children to eat candy, as children want what they can't have. It is better to regulate how much and how often instead of saying absolutely not.

Booster Thoughts

Sometimes all the education and work you do with your children is challenged when they are away from home. In a family where consequences and choices were stressed and rewards and punishment frowned upon, a child in kindergarten said to her mother, "Mom, I know you don't believe in rewards, but my teacher gives candy prizes if we behave. I don't want you to say anything to her, because I like prizes and I don't want you to ruin it for me. I know that candy isn't good for us, but I want to win a prize at school. If I do, I'll eat the candy on my candy day instead of buying any more candy."

5. At some point, when your children are older and have more freedom, they may choose to eat a lot of candy. You can't and don't want to follow them around, but you can tell them how you feel and let them know that if they have excessive dental work they may have to help pay for the treatment. Children do go through phases, especially in their early teens, when eating junk food and candy is a safe way to rebel.

Planning Ahead to Prevent Future Problems

1. Let your children know that eating candy may create dental problems. Talk about brushing after sugary treats. One family had a jar so the kids could put in an amount equal to the cost of the candy in order to save for the dentist.

2. Ask your dental hygienist or dentist to educate the kids about the effects of candy.

3. Talk to your children about the addictive nature of sugar and how it affects the body.

4. Don't leave bowls of candy around the house to tempt the kids.

5. Have plenty of healthy snacks available.

6. On Halloween, ask your children for their ideas on how they can limit eating the treats they get. For young children, take their candy bags and let them pick out one or two treats a day. In some cities, there are dentists who pay children by the pound to turn in their Halloween candy. Let your children know this is a choice.

Life Skills Children Can Learn

Children can learn what foods are healthy and what foods are not so they can decide what they want to put into their bodies. They can learn about moderation, making choices, and how to limit themselves.

Parenting Pointers

1. It's important to know that sugar can be addictive and can spoil a child's appetite for nutricious food.

2. Educate your children early that the choices they make have health consequences. Children need information and will listen when it is given in a friendly manner. They tune out hostile lectures.

Car Hassles

"Is it possible to go for a ride in the car with children who wear their seat belts, don't fight, and don't talk or chew in your ear? I can hardly stand getting in the car with my kids or my friends' kids."

Understanding Your Child, Yourself, and the Situation

If you recognize yourself in this picture, you aren't alone. This is a common problem for parents and children. It can even be dangerous. Who knows how many accidents have been caused by fighting children or by parents who are trying to hit their kids in the backseat while they drive. Since cars are essential transportation in most families, it is important to find ways to improve on this situation so everyone can be safe and comfortable.

Suggestions

1. Do not start the car until everyone is in a buckled car seat or has buckled a seat belt. Each child needs to have his or her own seat and a seat belt to ensure safety in the car. Kids know when you mean what you say, and they know if they can manipulate you to give in to their demands.

2. Decide what you will do. Let the kids know that when you feel it is unsafe to drive because it's too noisy, you'll pull over until things calm down. Have this discussion at a time other than while in the car. Then if the kids start yelling or fighting, simply pull over and wait without saying a word. Do it as many times as you need to until the kids learn you really mean it.

3. If you are having car problems with kids, leave plenty of time to get to your destination so you can have time for training. When children remove their seat belts, pull the car over at the first available spot and wait until they rebuckle. It is best not to say a word. When they know the rules in advance, it is disrespectful to assume

Booster Thoughts

The Jones family is very excited. They have just finished planning a day at the beach. Seven-year-old Jason and five-year-old Jenny have promised that they won't fight. Mr. Jones has warned, "If you do, we'll turn around and come back."

"We won't, we won't," promise Jason and Jenny again.

The Jones family hasn't gone two miles when a loud wail is heard from the back-seat. "Jason hit me."

Mrs. Jones says, "What did we tell you kids about fighting?"

Jason defends himself: "Well, she touched me."

Mr. Jones threatens, "You two had better cut it out, or we are going home."

The children cry out in unison, "Noooooo! We'll be good."

And they are—for about ten minutes. Then another wail is heard. "He took my red crayon."

Jason replies, "Well she was hogging it. It's my turn."

Mr. Jones says, "Do you want me to turn around and go home?"

"Noooooo. We'll be good."

And so the story goes. Throughout the day, Jason and Jenny fight, and Mr. and Mrs. Jones make threats. At the end of the day, Mr. and Mrs. Jones are angry and threaten never to take the kids anywhere again. Jason and Jenny feel bad that they have made their parents so miserable. They are beginning to believe they really are bad kids.

Now let's visit the Smith family. They have just planned their trip to the zoo during their weekly family meeting. Part of the planning included a discussion about limits and consequences. Mr. and Mrs. Smith have told Susan and Sam how miserable they feel when they fight. The kids promise they won't. Mr. Smith said, "I appreciate that, and I think we should come up with a plan for what will happen if you forget." The kids keep insisting they won't fight. Mrs. Smith says, "Well then, is it okay with you if we stop the car if you do forget? We don't think it is safe to drive when you are fighting, so we'll just pull over to the side of the road and wait for you to stop. You can let us know when you are ready for us to drive again. How do you feel about that solution?" Both kids agree with innocent enthusiasm.

Typically, it doesn't take them long to forget their promise, and a fight begins. Mrs. Smith quickly and quietly pulls off to the side of the road. She and Mr. Smith take out magazines and start reading. Each child starts blaming the other while whining about his or her innocence. Mr. and Mrs. Smith ignore them and just keep reading. It doesn't take long for Susan to catch on that Mom and Dad must mean what they said. Susan says, "Okay, we are ready to keep driving." Mr. Smith says, "We'll wait until we hear it from both of you." Sam says, "But she hit me."

Mom and Dad just keep reading. Susan hits Sam. "Tell them you are ready." Sam cries, "She hit me again." Mom and Dad just keep reading. Susan realizes that hitting Sam won't help, so she tries to reason with him. "We'll have to sit here forever if you don't say you are ready." Susan follows her parents' lead and starts to color. Sam holds out for about three more minutes before saying, "I'm ready for you to start driving." Mom says, "Thank you very much. I appreciate your cooperation."

About thirty minutes later, another fight starts. Mom starts to pull over to the side of the road. Both kids cry out in unison: "We'll stop. We're ready to keep driving." There was no more fighting for the rest of the day, and the Smiths enjoyed a wonderful day at the zoo.

Mr. and Mrs. Smith stopped using words and instead followed through with kind and firm action. It took a little longer for the kids to catch on, but once they did, it had a longer-lasting effect. Because they are kids, they just had to test the waters one more time. When their parents started to follow through again, the kids knew they meant what they said. They were left with the feeling, not that they were bad kids, but that they were clever enough to figure out a solution to the problem and that cooperation was the most effective alternative. Kind and firm are key words to remember to make follow-through effective.[11]

---

11. From Jane Nelsen, Cheryl Erwin, and H. Stephen Glenn, *Positive Discipline for Blended Families* (Rocklin, CA: Prima Publishing, 1997), 146–148.

they need reminding. Actions speak louder than words.

Planning Ahead to Prevent Future Problems

1. When you aren't in the car, ask the kids for their ideas of what will help make the trip more comfortable and fun for them. Then let them discuss rules for safety. Children cooperate better when they are involved in creating the rules.

2. If you are going on a long trip, have the kids bring toys and books to entertain themselves. Some families have special baskets or backpacks with toys that can be used only in the car.

3. If the trip is long, make frequent stops so the kids can get out, run around, and stretch. It may help to have a timer so the kids can see how much longer before you stop.

4. If the kids are fighting over who sits in the front seat—and what kids don't fight over this?—let them work out a system for taking turns. Have them inform you when they are ready to put their system into effect. You do not need to know their system; they do. If the fighting starts again, they can all sit in the backseat until they are ready to try again.

Life Skills Children Can Learn

Children can learn that the car is not a place to move about or create unsafe situations and that they can cooperate to help their family be safe. They can learn that parents mean what they say and will follow through with dignity and respect. They can learn that their parents also consider their needs.

Parenting Pointers

1. Take time for training. Leave for your destination at least ten minutes early. This allows time for you to pull over and read a novel while your children test you to see if you mean what you say.

2. Everyone is expected to wear a seat belt. It goes without saying that you need to wear your seat belt, too.

Chauffeuring

"Sometimes I feel like my biggest role in life is chauffeuring my kids all over the place. I don't usually mind, but I do feel resentful when the kids take advantage and expect me to drop everything to meet their last-minute demands."

Understanding Your Child, Yourself, and the Situation

It is important for children to be involved in healthy activities. The more healthy hobbies and interests they have, the less likely they are to engage in unhealthy activities. Transportation to these activities is necessary, but parents don't have to put their needs on the shelf entirely. The problem of transportation can provide an opportunity to teach children important life skills such as practicing give and take, planning ahead, respecting the needs of others, gratitude, and finding resources other than their parents.

Suggestions

1. Discuss the principle of give and take at a family meeting and work on a transportation plan that includes it. "I'm willing to contribute my time and car to help you with transportation. What are you willing to do to help me?" Be ready with suggestions about where you would appreciate some help.

2. Include calendar time at every family meeting. This is the time for everyone to put upcoming events on the calendar so transportation (and attendance) can be planned in advance. Include all people over sixteen and with a driver's license in the rotation for chauffeuring.

3. When planning for transportation, include other ways besides taking total responsibility yourself. Create car pools with other parents, encourage children to ride their bikes when appropriate, and check bus schedules.

4. Help your children help themselves by keeping them company while they call other parents and friends to plan alternate transportation. Don't expect your children to do this alone or think it is your job to do this for your child. Work together as a team. It takes a little extra time, but your children will learn a sense of responsibility for planning ahead.

Planning Ahead to Prevent Future Problems

1. Let children know in advance what you are willing to do and what you are not willing to do. For example, "I am willing to take you whenever I can if I have advance notice. I am also willing to take you at the last minute if it is convenient for me. I will not cancel my plans to take you at the last minute."

2. Encourage and support your child's efforts to engage in healthy activities and show faith in your child to organize some transportation that does not include you.

Life Skills Children Can Learn

Children can learn that their needs and desires are important and are treated with respect, encouragement, and support. They can learn that it is important for them to respect others, plan ahead, and use some of their own resources.

Parenting Pointers

1. It is difficult for children to associate time and the inconvenience of others with

Booster Thoughts

Twelve-year-old Janet loved ballet and decided she would like to take classes five days a week. She explained to her mother that her teacher thought she was good enough to increase her lessons from two to five days a week. Janet's mother was excited that her daughter wanted to continue with ballet and proud of how well she was doing. Janet's mother worked full-time and also knew that she wouldn't be able to get away from work to drive five days a week.

Mom: I'm willing to pay for the extra classes and pick you up from the lessons after work, but I can only take you to your classes on Tuesdays and Thursdays. You will have to find a car pool arrangement for the other days.

Janet: But Mom, no one in my classes lives near me, and their parents won't drive out here to pick me up.

Mom: Well, honey, I'd be willing to help you check out the bus schedule and figure out how to take the bus to class.

Janet: But that means I'll have to carry all my dance gear to school with me, lug it on the bus along with my homework, transfer downtown, and wait forever for the bus.

Mom: Janet, I'm not trying to think of ways for you to suffer, but I really can't leave work to take you. You need to think about how important dance is to you. I know taking the bus will be difficult, but it's up to you.

Janet ended up taking the bus. While it was very difficult, she decided the sacrifice was worth it. Years later, she realized she had acquired self-confidence and skills that came in handy when she decided to travel around the world.

things they want. They need your help to make this connection and plan for it.

2. Do not feel guilty when you respect yourself and your needs by saying, "I'm sorry, but I have other plans." You are doing yourself and your child a favor. It is not respectful to children to teach them that it works to be forgetful, thoughtless, and demanding.

3. It's okay to draw a line about the number of activities you are willing to support with driving. Sometimes parents overdo meeting their children's needs at the expense of their own.

Chores, Age-Appropriate

(See also *Chores, Getting Cooperation*)

"When are my children old enough to help with chores?"

Understanding Your Child, Yourself, and the Situation

It's never too early or too late. Kids need to know they are important, useful, contributing members of your family. If they don't find satisfaction in positive ways, often they find not-so-positive ways to feel important.[12] Working builds skills, makes them feel useful, and teaches appreciation for the work that needs to be done and for those who do it. It may be tempting for parents to do everything themselves, thinking it is easier and will get done "properly." When parents take that attitude, they deprive their kids of opportunities to learn cooperation and responsibility.

Suggestions

1. Get the kids involved in brainstorming a list of jobs that need to be done to help the family.

2. Take time for training and work with your children until they learn how to do the job. When they feel ready to do the job alone, let them know you are available if they need help. Step back and don't jump in unless asked. If there are problems, work them out at a family meeting instead of criticizing at the moment.

3. Provide kid-sized equipment, such as a small broom, a feather duster, or small gardening tools.

4. Create a chore time when everyone works together rather than handing out lists of chores for kids to do.

5. Notice the contribution instead of the quality of work done. If your very young child loses interest halfway through emptying the silverware in the dishwasher, thank her for the half she did instead of insisting she finish every last piece.

12. For more information on motivating family members of all ages to help with chores, see Lynn Lott and Riki Intner, *Chores Without Wars* (Rocklin, CA: Prima Publishing, 1998).

6. Don't feel sorry for kids and do their jobs for them because they have a lot of homework or play in a sport. Help them organize their time to continue helping the family.

7. Make sure the jobs are appropriate for the age, as suggested in the following lists.

Two- to Three-Year-Olds

- Pick up toys and put in the proper place
- Place napkins, plates, and silverware on the table (perhaps not correctly at first)
- Clear their own place at the table (put the dishes on the counter after cleaning the leftovers off the plate)
- Wipe up their own accidents
- Unload utensils from the dishwasher
- Fold washcloths and socks

Four-Year-Olds

- Set the table—with good dishes, too
- Follow a schedule for feeding pets
- Help make the beds and vacuum
- Help wash the dishes or fill the dishwasher
- Dust the furniture
- Prepare cold cereal
- Hold the hand mixer to whip potatoes or mix up a cake
- Get the mail

Five-Year-Olds

- Help with meal planning and grocery shopping
- Make their own sandwiches or simple breakfasts, then clean up
- Pour their own drinks
- Tear up lettuce for the salad
- Make the bed and clean their rooms
- Scrub the sink, toilet, and bathtub
- Separate clothes (white, color) for washing
- Answer the telephone and begin to dial it
- Take out the garbage

Six- to Eight-Year-Olds

- Shake rugs
- Water plants and flowers
- Peel vegetables
- Cook simple foods (hot dog, boiled egg, toast)
- Prepare their school lunches
- Gather wood for the fireplace
- Take a pet for a walk
- Clean out the inside of the car

Nine- to Ten-Year-Olds

- Change sheets on the bed and put dirty sheets in the hamper
- Operate the washer and dryer, measuring detergent and bleach
- Buy groceries, using a list and doing comparative shopping

Booster Thoughts

Three-year-old Kristin asked if she could help clean the house in preparation for company coming to dinner. Her mom asked if she would like to do the bathroom, and she said yes.

Kristin took a can of cleanser and a cloth into the bathroom. When Kristin was finished, she said to her mom, "The bathroom is all cleaned up! I like helping you clean." Her mom got busy and forgot to check Kristin's work.

The guests used the bathroom several times during the evening without comment. After they left, Kristin's mom went into the bathroom. To her shock, she saw that Kristin had used an entire can of cleanser. There was white powder everywhere. Kristin's mom laughed to herself as she thought about what her guests might have been thinking when they took their turn in the bathroom. She realized Kristin needed more time for training in the use of cleanser.

- Keep their own appointments (dentist, doctor, school) if within biking distance
- Prepare a family meal
- Do neighborhood chores
- Wash the family car

Ten- to Eleven-Year-Olds

- Earn their own money (baby-sit, do neighborhood yard work)
- Pack their own suitcases
- Be responsible for a pet, i.e. caring for a hamster or lizard

Eleven- to Twelve-Year-Olds

- Run their own errands
- Mow the lawn
- Help a parent build things
- Clean the oven and stove
- Be responsible for a paper route
- Help with family errands

Planning Ahead to Prevent Future Problems

1. Refrain from nagging and reminding. If a job is forgotten, ask the kids to look at the chore list to check if everything is done.

2. If the kids forget to do a chore, use a sense of humor. One mother brought a pot of soup to the table and pretended to ladle the soup into imaginary bowls. The table setter for the evening suddenly realized he had forgotten his job and ran quickly to

bring the bowls before the soup hit the table.

3. Use mutually agreed-upon nonverbal reminders if a chore is forgotten. Many kids like the signal of an upside-down plate at the table. When the plate is upside down, it reminds the kids that part of the routine needs to be completed before sitting down to eat.

Life Skills Children Can Learn

Children can learn that they are part of the family and people need their help. They're capable and skilled and can be useful, for themselves and others.

Parenting Pointers

1. Children aren't born with the competency to do jobs efficiently and quickly. As a matter of fact, it's usually more work to have them help. If, however, you send them out to play so you can zip through the housework, you teach children they are not really needed. Later, you may complain that you have to do it all.

2. The extra effort it takes to involve and train children to help the family is worth it because they learn skills such as keeping commitments, planning ahead, following through, organizing their time, and juggling several tasks at a time.

Chores, Getting Cooperation

(See also *Chores, Age-Appropriate*)

"It is a constant battle to get my child to do his chores. He always says he will, but then he doesn't without constant reminders and hassles that usually end in punishment. I feel like giving up and doing everything myself, but I know he needs to learn responsibility."

Understanding Your Child, Yourself, and the Situation

It is normal for children to avoid chores after the age of three or four. Remember when they were two and said, "Me help, Daddy!" "Me do it, Mommy!"? We discourage toddlers by saying, "No, you're too little. Go play. Go watch TV." Then we wonder why it is difficult to get them encouraged to help again. However, just because it is normal for children to avoid chores doesn't mean they shouldn't do them.

Suggestions

1. Use the "As soon as _____, then _____" formula. "As soon as your chores are done, then you can go out and play."

2. Use follow-through, as described in Part 1.

3. When you are in a power struggle, say, "Let's put this problem on the family-

Booster Thoughts

A two-year-old can scramble eggs and do a pretty good job if you allow him the opportunity and are willing to have some crunchy calcium in your eggs. Can you imagine how proud he will be after this accomplishment? Won't he believe, "I'm capable! I can contribute!"?

Some parents say, "I wouldn't let my child scramble eggs. He might burn himself." It is unlikely your child will burn himself if you have taken time for training and if you supervise the job. However, even if he did receive a little burn, it will heal. How much more damage we do to the confidence and self-esteem of our children when we don't allow them to learn how capable they can be!

meeting agenda and solve the problem when we both feel better."

4. Read *Chores Without Wars*[13] for suggestions on increasing cooperation, accelerating change, developing an encouraging style, handling money, working with teens, involving them, improving cooperation in blended families, and more.

Planning Ahead to Prevent Future Problems

1. Discuss chores at a family meeting so kids can get involved in the planning.

2. For children aged three to four, make a chore spin wheel. Find pictures that represent chores such as dusting, putting the silverware on the table, unloading the silverware from the dishwasher, cleaning the sink, or putting clothes in the washer or dryer. Paste these pictures around the edge of a paper plate. Make an arrow from heavy construction paper. Use a brad to punch a hole through the arrow and the center of the paper plate so the arrow spins around the plate. Let kids spin the wheel to see which chore they will do for the day.

3. For children aged four to six, make a list of chores kids can do at their age level. Put each chore on a piece of paper and put them in a box for each age level. As part of the family meeting, let kids pick out two chores they will do every day for that week. They can pick new chores at the next

13. Lynn Lott and Riki Intner, *Chores Without Wars* (Rocklin, CA: Prima Publishing, 1998).

family meeting so no one is stuck with the same chore all the time.

4. For children aged six to fourteen, use a kitchen whiteboard to list chores that need to be done that day (at least two for each child). Each child (on a first-come basis) chooses the chores he wants to do and then crosses them off the board after they are done.

5. Teens aged fifteen to eighteen may have strong problem-solving skills. Have regular discussions at family meetings to agree on what chores need to be done and to put in place a plan that works for everyone.

Life Skills Children Can Learn

Children can learn that they are capable and can contribute in meaningful ways. They are part of the family and it is important to do their part to keep the family running smoothly.

Parenting Pointers

1. It is important to take time for training to make sure children know what is expected and how to do it.

2. Do not use punishment when chores are not done. Keep going back to the family meeting to work out the problems and come up with plans.

Clothes, Choosing

"What should I do when my child refuses to wear the clothes I picked out?"

Understanding Your Child, Yourself, and the Situation

Parents want children to learn to think for themselves, yet too often they think for their children. We want children to develop self-esteem, yet too often we don't give them the opportunity to see themselves as capable people (a primary ingredient of healthy self-esteem). We may not be aware that sometimes we act more concerned about what others will think if our child is not dressed "properly" than about the well-being of our child.

Suggestions

1. Allow children to choose their own clothes. Ask yourself, "Is it more important that my children be neat and color-coordinated or that they be capable and confident?"

2. Some parents start giving up control by allowing children aged two to four a choice between two outfits.

3. Children between the ages of five and ten need more open choices. Grin and bear it when they leave the house in mis-

matched or "terrible" outfits. Allow them to experience the natural consequences of their choices. They will get plenty of feedback from their peers.

4. As children develop stronger tastes, allow them to go shopping with you and make some choices within your budget. Let them help plan what they need—how many pants, tops, shoes, socks, and underwear. Work on a budget together so they know that if they spend too much on one item they will have to give up another.

5. Ask your children if they would like your opinion about what to wear. They are often interested if it doesn't sound like a lecture.

6. When it is very important to you that your child dress a certain way (the president is coming to dinner), tell her why it is important and ask for cooperation. Strike a bargain: "I don't bug you six days a week, please do this for me one day a week."

7. If you are really concerned about how your child is dressing, sit in front of his school for ten minutes as the children arrive. You will probably find that he fits in perfectly with the other kids if he is picking out his own clothing—probably better than if you chose his clothes.

8. Before interfering in a choice your child is making, ask yourself two questions: Is there any possibility that someday she may need to make a choice when I'm not around? How serious will the consequences of her choice be? The answer to the first question is obvious, so if the consequences are not life-threatening, do not interfere. If she does not like the consequence of her choice, you can gently ask: "What happened? How do you feel about that? What can you learn from this experience? What ideas do you have about what you could do differently next time?"

Planning Ahead to Prevent Future Problems

1. Set up a time in the evening for children to choose the clothes they want to wear the next day. Children often use time restraints as a way to rebel. When they have plenty of time to choose, they usually choose quickly. When they have a limited time to choose, they often want the shirt at the bottom of the clothes hamper and insist that it be washed, dried, and ironed in twenty minutes because it is the only thing in the world that they can possibly wear.

2. During winter, put summer clothes in storage boxes (and vice versa). This reduces unreasonable choices.

3. If children share clothing with their friends, stay out of it. Many children extend their wardrobe by swapping. If clothing gets lost or isn't returned and your children are on a clothing allowance, allow them to experience the consequence of their behavior by waiting until the next financial installment to replace it.

Booster Thoughts

A father shared an experience he had with his style-conscious daughter. He gave her a back-to-school clothes allotment. She decided that instead of buying several interchangeable pieces of clothing, she would buy one Ralph Lauren original. Dad carefully explored the implication of that decision. "Honey, have you considered what kinds of things you will have to wear day in and day out?"

"Yes, I have, Dad. This is real neat and real important. This is what I want."

Dad asked, "Do you understand when your next school clothes allotment will come?" She verified that she understood it would be the following December and that it was now the beginning of September. That confirmed, she went ahead and bought her Ralph Lauren original.

Within a week, she was bored stiff with the outfit, and her friends were asking her if she at least washed it. This touched off a great round of creativity. Having no budget, she took over some extra-large shirts her dad had marginally worn out, got out the sewing machine, and decorated them with drawstrings, rickrack, ribbons, fancy buttons, and appliqués. Somehow, she made it until December.[14]

---

14. From H. Stephen Glenn and Jane Nelsen, *Raising Self-Reliant Children in a Self-Indulgent World* (Rocklin, CA: Prima Publishing, 1989), 200–201.

4. Respect the desires of your children so you don't invite rebellion. If you are worried about what your friends think about how your child dresses, ask yourself if your friends would really think you picked out those outfits.

Life Skills Children Can Learn

Children can learn that their choices are respected as long as they are not harmful to themselves or others. They can learn from their mistakes and develop their judgment.

Parenting Pointers

1. Respect invites respect. When you show respect to your children, they are more likely to respect your reasonable wishes.

2. Children need to rebel a little to test their powers and find out who they are,

separate from their parents. When we allow them to rebel in safe areas (like choosing their own clothes even when we can't stand their choices), they have less need to rebel in areas that are not safe, such as drugs.

3. Allow your children to make choices and mistakes while you are around to give support and have some influence, instead of having them wait until they are on their own and make bigger mistakes because they haven't learned.

Computers and Other Electronic Equipment[15]

"I know that computers are supposed to be wonderful learning tools, but I draw the line when my ten-year-old refuses to do anything other than play computer games from morning till night and sneaks into the chat rooms when I'm not around. I want my kids to have a computer to help them with schoolwork, and I don't even mind if they use it to play some games in moderation. What I am uncomfortable with is all the inappropriate information for children on the Internet, the fighting over who gets to use the computer, and the lack of balance in my children's lives. I'm wondering if we wouldn't be better off going back to our typewriter."

Understanding Your Child, Yourself, and the Situation

There is nothing inherently wrong with a computer. It is simply a tool that can be used to accomplish wonderful things or can be misused. Computers are here to stay, and they continue to find their way into more parts of our lives. The new technology is like a train that is moving forward, and the choice you have is not whether to get on board, but when and how.

15. Thanks to Elisa, Neil, Steve, Rick, Debbie, Devani, Diane, Barbara, Lee, and Jan for their help putting this section together.

Booster Thoughts

The front page of the *San Francisco Chronicle* (February 24, 1998) stated that "Within a few years, students taking college admission exams won't be shading in circles in neat little rows anymore. They will be sitting at computer workstations . . . " and that "pencil and paper already have been eliminated for high-stakes tests such as the Graduate Management Admissions test used by business schools." Many colleges require incoming freshman to have computers as part of the entrance requirement.

The following online rules will help children learn to be respectful with this new tool while preparing them for the future:[16]

- I will not give out personal information such as my address, telephone number, parents' work address/telephone number, or the name and location of my school without my parents' permission.
- I will tell my parents right away if I come across any information that makes me feel uncomfortable.

Your children probably don't remember a time without computers and have been using one kind of electronic device or another almost since birth, including many of their toys. They see and use computers at school, at their friends' homes, in the stores. Children are often quite comfortable learning about computers because they are like a toy or a game to them, and a nonjudgmental one at that. Children disappear into computers and software when they are new. It's how kids learn, but it can be scary for adults.

While your children seem as comfortable with the computer as if it were an old friend, you may be feeling awkward about the new technology and having trouble coming to terms with both using the computer and monitoring the children. You may be resistant to learning about computers because they seem overwhelming and defer to your child, who appears to know more than you. Perhaps you think your children will be deprived if they don't have the latest, top-of-the-line equipment like all their friends, so you let the children use the computer in excess so they can "keep up with the Joneses." Then again, you may have grown up with computers yourself and you realize how beneficial they can be

- I will never agree to get together with someone I "meet" online without first checking with my parents. If my parents agree to the meeting, I will be sure that it is in a public place and bring my mother or father along.
- I will never send a person my picture or anything else without first checking with my parents.
- I will not respond to any messages that are mean or in any way make me feel uncomfortable. It is not my fault if I get a message like that. If I do I will tell my parents right away so that they can contact the online service.
- I will talk with my parents so that we can set up rules for going online. We will decide upon the time of day that I can be online, the length of time I can be online, and appropriate areas for me to visit. I will not access other areas or break these rules without their permission.

16. Many thanks to John R. Lynch, L.C.S.W., Clinical Case Coordinator for County of Sonoma Department of Health Services, Mental Health Division, for sharing his list of "Online Rules" he uses with youth. Use them as they are or modify them for your family's needs.

and can't imagine a home without at least one machine. Like anything else, the problems you are experiencing with the computer can provide a wonderful opportunity for learning by getting the children involved in solving the problems.

Suggestions[17]

1. Don't be afraid to purchase a computer for your home. Even though the technology changes rapidly, the machine and software you buy today will help you and your family become part of the technological revolution. Make computer shopping a family event as you learn about what is available and how much it costs. Your children may be able to help you get exactly what you need. Don't be afraid to purchase a used machine, depending on how it will be used.

2. Have a family project to help earn money to pay for online services, computer

17. Even though most of these suggestions mention computers or the Internet, they could apply to almost any electronic device used in your home.

programs, and other computer products. Expect your children to save part of their allowance to pay for electronic games and accessories.

3. Use the family meeting to set up and troubleshoot schedules and other problems for sharing electronic equipment. If children fight over the equipment, set it or their use of it aside until they are ready to use the equipment for the purpose it is intended and not for fighting. The children can let you know when they are ready to try again, or they can use the family meeting to get help working out a problem.

4. Help your children see the importance of doing school papers on a computer for saving, editing, and neatness functions. Invest in an inexpensive typing program so your children can learn to type their own papers. You do not need to be their secretary.

5. If your children want to play games or visit web sites that you don't think are age-appropriate or that don't fit with your value system, let them know that you don't approve of them because they don't support your value system and that these are not games you want in your home. Do create a dialogue with your children as to your thoughts and feelings and listen to them express theirs.

6. Spend time with your children, helping them download age-appropriate material or games from the Internet. When the family gets a new game, sit down together to help each other learn to play it. Encourage your children to help each other learn how to use the computer or software. The more time you and your children spend together at the computer, the less you will see a computer as a separate world that your children live in without you.

Planning Ahead to Prevent Future Problems

1. Ask your children, friends, and relatives to show you what computers can do and to give you recommendations for age-appropriate software. Take a computer class or read computer information to familiarize yourself with the technology.

2. If at all possible, put in an extra phone line for online activities. You'll be surprised how much the phone line will be tied up without it. If someone is working on the modem and another person picks up the phone, it will disconnect the work being done, so if you don't have an extra line, have a system by which you don't disconnect each other.

3. Get the kids involved in setting up a schedule for using the computer, and stick to it. Work out the times and the length of time on the machine with input from your children. Review the "Follow-Through" section in Part 1 so that you can enforce what you agree upon.

4. If you feel the computer is being abused, unplug the machine or install a

password only you know to access the equipment. Leave the machine disabled until everyone can work out a new plan that the family can try out for a week.

5. Use a rating, shielding, and filtering service available on the net, such as Magellan, Net Nanny, CYPERPATROL, CYBERsitter, and SurfWatch, to help you protect your children from exposure to inappropriate material or harassment of any kind online. There are programs available that can screen and prevent kids from going to certain sites.

6. Create a space accessible to everyone where you keep the computer equipment.

Life Skills Children Can Learn

Children can learn to become excellent researchers and increase their thinking skills using the Internet. They can learn how to be independent and find help without having to leave the house. Resources abound online that help enrich school papers and projects without having to coordinate with an adult for the trip to the library. Children can also learn to find resources without spending money. The computer and its programs can provide hours of free entertainment and endless resources, such as free songs for the guitar, and more.

Parenting Pointers

1. When your children use computers, they are learning skills that will help them become competitive in the new age of social transformation.

2. Even if you are less comfortable than your children in using the equipment, you still have an edge in terms of helping your children to be reliable, responsible, and resourceful.

Cooking

"No matter what I cook, someone doesn't want to eat it. I spend a lot of time trying to feed the family healthy food, and they don't appreciate my efforts at all."

Understanding Your Child, Yourself, and the Situation

Children are more cooperative when they are involved. Cooking is one of the best opportunities in a family for children to contribute, feel a sense of belonging, and help the family. Getting children involved in cooking as early as eighteen months old is a way to share special time together, get help in the kitchen, and teach skills such as eye-hand coordination, sequential learning, creativity, and more. The parent's attitude is the most important part of this equation. If you think working in the kitchen is a chore or just your job, you may be missing out on a lot of fun you could have with your children. Kids love to help cook and are less likely to be picky eaters when they participate.

Suggestions

1. Start early. Let toddlers help stir, pour, measure, taste, and push buttons.

2. Provide your children with children's cookbooks with pictures and easy recipes.

3. Let the children work with you as assistant chef one night a week until they are trained, then be their assistant and let them cook at least one night a week, including choosing the menu.

4. Teach children how to use a microwave and stove safely. Be nearby to supervise them and help if needed until you know they can cook safely without you around.

Planning Ahead to Prevent Future Problems

1. Adopt an attitude that mistakes are wonderful opportunities to learn and grow, and show your children how to remedy mistakes instead of trying not to make them in the first place.

2. Allow for differences—your children may enjoy eating foods that are quite different from the ones you enjoy cooking.

3. Teach children how to make their own school lunches and let them pick out treats at the store for their lunches. When you

Booster Thoughts

Several parents were sharing their favorite stories of their children cooking. One mother remembered the time her ten-year-old misunderstood the directions and used one-fourth cup instead of one-fourth teaspoon of pepper in a stew he was making. When he realized his mistake, all by himself he threw out what he had made so far, searched the refrigerator, and created an entirely new meal in time for the family dinner.

Another parent shared how her eleven-year-old son decided to make ravioli from scratch for dinner. He sent his mom to the store for ingredients, but he didn't start cooking until 5 P.M. The family ate hors d'oeuvres until 11 P.M., when the ravioli was finally completed. Everyone raved about the food as the boy said, "Maybe I'll start earlier next time."

shop, provide them with a small basket and tell them how many treats they can find or how much money they can spend, depending on their ages. Children are old enough to make their own school lunches with your help by first grade.

4. Let children help plan menus during family meetings. They are more likely to eat if they have been involved in menu planning.

5. Make cleanup part of cooking and share that responsibility with the children.

Life Skills Children Can Learn

Children can learn how to plan, use their creativity and imagination, follow directions, help the family, and know what goes into prepared foods. They can learn how to find items in a grocery store, that working in a kitchen can be fun, and that their parents enjoy being with them.

Parenting Pointers

1. Remember that even preschoolers enjoy cooking if they are preparing simple food and if they get supervision and time for training. If you build experience using small steps, children will do just fine.

2. Be willing to let go of staying stuck in a role and thinking it is up to the parent to do the cooking. Don't label kitchen activity as for females only. With training, children can master many recipes and have fun in the kitchen.

Cruelty to Animals

"My little boy kicked the cat. I was so upset, I spanked him and told him he should never be cruel to animals. The very next day he was squeezing the cat and practically choking it to death. How can I teach him to be kind to animals?"

Understanding Your Child, Yourself, and the Situation

It is normal to feel angry and indignant when we see cruelty to animals. It does not help to treat children with the same kind of cruelty (spanking hurts children just as much as kicking hurts animals). Children often treat animals the way they are treated. Children also may show love by hugging too vigorously or experiment by kicking or poking just to see what will happen. Help them find other ways to express their love and curiosity. Chronic sadistic acts may indicate a more serious disturbance that requires professional help.

Suggestions

1. Allow for a cooling-off period and then apologize to your child for spanking him. Tell the truth. Tell him that you were angry about the way he hurt the cat but it was not an excuse for you to hurt him.

2. Get into his world and make a guess about how he felt when you spanked him: "I'll bet you didn't like it when I spanked you. It probably made you feel angry or hurt." Wait for a response, listen, and validate his feelings by saying, "I would probably feel the same way, and I'll bet the cat does, too."

3. If it happens again, take quick action. Separate the cat from the child and say, "It is not okay to treat animals disrespectfully. You can play with the cat again when you are ready to treat him respectfully." You may have to do this several times while breaking the cycle of disrespect outlined in the following suggestions.

4. Give a choice. "You can treat the cat respectfully, or we will find another place for the cat to live where he will be treated respectfully."

Planning Ahead to Prevent Future Problems

1. Decide what you will do. You may be using disrespectful methods with your pets, perhaps unconsciously or perhaps because you think that is the best way to train a dog or cat. Make sure you practice what you preach and stop using punitive methods with your pets.

2. Ask "what" and "how" questions. "How do you think the cat feels when you kick

Booster Thoughts

Rosie used to dress her cats in doll clothes. She would bend their little limbs this way and that as she squeezed them into their outfits. Her mother watched in horror as they scratched and bit her. The cats' behavior never discouraged Rosie, and her behavior never discouraged the cats. In fact, to Mom's amazement, they lived in her room, slept under her covers, avoided the rest of the family, and ran to her like a dog would when she came into view.

Sometimes the best solution to cruelty to animals is to let the child and the animal work it out—as long as the animal is not really being harmed.

him?" "What are you feeling when you kick the cat?" Wait for a response and listen. (Children under four cannot understand abstract reasoning. These children need supervision so parents can separate them from the animals if an incident arises.)

3. When your child feels listened to and that his feelings are validated, you will create an atmosphere of mutual respect and understanding that will help you work together on a solution.

4. Teach your child that feelings and actions are different. It is okay to feel angry. It is not okay to do things that hurt others. Help him find acceptable actions. "What else could you do when you are angry or hurt that won't hurt other people or animals? What could we do to make the cat feel safe and you feel safe?"

5. When children hurt animals or other people, they usually feel hurt themselves (unless they are too young to know that a hard squeeze hurts). See if you can guess what your child might be feeling hurt about. Share your guesses with him in a friendly manner to see if you're right. Work together on solutions.

Life Skills Children Can Learn

Children can learn that it is not okay to physically abuse animals and that they won't be physically abused. They can learn to be respectful because they are treated respectfully. Their feelings are valid and will be listened to. What they do is separate from what they feel.

Parenting Pointers

1. Children learn what they live. If they live with cruelty, they learn cruelty. If they live with respect, they learn respect.

2. Children deserve the same kind of compassion and protection from harm that we give animals.

Crying

(See also *Upset Child*)

"My child is so sensitive that he cries at the drop of a hat. I find this so annoying. How can I get him to change?"

Understanding Your Child, Yourself, and the Situation

Children are different. Every parent who has more than one child can verify this fact. We are sure this isn't news to anyone. Some children cry easily because they have a sensitive nature and this is their way of expressing themselves. Other children cry to seek attention, power, revenge, or as a display of inadequacy. Some children cry out of momentary disappointment, anger, or frustration. And, of course, babies cry because it is their only means of communication. The key is to know your child well enough to know the difference and to have the parenting skills to deal effectively with each situation.

Suggestions

1. You might use reflective listening, which can be done with your mouth shut ("Hmm. Umm"). Then allow him to work the problem out for himself—unless he asks for your help (see "Planning Ahead to Prevent Future Problems," item 4).

2. You could use active listening, which means hearing between the words and verbalizing his deeper feelings: "You feel really angry" (or hurt or upset—whatever you think he might be feeling). Again, that is enough. It can be so validating to a child to feel understood.

3. Never tell your children to stop their crying or call them names such as "crybaby" or "sissy." You might need to leave the room until you feel better and can deal with the crying in a loving, kind, and firm way.

4. Ask if he would like to sit on your lap while he cries. If he does, just offer comfort while he feels what he feels. Or give your child a big hug and wait till the crying ends.

Planning Ahead to Prevent Future Problems

1. Part of your aggravation could be that you think you need to protect him or to fix the problem. It may help if you change your attitude about crying. Allow your child to feel what he feels without thinking you have to fix the problem or change it.

2. Your child needs unconditional acceptance for who he is. If he is sensitive, accept this personality trait even though he is different from you or your ideal. It will also help if you focus on the positive side. Many women wish they were married to men who were more sensitive, and vice versa. Diversity in personalities is one of the things that makes the world interesting.

3. Teach your child about positive time-out (see Part 1). This means he helps design an area that would be comforting and nurturing to him. It might have cushions, books, soft music, or stuffed animals. Then, when he is crying, ask, "Would it help you to go to your comfort spot?" It won't help if you send him there. It is effective only if he chooses to go there. You could offer to go with him.

4. Anytime a behavior becomes a pattern, advance planning is appropriate. Tell your child that you respect his right to feel what he feels. If he would like your problem-

Booster Thoughts

Mrs. Sylvester was concerned because her nine-year-old son, Sam, cried so easily. In her parenting class, she took part in an activity where everyone in the class was given a plant. Some looked better than others. The class leader asked the group if it were possible to change a petunia into a rose. The group got the point. The leader then engaged them in a discussion about what would be needed to nurture the plants they received.

Mrs. Sylvester was touched by this activity and saw how important it was to accept her son just as he is instead of wishing he were different. Within three weeks, Mrs. Sylvester reported to her parenting class that Sam seemed like a different child. She said, "It is amazing. When I stopped wanting him to change, he changed. I don't mean that he stopped being sensitive. He still cries more often than some children. However, now that I simply listen to or comfort him instead of trying to change him, he recovers much quicker. Now that I accept him, he seems to accept himself. He has learned to solve most of his problems with confidence." Unconditional love is very powerful.

solving help, he can let you know when he is ready. Let him know that it is not effective to try solving problems at the time of upset but that you will be available if he wants your help to solve the problem later. (Helping a child solve a problem when asked is much different than trying to help because you feel the need to rescue or overprotect.)

5. Never compare one sibling to another or to anyone else. This is disrespectful and discouraging.

6. Have regular family meetings where all family members have an opportunity to share their feelings and to work on solutions together.

Life Skills Children Can Learn

Children can learn that they are accepted for who they are. They learn that it is okay to feel what they feel and that they can deal with their feelings.

Parenting Pointers

1. Crying is a natural, healthy process, along with laughter, for relieving stress—for both boys and girls.

2. Children should be allowed to cry in the interest of their mental health. However, if you think they are using water power to manipulate you, acknowledge their concern without buying into their manipulation.

Death

(See also *Grief*)

"My child and I were watching the news and saw a story that involved death. My child seemed agitated and confused. How do I approach this issue?"

Understanding Your Child, Yourself, and the Situation

Death is part of living, but in this culture we often avoid or deny the issue. The media sometimes makes death look so awful and violent that it becomes depersonalized. Even when death comes as a natural process for aging grandparents, it usually happens away from home and children are excluded. These issues make it difficult for them to have a healthy understanding of death. Coming to terms with death and dying can enrich living.

Suggestions

1. Don't try to hide death and dying from children. Help them learn to be part of it by talking openly about people who are dying and encouraging children to talk with the dying person.

2. Allow children to participate actively in acknowledgments of death, especially of people close to them, so they can achieve a sense of completion. This includes attending funerals, wakes, and memorial services.

3. When a pet dies, help the children plan an appropriate service and burial. Use this as an opportunity to discuss their perceptions of death as part of life.

4. When children are exposed to violent death, discuss openly their fears and apprehensions. Help them identify resources they have so they don't feel so vulnerable. These might include praying, writing in a

Booster Thoughts

A little girl was killed in a car accident. Her classmates held a class meeting and were invited to celebrate how this little girl had touched them. Each student had a chance to share an appreciation for this girl who had died.

Then the teacher asked her students, "What are your concerns now?" Some of them were afraid to go home. Many had never dealt with death before and didn't know what do to.

The students brainstormed and came up with several suggestions. One was to set up a phone tree so they could call each other, even in the middle of the night. They made a list of people they could talk to during the day—janitors, librarians, a lunchroom supervisor, counselors, teachers, the principal, and each other. It was decided that anyone could get a pass to go talk to someone whenever he or she felt the need. They put pictures of the little girl on ribbon pins, which they wore for a week in her memory. They planted a tree and nurtured it throughout the year to remind them of the girl. The kids became role models for the adult school personnel on the many alternative ways to deal with grief.[18]

18. From Jane Nelsen, Lynn Lott, and H. Stephen Glenn, *Positive Discipline in the Classroom, Revised and Expanded Edition* (Rocklin, CA: Prima Publishing, 1993), 98–99.

journal, drawing, and talking to family members and friends.

Planning Ahead to Prevent Future Problems

1. Talk with your children about preparation for natural disasters that could happen in your area. Make sure they are prepared with a fire, earthquake, or tornado or hurricane safety plan for your home. This may help them feel less vulnerable because they know what to do.

2. If children are worried about international events that could lead to war, encourage them to write letters to their members of congress and the president.

3. Seek out opportunities for children to be involved in the care and support of the elderly or sick.

Life Skills Children Can Learn

Children can learn that death is part of life and that they can face their fears about the future with help and courage. They have many personal resources for dealing with traumatic events. They can also learn to value life more when they know that death is part of it.

Parenting Pointers

1. Work through your own attitudes about death and dying.

2. Share your own thoughts and fears about your mortality.

3. Welcome each day as a gift and share that with your children.

Defiance

"If I say yes, my child says no. If I say, 'Don't run into the street,' my child looks at me and runs into the street. It's like this all day. I'm angry and don't know what to do."

Understanding Your Child, Yourself, and the Situation

You and your child are in a power struggle that can easily turn to revenge. The more you try to force your will with your child, the more she will defy you and the more deeply discouraged you will both become. Some children have a tendency to react to life with optimism, while others tend to react with pessimism. A child may unconsciously find a sense of belonging and importance in a family by being the "grouch" or the "problem," especially if there is an angelic sibling close at hand. Defiant children are a gift sent to parents who need to practice inviting cooperation instead of practicing power over others.

Suggestions

1. The first thing to do is to look at your own behavior. Defiance is often a direct response to parents who are excessively controlling or overly protective.

2. If your child is an arguer, she may have someone nearby who gives her arguing practice. If it's you, practice letting your child have the last word. (This is harder than you think. Try it.)

3. Get into your child's world and make some guesses to learn what is behind the defiance. For example: "Could it be that you are angry because you think I boss you around too much?" "Could it be that you feel hurt because the baby gets so much attention?" You can usually guess what is going on in your child's life that may be provoking defiance. Your child will

feel validated and understood when you guess correctly. If you guess incorrectly, try again.

4. Let your child take the lead whenever possible by offering limited choices. For instance, ask your child, "Do you think you are ready to cross the street by yourself, or would you like me to hold your hand?" "Would you like me to hold onto the back of your bike and help you practice, or can you ride it by yourself?" "Would you like to set the table or carry the dishes to the table so I can set it?"

5. Some children will push and push until they get a spanking. Then they settle down. They have been trained not to settle down until they are spanked. Instead of spanking, hold the defiant child firmly on your lap. No matter how much she struggles, do not let go until she settles down. With an older child, say, "I'm not going to spank you or use any form of physical abuse with you. I am sorry I have used those methods in the past and wish to change our relationship. I'm not happy with what you are doing, but I love you and would like your help so we can stop fighting with each other and work things out together, instead."

6. Instead of telling your child what to do, try asking her what needs to be done. "What do you need to do before you cross the street?" This often invites a child to think and use his power to solve the problem instead of defying your direct orders.

7. Let your child know that you need her help and say, "I would appreciate anything you could do to help." This invites cooperation instead of defiance.

8. Emotional honesty is another help. Remember to use the "I feel ________ because ________ and I wish ________" formula. (See Part 1, page 5.)

Planning Ahead to Prevent Future Problems

1. This is an opportunity for you to learn how to invite cooperation. Pay attention to how much talking you are doing. Are you barking orders, nagging, and scolding? Your child may be "parent-deaf" because you talk more than you act. Talk less and act more if this is the case (see also Listen, Refuses to). Don't say anything unless you mean it, and if you mean it, give the matter your full attention. Say what you mean kindly and firmly, then follow through on what you say (see the "Follow-Through" section in Part 1).

2. For a child who has a pattern of defiance, create time for training. (This includes your training in kindness and firmness.) Take your child someplace, such as the park. The moment he starts defiant behavior, take him by the hand and take him home, saying, "We will try again tomorrow." If you are with other people and don't want to spoil their fun, take the

Booster Thoughts

Thirteen-year-old Billy was called a defiant child by people who spent time with him. He did act like a know-it-all, refusing to listen to anyone. The more others yelled at him, the more he tuned them out and did the opposite. (He did listen long enough to hear what they wanted, so he could do the opposite!)

Billy, his family, and friends went skiing. The ten people in the group spent a lot of time looking for Billy, who took off ahead of everyone and seemed to get "lost" a lot. Everyone was angry with Billy and alternated barking orders at him, threatening him, or whispering behind his back how difficult he was. No one was having any fun.

Billy's older cousin rode up the lift with him and said, "Billy, there's something I want you to think about as you ride up the lift. I'd like your opinion about an idea I have, but I don't want you to tell me what you think until we get to the top of the hill. I was thinking that it might work best, since we're such a large group, to suggest that everyone wait at the top of the hill for the entire group before starting down. I'm not sure if this is a good idea, so please give it some thought and let me know your ideas at the top of the lift." The two boys continued up the long lift talking about baseball, school, and friends.

Billy never said a word at the top of the lift, but the rest of the day he waited patiently for the group to assemble before skiing. He stopped more frequently to look back and wait for stragglers. He had a big smile on his face.

Billy's cousin invited cooperation, and Billy felt important because his cousin asked for his opinion instead of telling him what to do or scolding him one more time. Inviting cooperation works wonders with a defiant child.

defiant child to the car. Have a book handy so you will have something to do while you wait for him to say, "I'm ready to try again." Let your child know in advance that this is what will happen.

3. Give limited choices and ask questions instead of giving lectures. Ask for your child's opinion and input. Really listen to what he tells you.

4. Get your children involved in the planning of events and in problem solving during family meetings. Children are seldom defiant when they have been respectfully included in the decision-making process.

5. Watch out for the "no monster." Are you saying no without thinking every time your child asks you a question or makes a request? Do you say no every time your toddler touches a forbidden object? When children are very young, use distraction to show them what they can do instead of teaching them to say "no" through your example. When they are older, find a way to say yes. For example, when your child says, "I don't want to do what you say," reply with "Yes, I can understand that. How about putting the item on the agenda for the family meeting or telling me your idea of what you think would work better so I can think it over?"

6. Often preschool-age children will say no to everything. If you don't find this cute and adorable, stop asking them questions that can be answered by a yes or no.

7. Choose your battles and let things go that aren't that important. Ask yourself if you will remember or care a week or a month or a year from now about the issue that seems so important to you in the moment. It takes a lot of energy to plan ahead and follow through to make real changes, so don't waste your energy on issues that aren't that important.

Life Skills Children Can Learn

Children can learn that cooperation works better than arguing when everyone is treated respectfully. They can learn that parents mean what they say but also allow and respect appropriate choices

Parenting Pointers

1. Children prefer to cooperate and do what's in their own best interest, but if you treat them disrespectfully, they are willing to suffer great personal pain to show you that you can't boss them around.

2. If you wait and watch before jumping in and controlling, kids will usually do the right thing. If they make a mistake, it's okay to help them correct it or ask how they might do it differently next time. Often it's enough to ask, "Would you like to try again?" instead of becoming controlling or punitive.

3. Children who defy see punishment as an excuse to defy more. Natural consequences work best whenever possible (see "Natural Consequences" in Part 1).

Demanding

"My three-year-old son wanted his milk in a special glass instead of the one I gave him. I was tempted to get the glass for him, but I wondered if I would be teaching him to be spoiled and demanding and to expect special service from others based on capricious whims. On the other hand, if I didn't respect his request, would I be damaging his self-esteem by teaching him that his desires are not important?"

Understanding Your Child, Yourself, and the Situation

This is an excellent question that could be asked by all parents who are interested in developing healthy self-esteem in their children. One of the major causes of deterioration of self-esteem in a child is not being listened to, taken seriously, and affirmed. However, some children become demanding because parents do too much for them, so children develop the expectation that their demands will be met. It is important to understand that fine line so we don't pamper and become a slave to every demand but don't discount children's wishes by negating their importance.

Demanding children are often referred to as "difficult children." (Be careful of labels. This comment is to help you understand, not to label.) Punishment does not help these children, nor does giving in. All of the following parenting suggestions help parents avoid power struggles and to use methods that teach children important life

Booster Thoughts

After Kevin's mother learned the skills we've discussed, Kevin gave her the opportunity to practice the very next day (just to make sure, she gave him a glass she knew he would hate).

Kevin: I don't want this glass.

Mother: If you want another glass, what do you need to do to get it?

Kevin: I can't reach it.

Mother: What would happen if you pushed the chair over to the cupboard? Then what could you do?

Kevin (grinning): I could climb up on the chair and reach the glass.

Mother: Do you need my help pushing the chair over to the cupboard, or can you do it by yourself?

Kevin: I can do it.

He pushed the chair over to the cupboard, got the glass, climbed down, and took the glass over to the table, looking very proud of himself. He spilled quite a lot of milk while pouring it from the old glass into the new.

Mother: What do you need to do now to clean up the milk you spilled?

skills, such as problem solving. This does not mean that demanding children will be "easy" to work with, but punitive methods will only make things worse by inviting power struggles or revenge cycles.

Suggestions

1. Help the child fulfill his own desires by giving him whatever training he needs to get his own glass and pour his milk by himself. (The glass of milk is just an example. You may translate the concepts into other demanding situations.)

2. Ask "what" and "how" questions. (See the "Booster Thoughts" below.)

3. Offer a limited choice: "Can you get another glass of milk by yourself, or do you need my help?" If the choice is help, be sure you just help instead of doing it yourself.

4. With children four years of age and older, simply say, "Sounds like a reasonable request to me, and I'll bet you can figure out a way to get what you want." Then let them do it, instead of feeling it is your job to do it for them.

Kevin jumped down from the table, got a sponge from under the sink, and cleaned up the spilled milk. He left the sponge on the table.

Mother: Do you know what happens to milk when it is left in a sponge?

Kevin: No.

Mother: It turns sour and smells very bad. You'll need to rinse the sponge out in the sink really well before you put it back under the sink.

Kevin happily moved the chair over to the sink, climbed up, and rinsed the sponge out. His mother taught him how to squeeze it thoroughly to get all the milk out.

Mother: Do you want me to bring the old glass over for you to wash while you are at the sink, or do you want to get it?

Kevin: I'll get it.

After the glass was washed, Kevin moved the chair back to the table and sat down to drink his milk out of his special glass.

Time consuming? Yes! Is it worth it? Yes! What has Kevin learned? That his needs and desires are valid and that he is capable of taking care of them. His mother took the time to teach him the skills he needed.

5. When it seems you are in a power struggle, think of your demanding children as cute and adorable. Then go to another room and ignore their demands. Explain that you will be happy to work together on polite requests (perhaps by brainstorming for solutions), but you will ignore impolite requests.

6. When your child asks you to do something he or she can easily do, smile and say, "Good try!" Then let your child do the task without your help.

Planning Ahead to Prevent Future Problems

1. When your child is a preschooler, create solutions to recurring problems. For example, set up a place in a low cupboard for his dishes and a low shelf on the refrigerator with milk and juice in small pitchers, so he can help himself.

2. Take time for training—teach children to clean up spills and to wash their dishes before returning them to the cupboard.

3. Give enough information so that children understand the needs of the situation. For example, milk needs to be cleaned up so it won't sour and smell bad and you can all enjoy a clean kitchen.

4. Be very clear when you will be available to help your child. For example, if your child demands you do laundry at the last minute, tell your child you will be happy to wash clothes that are in the hamper on your laundry day. All other clothes will have to wait, or (if the situation is age-appropriate) you will be happy to show your child how to use the washer. As another example, tell your child you will be available to help with homework from 6 to 8 P.M.; after that, you are busy doing things for yourself.

5. Have faith in your child and verbalize encouragement: "I have faith in you. You can do it. You are a good problem solver."

6. As soon as your children reach the age of four, family meetings provide an excellent opportunity for them to learn cooperation skills (see "Family Meetings" in Part 1).

Life Skills Children Can Learn

Children can learn that it is okay to want what they want but it is not okay to demand special service from others. They feel better about themselves when they learn to be self-reliant and respectful to others.

Parenting Pointers

1. Some parents give in to the demands of their children in the name of love. It is an unloving thing to do for yourself and for your child.

2. When parents give in to children's demands, they are teaching their children that "Love means getting other people to take care of my demands."

3. Be kind and firm at the same time. Your confidence and tone of voice will convey that it is possible to respect yourself and

the needs of the situation (firm) and the needs of your children (kind). Kind does not mean that you give in but that you are respectfully firm.

Depressed Child

"My child seems so depressed all the time. Is this a physical problem?"

Understanding Your Child, Yourself, and the Situation

Everyone feels depressed at one time or another. There is a difference between feeling depressed from time to time and consistently acting in a depressed fashion. When children are depressed, it may be a sign of something disturbing happening in their lives. They may be being abused or molested or neglected by a parent who is addicted to alcohol or drugs. It is important to keep your perspective and look for the pattern. If depression is a recurring symptom, get professional help for yourself and your child. Stay away from therapists and doctors who treat depression in children with antidepressants. Your child's feelings are an important indicator of something serious, and putting a drug Band-Aid on them won't get to the deeper issues. Some children have learned that acting depressed is a way to get special service or extra attention (read about the four mistaken goals of misbehavior in Part 1).

Suggestions

1. Be curious. Ask your child open-ended questions about what is going on, such as "Is there something happening that you are feeling bad about? Can you tell me about it?" "I see a big gloomy face. Anything I can do to help?"

2. Sometimes you can get information from your children by asking silly questions or guessing how they feel, such as "Are you angry because your teddy bear won't play with you?" "I bet I know why you're sad—because I forgot to tickle you today." "You're feeling unhappy because I spent more time with your sister than with you, and you wish I would play with you more."

3. Stay open. Don't assume you know why your child is unhappy. Parents often assume that children are unhappy for the same reasons they might feel bad. Where there has been a divorce or death, parents might think that is causing their child to be unhappy. When they ask the child what is bothering her, they may find out that she wishes she had a friend to play with or money to buy a special outfit instead.

Booster Thoughts

Two children in the same family displayed depression quite differently. The eight-year-old girl was threatening to kill herself by mixing various concoctions together and then threatening to eat them. Her family came in for counseling, and in the course of the session she admitted that she liked it when her parents noticed her and that they were very attentive when she threatened suicide. The counselor suggested that perhaps her parents could each spend fifteen minutes a day doing something fun with her as a way for her to get attention.

She loved the idea. After a week of special time, her depression in the form of "suicidal" tendencies disappeared.

Her ten-year-old brother, on the other hand, seemed sullen and angry all the time. His depression was anger turned inward. When the counselor asked him to describe a typical day, it involved six or more hours of watching television by himself. The counselor expressed concern to the parents that his television viewing was addictive and harmful and that he needed some help creating other ways to spend his time. When his parents agreed to limit the time their son spent watching television, he said he didn't know what else to do. His family, the boy, and the counselor brainstormed a list of other activities he could do instead of watching television.

The first week, the boy just watched the blank television screen. The next week, he would walk over, look at the list, and then sit down with his head in his hands. By the third week, he realized his parents weren't going to weaken on the television limitation rule, so he tried out some of the activities on the list. It took him over six weeks to shake his depression, smile, and enjoy other ways of amusing himself.

Planning Ahead to Prevent Future Problems

1. Keep the lines of communication open with your children. Let them know they can tell you how they feel without your making fun of them or telling them they shouldn't feel the way they do.

2. Some children get depressed when they think their parents will be disappointed in

Twelve-year-old Mitchell couldn't sleep. He started to go downhill in school and refused to eat. He generally seemed gloomy and grumpy all day. His mother worried about him and took him to the family doctor, who listened to the symptoms and immediately wrote a prescription for antidepressants for Mitchell. No one took the time to find out what was bothering him. Instead, they looked for a cause, made a diagnosis, and came up with a treatment.

One day, Mitchell was spending the night at his father's house. (His parents were in the process of getting a divorce and had been in an acrimonious battle for over two years.) He and his dad were watching TV together when Mitchell asked, "Dad, are you planning to marry someone else and leave us with Mom?"

"Mitchell," Dad responded, "what are you talking about? You sound pretty worried. What brought this on? You know I love you and would never leave you kids. Mom and I won't be living together anymore, but you'll always be part of my life and we'll always find ways to be together. I thought you knew this."

"Well, Dad, Mom said that you had a new girlfriend who doesn't like kids and that she'd probably tell you we couldn't come over and make you move far away. I didn't think it was true, but then I overheard you on the phone the other day talking to someone about relocating to another state."

Dad put his arms around Mitchell and said, "No wonder you've been worried. If you ever feel this way again, please check things out with me right away. The conversation you overheard was me complaining to my friend. I wasn't serious. You know how when you are mad you sometimes say things you don't really mean? That was what you heard—me exaggerating. I'm here to stay, Mitch, and if there are ever any big changes in the future, you and I will discuss them at length before anything happens. I love you."

them. Be sure your children know they are loved unconditionally.

3. Anger turned inward creates depression. Children may be angry about things they don't realize it is okay to be angry about. Look for ways you may be overcontrolling, overly protective, or having overly high expectations for your children. These situations may create unconscious, hidden anger.

4. Be sure you are not taking sides in your children's fights or labeling a child as a troublemaker or bad child. Children may end up feeling hopeless and helpless if they think they are unloved and have no one who will take their side.

5. Don't make threats you don't mean. Children can get scared and take you literally if you say things like "You kids are making me so angry, I'm going to pack my bag and run away from home." Your children need to know that they are secure, and threats made in the heat of anger can cause a lot of harm if your kids take you seriously.

6. Stop overprotecting your children. Overprotection invites children to feel depressed when they don't get their way or when they lack the skills to do what is needed (because everything has always been done for them).

Life Skills Children Can Learn

Children can learn that they can tell adults what is troubling them and that there is someone for them to talk to. They don't have to figure everything out themselves or carry secrets around. They can learn appropriate ways to express anger so it isn't transformed into depression (see *Angry Child*).

Parenting Pointers

1. Don't try to talk children out of their feelings or think you know how they really feel better than they do.

2. It's okay for children to be unhappy and depressed at times. If you let them have their feelings, they will probably cycle out of their mood quickly. If you try to make them happy when they aren't, they may stay upset to show you that you aren't in charge of their feelings.

Disagreements Between Parents

"Everyone says my wife and I should maintain a united front with the children. I think she's too strict, and she thinks I'm overindulgent. I don't see how we could ever agree on anything about our kids."

Understanding Your Child, Yourself, and the Situation

Where did we ever get the crazy notion that coparenting means both parents have to think and act exactly alike with the children? If there is mutual respect in a relationship, then both parents respect themselves as well as each other and know that it is okay to agree to disagree. Children have no trouble learning that Dad does things one way and Mom another. This is not confusing to children. What is damaging is when parents try to overcompensate for the other parent instead of being themselves or when they allow children to manipulate the parents against each other and run the family. Once parents learn to value the differences and work with them, there can be joy and shared responsibility in coparenting. (The ideas in this discussion apply to blended families, divorced families, families where several generations are helping parent the children, and families with two parents living together.)

Suggestions

1. Agree to disagree. Let the other parent know that while you may not like the way he or she does something, you are willing to respect his or her relationship with the children. Feel free, when the children aren't around, to discuss your ideas, thoughts, and feelings about parenting.

2. If the children need a decision, let them know that they need a yes from each parent before they can proceed.

3. Do not interfere with what the other parent is doing. Discuss your thoughts later. (This advice does not apply if safety or any form of abuse is involved. See *Sexual Abuse* and *Fears* for more information.)

4. Get out of right/wrong thinking and appreciate differences. Look at what each parent contributes to the family and focus on strengths.

5. Don't bad-mouth the other parent in front of the children or ask them to carry messages from one parent to another. Don't complain to the children about the other parent and expect them to help you work out your relationship with your mate or ex-mate.

6. If your children tattle about the other parent, suggest they put their complaint on the agenda for the family meeting or let them know you will go with them while they tell the other parent their concern. Don't try to fix things for the kids without them being part of the solution.

7. Do not make threats to your spouse around the children, such as "I'm going to divorce you" or "I'm going to run away from home if you keep acting like this." You don't want to scare your children or teach them that threats are a way of settling disagreements. If necessary, tell your children that you and their other parent disagree and can't seem to work things out without help. Then seek a counselor or conflict management class to improve the situation.

Booster Thoughts

Ten-year-old Brett told his father, Sam, "Mom said I can stay overnight at Skip's house and that I don't have to play in my baseball game tomorrow morning."

Sam was enraged and said, "You'll be at that game, and I don't care what your mother said."

Later that day, Brett's mom, Helen, said to her husband, "Why did you tell Brett he can't stay at Skip's house?"

Sam asked, "Why did you give Brett permission to miss his baseball game?"

Helen was dumbfounded. "Sam, why would I say a thing like that? I thought we stressed how important it was to be at all the games if the kids decided to play ball."

"Well, I thought so, too," replied Sam.

"I think someone is taking advantage of us, and it's time we stopped Brett in his tracks."

"What do you suggest?"

"Well," said Helen, "let's tell Brett that he has to get two yes answers before he can do what he is asking. If you think he's making up stories, bring him to me while he asks for the second yes."

Planning Ahead to Prevent Future Problems

1. Before having children, discuss the baggage you bring with you about parenting roles and responsibilities. Negotiate solutions for child care that you can both live with.

2. Hold regular family meetings to discuss problems instead of trying to maneuver behind the scenes or keep secrets from other family members.

3. Take parenting classes. Many parents lack skills and information that are easy to pick up in parenting classes.

4. Make clear what you want from your partner instead of expecting him or her to read your mind.

Life Skills Children Can Learn

Children can learn that it is okay to be different and that they have the skills to handle the differences. Their parents are the leaders

Sam smiled. "I like that idea. I think Brett has been playing games with us."

Later that day, Brett approached his father and said, "Mom said I can go to the store by myself. See you later, Dad."

"Wait a minute, son. Let's go check that out. It's okay with me if you go to the store by yourself, but let's see what Mom says."

"But Dad, Mom always lets me go to the store."

"Great. Then this won't be any problem at all."

Brett looked sheepish as he reluctantly followed his dad.

"Helen, Brett says it's okay with you if he goes to the store. It's okay with me, too."

"Excuse me," exclaimed Helen. "I just told Brett that he has to clean his room before he can go anywhere. When he's done with his room, it's okay with me for him to go to the store if it's also okay with you."

Brett grinned and said, "That's what I meant, Dad." He ran up the stairs to begin cleaning his room, while Helen and Sam chuckled quietly.

in the family, and there are ways to work out differences without manipulation and game playing. Children can learn the joys of cooperation and the fun of having many different personalities loving and caring for them.

Parenting Pointers

1. Think about what your children are learning about conflict resolution from your couple relationship. If you practice manipulation and disrespect, your children will learn that. If you practice shared decision making, joint problem-solving, and win/win conflict resolution, your children will learn that.

2. If there is violence of any kind in the family—such as physical abuse, sexual abuse, or substance abuse—call for help. These situations can't be solved alone. Most communities have groups and programs to assist families with these problems so that you don't have to feel alone or walk around carrying secrets that damage everyone's self-esteem.

Divorce

"I want to get a divorce, but I'm so afraid it will hurt my children. Should I stay in my marriage for the sake of the children?"

Understanding Your Child, Yourself, and the Situation

Many situations in life can be hurtful for children, including divorce. There is evidence, however, that a bad marriage is more difficult and hurtful for children than an amicable divorce is. There are many things parents can do to reduce the pain of divorce for children.

Suggestions

1. Your attitude will greatly influence your child's attitude. If you feel guilty, the children will sense that a tragedy is taking place and will act accordingly. If you accept the fact that you are doing the best you can under the circumstances, children will sense this and act accordingly.

2. Encourage your children to express their feelings and show that you understand.

Booster Thoughts

In their book, *For the Sake of the Children*, Kris Kline and Dr. Stephen Pew point out that the anger and resentment accompanying divorce don't dissolve when the papers are signed.[19] Instead, the bitterness lingers on, sometimes for many years. This can cause tremendous harm to the children, who still love both parents and may feel caught between them. Parents going through a divorce may unconsciously torment their children in various ways. Sometimes, the custodial parent uses the children as a sounding board for his or her anger toward the other parent. At other times, mentioning the absentee parent becomes taboo. The child feels that the love he or she has for the absentee parent is almost illicit.

In this wise and practical book, the authors offer effective ways to break the pattern of behavior that leads to further pain. They asked children if they had any recommendations for divorcing parents, which, if followed, might make the process of divorce less painful for other children going through it. Here are some of the suggestions they received:

Frankly discuss that the change is painful for all of you and express confidence that you will all be able to handle it with time. If your children don't want to talk, don't badger them. Talk about your feelings, and trust that theirs will unfold if you are available for listening when they are ready.

3. Do not fight over the children. Children want to love and respect both parents. It is easier for children to love several parents (in the case of remarriage) than it is for them to have to choose between their two natural parents.

4. Do not say degrading things about each other in front of the children. You will probably be in pain yourself. It may be tempting to seek revenge through the children. Be aware of how much this hurts your children and avoid the temptation.

5. Encourage your children to love and respect both of you. Let them know they are not being disloyal to you by loving their other parent too.

6. Children benefit when the parent who does not have custody of the children maintains contact with them on a consistent

- "Try not to talk about each other in a negative way in front of your kids. Keep your problems between yourselves."
- "Even though you're going to be apart, make an effort to get along, I mean, like anybody else; if you needed to get along with somebody at work or whatever. You know, just for the child, so the child can have both parents around. Just make an effort to get along."
- "It isn't fair when your mom says that if you love her you won't love your dad, or you have to love her more than you love your dad."
- "Allow the children to like the other parent. Make it okay to like the other parent. And if you don't like them, so what? Grin and bear it."

The one strong theme that seemed to consistently emerge from conversations with young people was a desire to be allowed to love both parents equally without having to take sides.

---

19. Kris Kline and Stephen Pew, *For the Sake of the Children* (Rocklin, CA: Prima Publishing, 1992), 202–203.

basis that they can count on. This is not always possible, but do not discourage contact if it is possible. Don't forget to spend one-on-one time with each child even if you have them for only a limited time.

7. Do not try to be the "good" parent. Often the parent who does not have custody fights for the children's loyalty by providing special treats and outings every time they are together. This makes it difficult for children who need order and routine, and eventually the children expect special treats all the time.

Planning Ahead to Prevent Future Problems

1. Children often wrongly assume that something they did caused the divorce. Reassure them that the divorce is not their fault.

2. Maintain the family's regular routines. A parenting class or support group can be helpful at this time.

3. At family meetings, share feelings and solutions to problems.

4. Seek outside help. Because of the pain and trauma you are experiencing yourself, it may be very difficult to be objective enough to accomplish these guidelines without support.

Life Skills Children Can Learn

Children can learn that they can handle whatever life presents with courage and optimism. They can see the opportunity to learn and grow from experiences instead of seeing problems as failures.

Parenting Pointers

1. Studies on children of divorce have shown that when parents handled divorce effectively, their children did better socially, academically, and emotionally one year after the divorce.[20]

2. Don't expect instant adjustment—adjusting to divorce is a process.

---

20. ". . . when the divorce is undertaken thoughtfully by parents who have carefully considered alternatives; when the parents have recognized the expectable psychological, social, and economic consequences for themselves and the children; when they have taken reasonable measures to provide comfort and appropriate understanding to the children; where they have made arrangements to maintain good parent-child relationships with both parents—then those children are not likely to suffer developmental interference or enduring psychological distress as a consequence of the divorce. Even though the children may still regret the divorce and continue to wish that their parents had been able to love each other, some of these children may nevertheless grow in their capacity for compassion and psychological understanding." Judith S. Wallerstein and Joan Berlin Kelly, *Surviving the Breakup: How Children and Parents Cope with Divorce* (New York: Basic Books, 1980), 316.

Eating, Picky

(See also *Mealtime Hassles*)

"I have a daughter who just turned five. She is a very picky eater, and I cannot remember the last time she ate the same thing we ate during a meal. All she wants to eat is peanut butter sandwiches and cereal. I know this isn't good nutrition. What should I do?"

Understanding Your Child, Yourself, and the Situation

We don't understand how most children survive on the diet they eat. So many get too much sugar, soda pop, and junk food. However, they seem to survive and even thrive. The problems occur when parents engage in power struggles or try to overprotect their children. This invites children to develop one of the four mistaken goals around eating—to seek undue attention, to win the power struggle, to hurt themselves (through poor nutrition) in an effort to hurt back when they feel hurt by conditional love or overcontrol, or to believe they are inadequate due to pampering.

Suggestions

1. Don't try to make your children eat anything, as that will only invite power struggles.

2. Do not give your children undue attention for not eating.

3. Avoid lectures about starving children. Instead of having the effect you want, your children will probably tell you to send the food to them.

4. Do not make special meals for your children (see "Planning Ahead to Prevent Future Problems," item 7).

5. Decide on a beginning time and an ending time for meals. Ten to fifteen minutes is usually plenty of time for young children. At the end of the agreed-upon time, clear the table. If children complain that they are still hungry (because they have been dawdling), say, "I'm sure you can make it until our next meal." Children will learn from your actions that mealtime is not a time for manipulation.

6. Follow the suggestions in "Planning Ahead to Prevent Future Problems." Then

Booster Thoughts

One of our toddlers participated in a university preschool program in which all kinds of foods were placed on the lunch table and kids were allowed to eat what they wanted. Sometimes the toddler would eat cake first, and sometimes he would eat broccoli first. The main thesis of this program was that children would naturally choose foods that would balance out to good nutrition (over time) when they were allowed to choose from a variety of nutritious foods—without anyone making a fuss.

One mother thought it was her job to control what her daughter ate. If her daughter didn't eat her oatmeal for breakfast, Mom would give it to her for lunch. If she didn't eat the oatmeal for lunch, Mom would give it to her for dinner. Of course, her daughter refused to eat it. The daughter became sick. A doctor discovered she was developing rickets. It was more important for the daughter to win the power struggle than to eat.

When the doctor learned what was happening, he said, "Please put good food on the table and then leave your daughter alone." When the mother did this, her daughter started eating better. Not perfect, but better. Today, that daughter worries about eating too much because, like so many normal people, she is gaining weight.

---

be sure your children get a good multiple vitamin and relax.

Planning Ahead to Prevent Future Problems

1. As with every issue, children are more cooperative when they are respectfully involved. Even toddlers can help wash and tear lettuce, set the table, or help in many other ways (see *Chores, Age-Appropriate*).

2. When children reach the age of three to four, let them help plan meals. They are more likely to eat what they have helped plan. They can also help with the shopping and meal preparation.

3. Do not bring junk food into the house. Of course children won't eat regular meals

As frightening as eating disorders can be, most of them can be prevented if we just turn eating over to the child. One mother learned that when her teen says she's going on a diet, it's better to say "That's nice" and see what happens than to lecture, panic, or even help. Usually, her already-trim daughter diets for a few days and then goes back to her normally balanced and healthy eating patterns (which include a certain amount of junk food).[21]

All eating disorders have to do with control issues. Some kids lose their sense of power over their bodies and either eat out of control (obesity) or use starvation or vomiting (anorexia and bulimia) to overcompensate for their lack of power.

To say that teens with eating disorders are discouraged is an understatement. The reason they choose to act out their discouragement through food, though, is usually a function of the atmosphere created by the parent or society or by the parental style of nurturing.

Since any discouraging behavior tends to be a mistaken way of dealing with thoughts and feelings, it is important to listen to your kids and to not discount or ignore their feelings. We can also help our kids learn to express their feelings in words rather than through discouraged behaviors. If we find ourselves focusing on achievement rather than on building competence, we need to back off, since such pressure gives the message that we only love our kids if they are perfect.

21. From Jane Nelsen and Lynn Lott, *Positive Discipline for Teenagers* (Rocklin, CA: Prima Publishing, 1994), 323.

when they have filled up on snacks or junk foods.

4. Especially avoid products that contain sugar. Sugar can really mess up the body's natural craving for good foods.

5. Provide healthy snacks. It is fine if your children don't eat because they have filled up on cheese, carrot sticks, or other healthy snacks. Who said good food should be eaten only at mealtimes?

6. Plan meals around simple foods that children usually enjoy, such as spaghetti, macaroni and cheese, tuna casserole, tacos, hamburgers, mashed potatoes and gravy, Jell-O fruit salad, and toasted cheese sandwiches. Most children do not like the "gourmet" foods that adults enjoy.

7. Teach children how to make their own peanut butter sandwiches or tortillas with cheese. Continue including them in the planning and preparation of meals. Let them know that in the future they can choose between eating what is on the table and making their own sandwiches or tortillas. Then, without making a fuss, let them choose. If they complain about what is on the table, ask, "What do you need to do about that?"

Life Skills Children Can Learn

Children can learn that they can develop a taste for foods on their own schedule. They can learn that they will not be pressured to eat what they don't want, nor will be they be given special service. Children can learn that respect is a two-way street.

Parenting Pointers

1. We have talked to people who were raised during the depression. They say picky eating was never a problem. Parents didn't make a fuss when a child didn't want to eat because there often wasn't enough to go around. When children didn't get any mileage out of being a picky eater, they ate what was available or went hungry.

2. Most children change their eating habits in time—and much quicker when parents don't fuss and engage in power struggles.

Fabricating

(See also *Lying*)

"My child is constantly making up stories that other kids are hitting her. I thought this fabricating might be a stage, but it's not stopping."

Understanding Your Child, Yourself, and the Situation

Fabrication is a normal part of early childhood, as fantasy and reality tend to merge. Enjoy it and become part of the story whenever possible—you may end up with a creative child. Fabrication is sometimes a defense mechanism used when people fear that the truth will be ridiculed or dismissed or will reflect badly on them. Whenever possible, look behind the fabrication to see its intent. There might be

Booster Thoughts

As a four-year-old, Harold was afraid of the dark. His three-year-old sister used to tease him about it and put him down. One night, they were staying in a place where they had to cross an outside porch to get to a toilet. The wind was blowing, and the night seemed quite frightening. Finally, Harold's fear of wetting himself overcame his fear of the journey to the toilet, so he set out for the other end of the porch. Halfway across, he stepped into the light from a streetlight and was startled by his own large, "powerful" shadow.

In Harold's childish mind, it dawned on him that if he were large and powerful like his shadow, he would always feel secure. A lifelong pattern developed in which Harold tried to appear bigger than life in order to feel secure and accepted. When people rejected his fabrications, he would feel more insecure and develop another fabrication. Finally, someone looked beyond the fabrications to see what they meant to Harold and helped him outgrow this pattern through acceptance and support. This person helped Harold know that he is much better than any shadow—no matter how large.

The octopus, when threatened, releases an ink cloud bigger than it is to hide and escape behind. A skunk believes that the bigger the stink it can create, the safer it will be. So fabricators have some company in the animal kingdom.

more to a story than meets the eye. There is a lot to learn from our kids if we aren't so quick to correct or ignore them and let them talk instead. Your child might be trying to tell you something really important and not have the words or the skill to do it any other way. Some children make up stories to impress or upset others, but before jumping to conclusions, act as if your child has something worthwhile to communicate.

Suggestions

1. Instead of saying, "That's not true," try, "Tell me more about it."

2. Address the child's feelings instead of the words by saying, "You sound really

upset. I'm glad you wanted to talk to me about it."

3. Play "Let's Pretend" and ask your child to role-play and show you what happened. Even very young kids like to put on a show.

4. If you really think children are playing games with you, let them know that it's okay to tell stories and you like hearing them. You might also swap tall tales.

5. Remind kids of the story of "The Little Boy Who Cried Wolf." Let them know that if it's a story and not true, they should tell you so you can be there for them when they really need you.

Planning Ahead to Prevent Future Problems

1. Let children know that there may be times when kids or grown-ups tell them not to tell their parents about something. Assure your children that they can always tell you, that they won't get in trouble, and you will always love them.

2. Spend time each day with your child just hanging out, especially before bedtime, to create a time when your child knows you are available and it's safe to talk to you.

3. The child's world is one of play, and storytelling can be a great way to play. Every story, even if it's made up, has an element of truth hidden in it. Look for the deeper meanings.

Life Skills Children Can Learn

Children can learn that it is okay to be creative and that there is a difference between storytelling and facts. They can learn that they can tell the facts without getting into trouble and that their parents care about what they have to say.

Parenting Pointers

1. If your kids are afraid of getting in trouble or getting a friend in trouble, they may test you with partial details or made-up stories to see how you will handle things.

2. There are instances of child abuse and sexual assault that have gone unnoticed because a parent was too quick to tell a child, "You must be making this up." Kids need our protection and need to be taken seriously.

3. Fabrication is sometimes a form of self-enhancement used by insecure people. They have found that they can gain attention and recognition by embellishing or fabricating tales of their experiences.

Fairness

"My oldest is always complaining that his sister gets more than he does and is treated better. He says I'm not being fair. I try to make everything even, but he still thinks I love his sister more and that she is spoiled and he is deprived."

Understanding Your Child, Yourself, and the Situation

Many parents bring issues of fairness with them from their own growing up. We call these "justice issues." Our justice issues can get passed on to our children and create problems if we are unaware of them. The more a parent tries to be fair, the more children make an issue of fairness. Fairness is a very personal, selective idea—what is fair to one person may seem unfair to another. It is normal for children to compare themselves with their siblings or feel jealous. This doesn't mean that the parent's job is to fix everything or to try to control the family so a child never feels these feelings.

Suggestions

1. When children say, "It's not fair," listen to their feelings and validate them. Avoid the temptation to do more. Just feeling validated can be enough. Tell your children, "You're feeling jealous and hurt because you think someone is getting more than you. You wish you were being treated the same." Children will let you know if that's not what they're upset about.

2. Encourage a deeper level of sharing by asking curiosity questions: "Can you tell me more about that? Can you give me some other examples? Is there anything else that is bothering you? Anything else?" This last question can be repeated until the child says no. Again, it is often enough just to be listened to, thoroughly.

3. Use a sense of humor. For instance, if your child says, "He gets to stay up later and that's not fair," you could say, "Of course he gets to stay up later. That's because he has more freckles than you do." Then give your child a big hug. Another response is, "Good try! Now off to bed. See you in the morning."

4. Let children tell you why they think things are unfair and how they would fix things to make them fair. Suggest that they pretend they have a magic wand that can make everything fair. If they waved the wand, how would things change? You may or may not wish to act on their ideas.

5. Ask your child, "If you were the parent, what would you do about this situation?" Listen carefully to the ideas.

6. Help your children appreciate differences and uniqueness. For example, you might say to your younger child, "If your older brother goes to bed later, are you saying it's only fair that you do, too, because you think everything should be the same? I consider your differences and decide what

Booster Thoughts

Two kids, aged seven and five, were always fighting over who got to sit in the front seat of the car. No matter how many times their father explained to them why it was fair that one or the other sit in front, there were always hurt feelings and complaints. One day, in exasperation, the father said, "The front seat is off-limits until the two of you come up with a plan you can both live with for sharing the front seat without fighting. I am tired of hearing you argue about who sits where and getting mad at me for trying to come up with something I think is fair. Please work out a plan when I'm not around. I don't want to know what it is, either. Just let me know when you are ready to share the front seat without fighting, and we'll all try again."

A few days later, the two children came to their father and said, "We have a plan for the front seat, and we're ready to try again." Their father said fine, and he watched as they buckled their seat belts in the seat of their choice. For weeks, the children, as if by magic, took turns based on some kind of mysterious system that the father never figured out.

One day, the kids started bickering over the front seat again, and their father said, "Both of you in the back. Your plan for sharing seems almost perfect, but it looks like you have a few kinks in it. Work them out and tell me when you're ready to try again." Later that day, the kids said all was worked out, and from that day on the seat changing operated without a hitch.

Too often, as grown-ups we think we are the only ones who can make things fair, but until fairness fits our children's sense of justice, which may be very different from our own, the complaining and fighting persist. Have faith in your kids to work out many of the problems that you think only a parent can handle.

is best for each of you—because you are special in different ways. I'm willing to work with you on how much sleep you need, but the decision doesn't have anything to do with your brother."

7. Look for ways to let the kids decide how to make things fair. Some ideas include letting the kids serve themselves, letting one kid divide the items and the other choose first, and having the kids pick a number or a hand

held behind the back. Let the kids brainstorm for a solution they can all live with. (See the "Booster Thoughts" on previous page.)

Planning Ahead to Prevent Future Problems

1. Hold regular family meetings so the kids can place items important to them on the agenda. At the meeting, ask your children if they just want to complain or if they would like to have the family do some problem solving. Either would be fine.

2. Explore your own justice issues. Think of things you thought were unfair when you were a kid and see if you are teaching your children to hold the same opinions. Ask yourself if that is what you want to do.

3. If you have a "fair button," you might want to get rid of it. Children know how to push our buttons.

Life Skills Children Can Learn

Children can learn that "equal" doesn't mean "the same" and that it is more important to understand differences than to accept one person's notion of what is fair. They also can learn problem-solving skills and a variety of ways to make choices and decisions when there are differences of opinions.

Parenting Pointers

1. It's more important to try to understand why your children think the way they do and what their issues are than to try to rectify the situation or prevent injustices from happening.

2. "It's not fair" ceases to be an expression that manipulates parents to fix things when it is met with either curiosity or turning the problem back to the children. One father stopped complaints about unfairness simply by saying, "I don't do fair."

Fears

"My child has nightmares and complains about monsters in his room. He seems so fragile compared to other children his age. He's afraid to leave my side. This doesn't seem normal to me."

Understanding Your Child, Yourself, and the Situation

"A bruised knee can mend, but bruised courage lasts a lifetime."[22] Sometimes children have fears because we don't help them deal with the unknown by showing them

---

22. Rudolf Dreikurs with Vicki Soltz, *Children: The Challenge* (New York: Plume Books, 1990), 36.

Booster Thoughts

Sometimes children just need a little jump-start, like six-year-old Jane, who became fearful in her first-grade class. She developed the irrational fear that the doors and windows would lock and she wouldn't be able to get out. Periodically she would look at the windows and the door and start to cry. The teacher couldn't understand why she was crying and would get exasperated. The teacher tried sitting her on her lap and called her a baby. Jane cried louder. The teacher put her out in the hall. Jane cried for a while and then left the building. The principal saw her and told her she had to go back into class. Jane started crying and refused. The principal picked her up and carried her (kicking and screaming) back into the class. Jane cried so loudly that the principal had to come get her and take her to his office until it was time to go home.

The next day, Jane's mother helped her pick a rose from their garden to take to the teacher. Then Mom went to school with her and sat in the classroom all day. Jane felt comforted that her mother was there and didn't experience any fear. She

how to do things in small steps. Most of us have some fears, but they become bigger when others make fun of us, call us babies, or tell us that it's not okay to be scared or to cry. Fear is usually about the unknown, although children have good reason to be afraid at other times. It's not our job to protect children from every discomfort in life. If we do, they don't develop the confidence that they can handle some discomfort. If they have been abused, molested, or hurt in some way, their fears are healthy and justified. Then it is our job to do what we can to eliminate the scary situation from their lives.

Suggestions

1. Don't laugh at, minimize, judge, or discount your children's fears.

2. Listen when your children tell you what they are afraid of. Verify their feelings, such as saying, "You're afraid of dogs because they might bite you, and you wish the dog would go away and leave you alone." Sometimes just having their feelings validated is enough to lessen the fear.

3. Help your children find ways to handle situations when they are afraid instead of being manipulated by their fears. Offer

enjoyed her day in school. From then on, she went to school by herself and didn't experience any more fear about being locked in.

Ten-year-old Lisa decided she wanted to watch *Halloween III,* an extremely scary movie. Her parents said they thought the movie was too scary, but she insisted on watching it. No one in her family wanted to watch the movie with her, so Lisa decided she would watch it by herself. Her parents said they would be in the next room, and if she got scared, she could come in for reassurance.

Lisa's mother made her a bowl of popcorn, and her father helped her carry in her stuffed animals and special quilt. He turned on all the lights at Lisa's request and left the room as the movie began.

About ten minutes later, Lisa came into the living room and said, "I don't think I'm really in the mood to watch that movie tonight. Maybe I'll watch it another time."

Some children do what they really don't want to do so they can win the power struggle with their parents. Lisa's parents supported her to learn for herself how much she could handle.

comfort, but don't give them special service or try to fix their feelings for them. Help your children explore several possibilities so they feel that they have some choices. You might ask, "What would help you the most right now—a flashlight, a teddy bear, or a night-light?" Telling them not to be afraid isn't helpful; looking for solutions is. Letting children sleep with you when they are afraid is a subtle way of saying "You can't handle this. Let me fix it for you."

4. Encourage your child to deal with difficult situations in small steps. If he is afraid of the dark, put in a night-light. If he doesn't think he can sleep in his own room, fill his hand with your kisses and tell him every time he misses you to open his hand and take out a kiss. If he thinks there are monsters in the closet or under the bed, do a search with him before bedtime and let him sleep with a flashlight.

5. Listen carefully. Are your children trying to tell you that someone is hurting them or that you are doing something that is frightening them? Take what they say seriously.

6. Sometimes children's fears are irrational and they can't explain them. They may need your support and reassurance until the

fear goes away. This may be time consuming on your part, and that is what parenting is about. (See the "Booster Thoughts" on previous page.)

Planning Ahead to Prevent Future Problems

1. There are many wonderful children's books dealing with fears that you can read with your children so they can see they aren't alone.

2. If there is a scary show on television or a scary movie, discuss ahead of time with your child whether it is a good idea for him to see it. If you both agree he is ready to watch, discuss how you can be supportive. (See the "Booster Thoughts" on previous page.)

3. If your children seem overly fearful, you may be creating this by constantly expressing your fears or you may be pushing them to do something before they are ready. If your children decide they are ready to try something, work with them in small steps to make it safe and then let go instead of stopping them from doing things you are afraid of yourself or by pushing them too soon.

4. It's okay to share your fears on occasion, but don't expect your children to have the same ones you do. Telling your children about a fear that you conquered may be comforting to them. It will assure them that fears are normal.

5. If your children are afraid of a new situation because they have never done it before and don't know what it is, suggest they try it out two to three times before deciding against it.

Life Skills Children Can Learn

Children can learn that it's okay to feel fear but they don't have to be immobilized by it. There is someone who will take them seriously and help them deal with their fears so they aren't so overwhelming. They can handle difficult situations and go to their parents for comfort.

Parenting Pointers

1. If your children are afraid to leave your side, spend time with them, but also create situations where they can be away from you for short times. Many a preschool teacher has had to pull clinging, screaming children off their parents' legs. Minutes later, with the parents gone, the children have settled in and are happily playing with the other children.

2. Don't force your children into situations that are overwhelming to them just so they will be brave. Some children learn by jumping into the pool, and others watch from the sidelines for a summer before they put their faces in the water. Respect their differences and have faith.

Fighting, Friends

"My child seems to fight a lot with her friends. How can I help her?"

Understanding Your Child, Yourself, and the Situation

As parents, it is painful to watch our children suffer hurt, rejection, and isolation when they fight with their friends. However, this too seems to be a part of the growing-up experience. Even though children seem to suffer terribly when they fight, they usually get over the pain much more quickly than adults do. It is a mistake for parents to think they should protect their children from experiencing problems in life. Instead of playing the rescuer, parents can help their children more by being observers, listeners, coaches, and cheerleaders. In this way, children learn they can deal with life experiences in productive ways—or that they can simply deal with the pain and that it goes away when they get on with their lives.

We are talking about normal life experiences—not pain inflicted by abnormal experiences or safety issues, such as sexual abuse, gangs, bullies, or racism. There is a difference between friends fighting and our children becoming victimized and powerless. If the latter is occurring, parents need to take a very active role in getting outside help and/or helping children cope with a situation that may be beyond their ability to manage safely.

Suggestions

1. Be empathetic and listen without trying to rescue your child or solve the problem.

2. Show faith in your child. "Honey, I know this hurts, but I know that you can deal with it somehow."

3. Offer support. "Let me know if you need a sounding board or if you want any suggestions. My suggestions will be just brainstorm ideas. You can decide if any would work for you."

4. Don't treat your child like a victim, or he will learn to think of himself as a victim.

5. When your child doesn't want to see or play with a friend, support her in that

decision and don't push her to make up. If your child decides to cut off a relationship with a friend, trust her. She may have very good reasons why she doesn't want to play with that friend anymore (see *Friends, Choosing*).

6. If you have more than one child, don't expect friends to like playing with all of the children. It is important that each child be allowed to make and maintain separate friendships and play uninterrupted by siblings, if that is his or her preference.

7. Know that it is normal for many boys aged ten and up to roughhouse and "mock" fight with their friends. Don't exaggerate and assume this means your child will grow up to be a violent adult.

Planning Ahead to Prevent Future Problems

1. Share information about accountability without blame. "When we look at what we might have done to create a situation, we have the power to change our part if we want to. Knowing that you and your friend are each totally responsible for what happened, can you think of what you might have done to create the problem?"

2. Share your own stories of childhood fights—what happened and how you felt.

3. While tucking your children in bed at night, ask about their saddest and happiest times of the day. They will know they can share their experiences—both happy and sad—with you.

Booster Thoughts

We frequently talk with parents who are worried that their children don't have enough friends. Often when kids are in the sixth through the eighth grade, they go through a change in friends. When we talk with the kids, we learn that sometimes they don't want to hang out with their old friends because they've started using drugs. They don't want to tell their parents the reason because they are loyal to the old friends and don't want to get them in trouble with their parents. They resent being pushed to hang out with kids they no longer enjoy or respect. They wish their parents would back off and trust their judgment. Often the kids they have broken with have a polished public image saved for parents but in private act out and are rebellious.

Life Skills Children Can Learn

Children can learn that they have the courage and confidence to deal with painful experiences in life. They can take responsibility for their part in creating the pain and can choose to make changes. It is nice to have someone who can listen without rescuing or blaming them. In the case of safety issues, children will learn that you are there to make sure they have the help they need.

Parenting Pointers

1. Accept that fights among friends are normal and view them as a necessary part of your child's experiences. Know that the conflict will pass, usually in less time than you think. Children usually finish a fight much quicker if adults stay uninvolved.

2. Remember that children, like adults, often need a sounding board more than they need solutions imposed on them.

3. Keep in mind that there is a difference between normal fighting and safety issues or violence against a person, and adjust your role appropriately.

Fighting, Siblings

(See also *Sibling Rivalry*)

"What should I do when my children fight with each other?"

Understanding Your Child, Yourself, and the Situation

Most siblings fight. Most parents interfere in ways that increase competition and the need to fight. When parents interfere, they may stop the fight for the moment, but they feel frustrated because the kids are fighting again two minutes later. Maybe they are just entertaining themselves and having fun together. It is important to deal with the purpose of the fight as well as the behavior. Are kids symbolically fighting for their place in the family, because they think they have to win to be significant? Or do they feel hurt and want to hurt back? Or do they feel they are being treated unfairly and that fighting is the only way to gain justice? We need to help children change their mistaken beliefs about belonging and significance and teach them alternatives to fighting.

Suggestions

1. Do not take sides. This reinforces the belief about the need to compete.

Booster Thoughts

One father would stick his thumb in front of his fighting children and say, "I'm a reporter for CBC. Who would like to be the first to speak into my microphone and give our audience your version of what is happening here?" Sometimes his children would just laugh, and sometimes they would each take a turn telling their version. When they told their versions of the fight, the father would turn to an imaginary audience and say, "Well folks. You heard it here first. Tune in tomorrow to see how these brilliant children solve this problem."[23]

23. From Jane Nelsen, *Positive Discipline* (New York: Ballantine, 1996), 205.

2. Say, "You can both go to separate rooms until you are ready to stop fighting." This can serve as a cooling-off period when fights get out of hand. Tell them they can come out and try again when they are ready.

3. Give both of them a choice. "You can stop fighting, or else go outside to fight. If you choose to fight, I don't want to listen to it."

4. When a baby is involved, pick up the baby first and say to the baby, in front of the older child, "You'll need to go to your room until you are ready to stop fighting." Then take the older child by the hand and repeat the same message. It may seem ridiculous to put an innocent baby in her room for fighting. However, it's important to treat children the same so you don't train one to be a victim and the other to be a bully.

5. It can be comforting to kids if you let them fight while you sit quietly nearby, trusting that they can work it out without involving you. (This is a tough one, because it is hard for parents to avoid getting hooked.)

6. If kids are fighting over a toy, remove the toy and let the kids know they can have it back when they are ready to play with it instead of fight over it.

7. Sometimes kids' fights are a way to play with each other. Think of them as cute little bear cubs.

8. Put all the fighters on a couch and tell them they have to stay there until they give each other permission to get off the couch and try again. This distracts them to work on cooperation instead of fighting.

9. Send those with the conflict to a room with the instructions that they can come out as soon as they have worked out a solution.

10. Leave the room. Believe it or not, a major reason kids fight is to get you involved. Kids want you to take their side by blaming and punishing the other child. Then they can feel important.

11. Interrupt the fight to ask if one of the participants would be willing to put the problem on the family-meeting agenda to work on a solution.

12. If real danger is imminent (such as a child about to throw a rock at another child), keep your mouth shut and act. Move quickly to stop the rock throwing. Then use any of the other approaches.

13. Use a sense of humor and play "Pig Pile." When you see your kids fighting, wrestle them to the floor and say, "Pig Pile." This is an invitation for everyone to playfully climb on the pile and see who can end up on top. This can become a fondly remembered family tradition.

Planning Ahead to Prevent Future Problems

1. Have a discussion on fighting during a family meeting. Get the children to share their ideas on why kids fight and on alternatives to fighting.

2. When tucking kids in bed at night, after they have had a chance to share their saddest and happiest moments of the day, ask, "Would this be a good time to talk about what is going on when you fight with your brother and to work on some solutions?" Then listen to the child's point of view. Ask if your child would like to work with you on some possible solutions.

3. Never compare children. You may think you are encouraging improvement by saying, "I know you can do as well as your sister." Instead, you are creating competition.

4. Talk about all of these suggestions during a family meeting and ask kids which one they would like you to use when they are fighting.

5. Use the candle story to show that love for one child doesn't diminish the love for another (see the "Beliefs Behind Behavior" section in Part 1).

Life Skills Children Can Learn

Children can learn that there are other ways to solve problems besides fighting. They have belonging and significance in the family without having to fight for their place.

Parenting Pointers

1. Be careful to treat older and younger fighters the same. Otherwise, it is easy for the younger one to believe that "the way to be special around here is to get my brother into trouble." Soon she will be provoking

fights in ways you do not see. If the older one is blamed ("You should know better! You are older!"), it is easy for him to believe that "I'm not as special as my younger sister, but I can get even." This is how victims and bullies are created.

2. Create an atmosphere of cooperation through valuing differences, encouraging individuality, involving children in solutions, and treating them with dignity and respect. Fighting is greatly reduced in an atmosphere of cooperation.

Forgetting

"My child is always losing things at her friends' houses. Her new ski parka has disappeared along with her expensive blue jeans. We can't afford to continually replace these things."

Understanding Your Child, Yourself, and the Situation

Everyone forgets things from time to time, but some children turn forgetting into an art form, especially when their parents replace the forgotten items, give them a lot of attention for being forgetful, or take all the responsibility for remembering. Forgetting can also be a form of passive power. Many children would never defy their parents openly and say, "I don't want to," but they find it easier to say, "I meant to, but I forgot." This problem presents many opportunities for parents and children to learn.

Suggestions

1. Show empathy, but don't rescue: "That must be frustrating for you." Most parents "forget" that empathy is enough and that they should stop there.

2. You might help the child explore what is happening through "what" and "how" questions ("What ideas do you have to solve this problem?") until she figures out her own solutions.

3. Stop giving special service if your children forget things. Let them do without, and they will learn to remember. If your children forget their school lunches once or twice, you might do them a favor and take the lunches to school, but if forgetting is a habit and they always expect special delivery, say no. They won't starve, and they might be motivated to solve the problem.

4. Children who habitually forget their homework may be in a power struggle with you or their teachers. Let them work out the problem with their teachers, and don't ask or nag them about it. It's better if you stay out of the loop and allow them to experience whatever consequence comes at school.

5. If your children have clothing allowances and they lose clothing, they can

replace the items out of their allowances, borrow from friends until they can afford the new item, or do without.

6. When your child doesn't keep an agreement and says, "I forgot," stick to the issue and ask, "What was our agreement?" Wait for the child's reply. Repeat the question until all excuses are gone.

Planning Ahead to Prevent Future Problems

1. If your children forget things at their friends' houses, let them know when you are available to take them to look for the lost items, but don't nag them or look for the items yourself.

2. Ask your children if they would like your help with scheduling. For school assignments, help them look at the deadline and then count backward how many days *they* think they need to complete the project. Plan in advance the days you are willing to help them do their research if trips to the library are part of the plan. Set them up on a calendar.

3. If your children are constantly forgetting things, ask them if they might be

Booster Thoughts

Chris came home from school and said, "I was really mad at you when you wouldn't bring my lunch to school when I forgot it, but it worked out just fine. My teacher felt sorry for me and gave me some money to spend at the snack bar. All my friends gave me stuff from their lunches that they don't like, so I didn't have to be hungry."

His mother said, "Chris, I really like your ingenuity and the way you work things out. Do you have any ideas of what you might do to help you remember to bring your lunch?"

"Mom," Chris said, "I really don't think it's a problem. Anyone can forget things every now and then. If I forget my lunch, there's plenty to eat, so don't worry about me."

saying "I forget" instead of "I don't want to." Let them know you are willing to work with them to create choices.

4. If your children forget to do their chores, refer to the "Follow-Through" and "Routines" sections in Part 1, as well as *Chores, Getting Cooperation.*

Life Skills Children Can Learn

Children can learn that they may have to do without or wait for a convenient time for their parents to help if they lose or forget things. (They can learn from the slight inconvenience of having to do without.) Children can also learn that they can be honest with their parents and say no instead of making up an excuse.

Parenting Pointers

1. Remember that we all forget things. Be flexible about doing favors without making it a habit.

2. Labeling children as forgetful only increases the amount they forget. Accepting that some children will forget a lot because they have different priorities raises their self-esteem.

Friends, Choosing

"I have one child who complains that she doesn't have any friends. Another child keeps choosing friends I don't like. How do I help my children become friends with children I approve of?"

Understanding Your Child, Yourself, and the Situation

We often forget to honor the different styles and personalities of our children and try to make them all fit one mold. This tendency can be most blatant when it comes to the secret dream of most parents—to have popular children. Some children are quiet and passive, some are active and assertive, some choose conventional lifestyles, and some choose unique lifestyles. The following suggestions focus on meeting the true needs of the situation—to help our children honor the uniqueness of each individual and feel comfortable with who they are.

Suggestions

1. Allow your children to choose their own friends. (They will anyway.)

2. If your child chooses a friend you don't like, invite that person into your home often and hope that the love and values you practice will be beneficial to him or her.

Booster Thoughts

Peers don't make children what they are. Children choose their peer group as a reflection of where they are at the time. Drop a skater into a high school, and he'll find the other skaters by noontime. The same is true for cheerleaders, jocks, and brains. (As adults, when we go to a party, we tend to seek out people who have similar interests and avoid those who don't.)

Sometimes teens think their lives are over if they don't have a friend. When we overemphasize the importance of having friends, children who choose to be alone will feel uncomfortable with that choice, believing they should have friends rather than learning to be a friend to themselves.

3. If you are afraid a friend you don't approve of will have a negative influence on your child, focus on being a positive influence through a good relationship with your child.

4. When your child has a fight with a friend, listen empathetically, but do not interfere. Have faith in your child to handle the fight (see *Fighting, Friends*).

5. Don't worry about whether your child has the right number of friends. Some prefer just one best friend; some like to be part of a large group of friends.

6. If your child complains that he or she has no friends, practice your listening skills. Try rephrasing your child's complaint using feeling words, such as, "You're pretty upset right now because you don't think you have any friends. Did something happen today between you and your friends at school?" Often children will exaggerate and speak in absolutes when what they are really trying to say is that they are having a problem with one of their friends. Be a good listener to help your child think through the situation out loud.

Planning Ahead to Prevent Future Problems

1. Help children who have difficulty making friends by exposing them to many opportunities, such as trips to the park, Scouts or other youth groups, and church groups.

2. Do not expect your children to enjoy the children of your friends or insist that they play together if your child doesn't enjoy their company. Find time to spend with your friends without subjecting your

children to feeling stuck having to play with kids they don't like or with whom they don't have anything in common.

3. Go along with your child's wishes about clothing styles so he won't be embarrassed about not fitting in.

4. Make your home a place where kids love to come because they experience unconditional love, safe and respectful rules, and plenty of fun, child-oriented activities.

5. If you have issues about having enough friends yourself, don't worry about your child having the same problem or project your experience onto your child. Be careful not to put your judgments about friendships onto your children. You may think friends are forever, while your child may enjoy moving in and out of different groups of friends. Be a good observer and see how your child handles friendships.

6. Children don't like to bring friends home when one or more of their parents is chemically dependent, because they are embarrassed and fear what they might walk into with their friend. If someone in your family suffers from chemical dependence, get help, because your children will be missing out on a lot if they are afraid to bring friends home.

Life Skills Children Can Learn

Children can learn that their parents are their best friends because they love them unconditionally, value their uniqueness, and have faith in them to choose friends that are right for them.

Parenting Pointers

1. If your child is consistently choosing friends you do not approve of, look at your relationship with your child. Are you being too controlling, inviting your child to prove you can't control everything? Is your child feeling hurt by your criticism and lack of faith in her and trying to hurt back by choosing friends you don't like?

2. Have faith in your children and honor who they are. Try to make the people your children choose as friends welcome at your home, even if they are not the friends you would choose.

3. Your children may be making decisions about friends based on how you treat your friends. Are you acting how you would like your children to act?

The "Good Child"

"I attended a parenting lecture, and the presenter said that 'good' children can be as discouraged as 'problem' children. What does that mean?"

Understanding Your Child, Yourself, and the Situation

Placing too much emphasis on children being consistently "good" has some potential dangers. It is easy for these children to create the belief that "I'm worthwhile only if I'm always good." Children who get too much validation for being good cannot handle the slightest mistake without feeling they are failures. The extreme danger of this belief is suicide.

The purpose of the good behavior is more important than the behavior. Is the child being good to win approval or because he sees the value of being good for self-fulfillment and because it is helpful to others?

Suggestions

1. Don't compare your children or say things such as "Why can't you be good like your brother?" Stress what is unique about each child.

2. Notice progress and effort instead of results.

3. Stop saying, "Good girl" or "Good boy." Be specific and say what it is that you like or notice.

Booster Thoughts

"If I could eliminate forever four phrases from our language in the interest of healthy people, it would be 'good boy,' 'bad boy' and 'good girl,' 'bad girl,' and all their related derivatives. Keep what people do separate from who they are so that a bad act doesn't make a person bad nor a good act make a person good. This is an important key to healthy self-esteem."[24]

---

24. From H. Stephen Glenn, *Developing Healthy Self-Esteem* (Orem, UT: Empowering People Books, Tapes, and Videos, 1989), videocassette.

4. Notice if you blame or pick on one child excessively. Behind most "problem" children are "good" children trying to look or be good so you'll notice how "bad" their siblings are.

5. Use encouragement instead of rewards and punishment.

Life Skills Children Can Learn

Children can learn that they don't have to be good all the time. They are valuable no matter what they do. It is okay to make mistakes because so much can be learned from them.

Planning Ahead to Prevent Future Problems

1. Consistently emphasize that mistakes are wonderful opportunities to learn.

2. Instead of praising your child for being good, joke with him that he might not be taking enough risks so he can learn the valuable lessons of mistakes and failure.

3. When you send your child off to school in the morning, don't say, "Bye, honey. Be good." What a burden for a child. Instead, say, "Bye, honey. Make a lot of mistakes and see what you can learn from them." Wow! Think of the opportunities for learning and growth.

Parenting Pointers

1. Children need to know they have your unconditional love, no matter what, so they don't worry too much about disappointing you.

2. It is much easier to live with a good child, but what is easy for you may not be healthy for the child.

3. This does not mean you should worry if you have a good child. It simply means you should be aware of decisions your children might be making about what being good means and how important it is to prepare them with the skills they need to handle mistakes.

Grief

(See also *Death*)

"My wife died, and I'm having so much trouble handling my own grief that I don't know how to help our three children. I know I am neglecting them during this terrible time because I can't hide my sorrow, so I avoid them."

Understanding Your Child, Yourself, and the Situation

The loss of a loved one is probably the most painful experience in life. It does not help you or your children when you try to protect them from the experience by minimizing your own pain in front of them. It does help when you understand that children process grief differently than adults do. Some may only deal with the grief for five minutes at a time and be able to play the rest of the time. Some may hang on to fears about their own mortality or that they will lose both parents and not have anyone to take care of them.

Suggestions

1. The most important thing is to use emotional honesty to share your grief and to let your children share their grief with you. Understand also that children are not callous if they do not hang on to their grief once they have reassurance and some time.

2. Reassure small children that they are not going to die. (This is not the time to teach them that they will die some day.) They also need reassurance that you are not going to die or abandon them. They may need this reassurance several times before they stop wondering, "Will it happen to me? Will it happen to you? Who is going to take care of me?"

3. Do not tell children that the deceased person has just gone to sleep for a long, long time. They will be terrified to go to sleep. It is easier for them to hear the word you may want to avoid—the person is dead.

4. If you have religious or spiritual convictions, share them. It can help to believe dying means going to a more beautiful place and that even though we miss people who die very much, they are happy where they are. When it feels appropriate, you might want to share some stories from *Life After Life* by Raymond Moody.[25]

5. Explain the funeral procedure and allow your kids the choice of participation or not. Respect their wishes. Do not force them or manipulate them through guilt to do what you think is proper. Do not overprotect them by deciding they can't handle the funeral or memorial service. Have faith in them to know what they can handle.

6. Balance the expression of pain by encouraging everyone to talk about the happy times and the good memories. Do not remove photos of the person who died or treat the death as though the person never lived.

7. Another way to balance the expression of pain is to express gratitude for the time you did have together.

8. Let the children help you plan a private ceremony that will symbolically demonstrate the love and caring you all have. This could be planting a tree or placing a

25. Raymond Moody, *Life After Life* (New York: Bantam Books, 1975).

special box on the mantle with everyone's favorite memory written down and placed in the box.

9. Let your children comfort you as you comfort them. This could be an opportunity to strengthen your bonds through mutual giving and receiving.

10. If your children are old enough, encourage them to keep journals to record their feelings or photo albums to hold memories of good times.

11. Encourage children to express any anger or unfinished business. (We tend to idolize people after they die.) Children may think the death was their fault if they were angry at their parent. If they have an opportunity to talk about all their feelings, you can reassure them and correct their misunderstandings.

12. Encourage everyone in the family, including yourself, to talk with other people who can be supportive. You don't have to do it all yourself.

Booster Thoughts

A single mother, Susan, and her young son, Drew, were worried about who would die first, so they made a pact. The pact was that whoever died first would somehow come back and let the other person know he or she was okay, whether it was in dreams or in a special sign.

When one of Susan's friends lost a baby, Susan comforted her by saying, "I have a theory about babies who die. I think that all babies bring love, and they all have a mission. Sometimes it takes them years and years on this planet to accomplish that love and that mission, and sometimes it's accomplished while they're still in the womb. I believe that when they leave us early, it's because they came and did their mission and taught us a lesson. Now it's our job to figure out what that lesson is."

When Drew's friend since second grade shot and killed himself, Drew's theory was that even though he was really sad his friend wasn't here anymore, now he had a personal guardian angel. Drew was sure he had other guardian angels, but he didn't know them personally. Now when something good or exciting happens in Drew's life, he pictures his friend—his guardian angel—smiling and helping from above.

Planning Ahead to Prevent Future Problems

1. Grief takes time. Do not assume that one time for expressions of pain and caring or one ceremony is enough. Have regular sessions where everyone can continue to express feelings.

2. Once a year, perform a community service or service to another person with your children in memory of the person who died.

Life Skills Children Can Learn

Children can learn that all feelings are legitimate. It is okay to cry when they feel pain and to share their feelings with others. Even when the worst thing in life happens, life goes on and they can too.

Parenting Pointers

1. The balance of sharing feelings of pain with feelings of gratitude and focusing on special times helps people avoid getting stuck in grieving.

2. Children will handle their grief in direct proportion to how adults around them handle their grief. If you need help, find a therapist or a grief support group.

Guilt

"I feel guilty when I leave my child at child care, when I'm too busy to respond to demands for attention, when I have to say no, and so on."

Understanding Your Child, Yourself, and the Situation

Guilt comes from an environment filled with "shoulds" and "oughts." "You should be nice." "You should always take care of your child." "You ought to spend more time with your child." Then you even get contradictory messages. "You should not spoil your child." "You should respect your own needs." When people hear these messages often enough, they believe them and repeat them to others—thus perpetuating the guilt syndrome. Many parents have guilt buttons, and children know it. When you have a guilt button, children will be happy to push it. This helps children develop negative manipulation skills.

If you are feeling guilty, this could be a sign that someone around you is demanding undue attention (see "Beliefs Behind Behavior" in Part 1 for more information).

Booster Thoughts

One parent tells about her experience with guilt: "I had a distinct guilt button about working, and my kids learned how to push that button. When I dropped three-year-old Mark off at his nursery school on my way to work, he would cry, and I would leave with a heavy heart. My first clue that my guilt button might be creating the problem was the fact that Mark usually did not want to leave his nursery school when I came to pick him up. He was having a good time.

"I decided to take time for training. That evening, I sat down on the living room floor with Mark and said, 'Want to play a game with me?' Mark was eager. I said, 'Let's pretend it is time for me to leave you at your school. You can pretend you are crying and begging me not to leave. I'll show you what I mean.' I demonstrated. Mark laughed. I said, 'Now let's see you do that.' Mark pretended he was crying and begging me not to leave.

"I said, 'Wow, you really know how to do that well. Now let's see if you can try this one. Pretend I'm leaving and you give me a big hug and say bye Mommy.' I demonstrated and then said, 'Your turn.' Mark gave me a big hug and said, 'Bye, Mommy.'

"I said, 'Wow, you really know how to do that one, too. Tomorrow morning you have a choice. You can either cry or give me a hug.' The next morning, when I dropped Mark at school, he gave me a big hug and said, 'Bye, Mommy.'

"Why did Mark choose the hug instead of crying? I speculate that the time for training helped Mark learn a new skill. However, I think it was even more important that he could tell I had given up my guilt button. Don't ask me how, but I think kids know."

(Years later, this mother's guilt button reappeared. For a continuation of the story, see *Working Outside the Home*.)

Welcome the feeling as a signal that you may be discouraging one of your children by doing things for the child that she could do for herself or that you are spending a lot more time with your child than is healthy. Some children feel empty and threatened when the focus is off of them. Your job is to help your child feel belonging and significance without having to be center stage at all times.

Suggestions

1. Make a list of all the "should" and "ought" statements that are going through your mind. Review your list and see which of these things you would want to do even if there were not a "should" or an "ought" in front of it. Disregard the other items on the list.

2. Give yourself permission to be less than perfect, nice, or wonderful all the time. This will help your child avoid the trap of perfectionism based on your example.

3. Do your best to maintain a reasonable balance between taking care of your needs and priorities and those of your child.

Planning Ahead to Prevent Future Problems

1. Trust yourself to know what is best for you, your child, and the needs of the situation and follow through on your decisions with dignity and respect.

2. Realize that it is healthy for your child to spend time away from you. Leave your child with a child care person, say goodbye, tell him you will return, and then have faith in him to deal with the situation, even if that includes some crying.

3. Help children learn not to expect to always be the top priority or center of attention. This will prepare them for healthy relationships based on give and take. Say, "I'm busy right now. I'm looking forward to our time together later."

4. Have regular family meetings where needs and priorities can be discussed and solutions found that respect the needs of everyone.

Life Skills Children Can Learn

Children can learn that there is a time and a place for needs to be met. They can become less judgmental by avoiding the use of "should" and "ought" statements with themselves and others.

Parenting Pointers

1. Shoulds, oughts, and manipulation add needless stress that is counterproductive to healthy self-esteem.

2. When shoulds and oughts are dropped from your thinking, you will have room to find effective solutions.

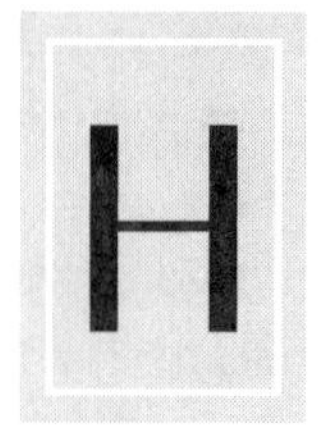

Habits, Annoying

"Our daughter is constantly clearing her throat, and it drives me crazy. I told her I'd let her know when she was making that noise so she'd be aware of it and stop. That isn't working."

Understanding Your Child, Yourself, and the Situation

If you try not to think about elephants, what happens? You think about elephants. The same applies to irritating habits. The more we remind, mention, nag, and suggest, the worse the habit gets. Throat clearing, nose picking, and other habits that may be annoying to adults usually start off quite innocently and then gather force as your child is reminded a thousand times not to do that. Parents worry that their child is reacting to stress and often give more attention to the child. The more attention children get around their habit, however, the more they persist. Kids don't plan bad habits to keep adults busy with them, but they are willing to play that game when adults start it.

Suggestions

1. Ignore the habit and let children decide if or when they want to stop. Leave the room if that helps you ignore it.

2. Let children know you understand that they may not be able to help it that they make a particular noise or have a particular habit. Also tell them that it's hard for you to be around when they do that, and if you feel bothered, you'll go somewhere else for a while.

3. If your children are concerned about a habit and want your help to deal with it, reassure them that you love them just the way they are. If you have a suggestion, share it with them. Some nail biters stop when they keep their nails filed and polished. Kids who carry blankets around will often let their parents put the blankets in a special place for certain times of the day until they want to use them again.

4. Encourage your children to express their feelings while you simply listen, as an indirect way of dealing with stress that may be contributing to the habit.

Planning Ahead to Prevent Future Problems

1. Throat clearing and other habits that make noise might be related to a physical condition. It would be helpful to have a general physical for your child without drawing attention just to the throat.

2. If children bite their nails or engage in other habits that annoy you, do not refer to them as problems or nag about the behaviors. If you can think of these habits as cute and adorable, the habits will probably take care of themselves in time.

3. Let your child know that there are some behaviors that are private and best done away from other people because others may feel uncomfortable (see *Masturbation*).

4. If you are creating stress in your child by making excessive and unreasonable demands for high performance in school, music, or sports, stop.

5. Realize that children can experience stress that has nothing to do with you, so don't take their behavior personally. Try to find out what is bothering them through discussion, games, role playing, and by asking questions. The best questions are the ones that seem silly. Your child will set you

Booster Thoughts

Four-year-old Betsy loved to spit. Every time someone said, "Hello, Betsy," she would pucker up and get ready to spray the person with a cloud of saliva. Her parents were embarrassed and couldn't understand how she started such a "bad" habit. They were both very respectful people and didn't understand where Betsy learned to do such a "naughty and disgusting" thing. All their efforts to get Betsy to stop fell on deaf ears.

One day, they visited their friend, and when Betsy puckered up to spit, the friend smiled broadly and said, "Betsy, I bet you love to spit. Let's both go in the bathroom and spit into the toilet. I think it's fun to do, too."

Betsy's parents watched in a mixture of shame and amazement as Betsy took their friend by the hand and the two disappeared into the bathroom. After a few minutes, they returned and Betsy stopped spitting. What Betsy's parents realized is that they had been creating a power struggle by trying to control Betsy's behavior. Now they had an option and could tell Betsy, "Spitting is okay as long as you do it in the toilet." It didn't take long for Betsy to give up her "habit."

We aren't sharing this story as a suggestion but to show how special our children may feel about their little idiosyncrasies.

straight and tell you what is really going on when you ask a really "stupid" question. For instance, if your child is handling stress with nail biting, you could ask, "I wonder if you bite your nails because you are trying to sharpen your teeth?" Most children will look at you like you are weird and tell you the real reason they bite their nails.

Life Skills Children Can Learn

Children can learn that they are not bad or neurotic. They have some special habits that they can choose to handle differently when other people do not pressure them. They can realize that while other people may not like their behavior, only they can decide to change.

Parenting Pointers

1. Children want to know they belong and are special. We can give them that message by loving them for who they are and spending time with them—or they can feel special because they get so much attention through nagging, scolding, or trying to control one of their habits. Kids will take attention in either form, but they may decide they are unlovable and don't belong when they get negative attention. Often they get caught up in a vicious cycle of seeking attention in increasingly negative ways.

2. Bugging children about sucking their thumbs by telling them they will have to wear braces or that they will ruin their mouths does more damage to their spirits than their mouths.

3. If children are biting their nails or engaging in any other bad habit due to stress, pressure to make them stop increases the stress. Unconditional love and faith in them to manage their lives reduces their stress and increases the chances that they may make different choices.

Hitting (Spanking)

"I have tried everything I can think of to get my child to stop hitting her little brother. Sometimes she hits me. This really makes me angry. Punishment doesn't seem to work. I have spanked her and made her say she is sorry, but the next day she is hitting again."

Understanding Your Child, Yourself, and the Situation

How are we ever going to teach our children it is not okay to hurt others when we keep hurting them? We are reminded of a cartoon depicting a mother spanking her child while saying, "I'll teach you not to hit someone smaller than you." When a child is hitting, usually his or her feelings are hurt. Your child needs help from you but may feel frustrated because he or she isn't getting the help needed. You probably feel frustrated, too, because you want your child to treat others respectfully and may even worry that your child's behavior is a reflection on you as a parent. Perhaps you are overreacting and treating your child disrespectfully out of shame and embarrassment, trying to prove to the other adults around that you won't let your child get away with this behavior.

Suggestions

1. Take the child by the hand and say, "It is not okay to hit people. I'm sorry you are feeling hurt and upset. You can talk about it or you can hit this pillow, but people aren't for hitting."

2. Help the child deal with the anger (see *Angry Child*).

3. Ask, "Would it help you to go to your time-out spot now?" Time-out is not helpful unless the child has helped create a positive time-out spot in advance (see "Planning Ahead to Prevent Future Problems," item 3). Also, time-out is not helpful if the child does not see the benefit and chooses it. If you make your child go to time-out, your child is likely to see it as punishment and may rebel.

4. After the child has calmed down, ask "what" and "how" questions. "What is upsetting you? How are you feeling?" See if you can get to the bottom of what is really bothering your child and then help the child discover what other things she could do besides hitting to deal with the problem. Lectures are ineffective at any age because they make children feel inadequate.

5. With children under age four, try giving them a hug before removing them from the situation. This models a loving method while showing them that hitting is not okay. Hugging does not reinforce the misbehavior.

6. Even though toddlers don't fully comprehend language, you can still use words (while you are removing the child from the situation), such as, "Hitting hurts people. Let's find something else for you to do."

7. When babies hit you, put them down and leave the room immediately for a minute or two without saying a word. At this age, they will understand actions better than words.

8. When your preschooler hits you, decide what you will do instead of trying to control your child. Let her know that every time she hits you, you will leave the room until she is ready to treat you respectfully. After you have told her this once, follow through without any words. Leave immediately.

9. Later, you might tell your child, "That really hurts" or "That hurts my feelings. When you are ready, an apology would help me feel better." Do not demand or force an apology. The main purpose of this suggestion is to give a model of sharing what you feel and asking for what you would like. People don't always give us what we would like, but we show respect for ourselves by sharing our feelings and wishes in nondemanding ways.

Planning Ahead to Prevent Future Problems

1. Teach children that feelings are different from actions. Feelings are never bad. They are just feelings. What we feel is always okay. What we do is not always okay.

2. Remind your children that it is okay to tell people what they don't like. They can also leave the scene if they are being treated disrespectfully.

3. Get your child involved in creating a positive time-out area (see Part 1). Teach her that sometimes we need time to calm down until we feel better before doing anything. Let her know that she can use the time-out area anytime she thinks it will help her feel better.

4. Find ways to encourage your children with unconditional love and by teaching skills that help them feel capable and confident.

5. Show that hitting is unacceptable by never hitting your child. If you make a mistake and hit your child, use the Three Rs of Recovery to apologize so your child knows hitting is not acceptable for you either (see Part 1).

6. Take time for training with your toddler. Help her practice touching family members or animals softly. This does not eliminate the need for supervision until she is old enough to understand.

7. Look around and see if there are ways you are hurting your child without realizing it. Are you sending your child to his or her room frequently, scolding and criticizing regularly, singling out the child when a problem occurs? If so, your child may be feeling really hurt and upset, and the hitting is a way to strike back at the world. Be more encouraging and positive and stop the hurtful behaviors, then see if there's a change in the hitting behavior.

Life Skills Children Can Learn

Children can learn that it is not okay to hurt others. Their feelings are not bad and they are not bad, but they need to find actions that are respectful to themselves and to others.

Booster Thoughts

He: There are times when it is necessary to spank my children to teach them important lessons. For example, I spank my two-year-old to teach her not to run into the street.

She: After you have spanked your two-year-old to teach her not to run into the street, will you let her play unsupervised by a busy street?

He: Well, no.

She: Why not? If the spanking teaches her not to run into the street, why can't she play unsupervised by the street? How many times would you need to spank her before you would feel she has learned the lesson well enough?

He: Well, I wouldn't let her play unsupervised near a busy street until she was six or seven years old.

She: I rest my case. Parents have the responsibility to supervise young children in dangerous situations. All the spanking in the world won't teach a child until he or she is developmentally ready. Meanwhile, we can gently teach. When we take our children to the park, we invite them to look up the street and down the street to see if cars are coming and tell us when it is safe to cross the street. Still, we don't let them go to the park alone until they are much older.

Studies show that approximately 85 percent of all parents of children under twelve years of age resort to spanking when frustrated, yet only 8 to 10 percent believe that it is dignified or effective. Sixty-five percent say that they would prefer to teach through consequences and encouraging improved behavior, but they don't know how. How often we resort to the familiar instead of learning a better way.[26]

---

26. From H. Stephen Glenn, *Developing Healthy Self-Esteem* (Orem, UT: Empowering People Books, Tapes, and Videos, 1989), videocassette.

Parenting Pointers

1. Be aware of the discouraged belief behind the misbehavior. A child who hits usually is operating from the mistaken goal of revenge, with the belief that "I don't feel like I belong and am important, and that hurts, so I want to hurt back." Children

will feel encouraged when we respect their feelings and help them act appropriately.

2. Many people use the biblical admonition "Spare the rod and spoil the child" as an excuse for spanking. Biblical scholars tell us the rod was never used to hit the sheep. The rod was a symbol of authority or leadership, and the staff or crook was used to gently prod and guide. Our children definitely need gentle guidance and prodding, but they do not need to be beaten, struck, or humiliated.

3. Toddlers are short on both language and social skills, and when they play together they can easily become frustrated. When they lack the ability to express what's wrong in words, hitting and other types of aggression sometimes result. It is developmentally normal for toddlers to hit. It is the parent's job to supervise and handle toddlers kindly and firmly until they are ready to learn more effective ways to communicate.

Hobbies

"I'd like my child to take an interest in a hobby, but he resists all my efforts to get him involved. Every book I read says that children who have hobbies and other interests tend not to get involved in drugs. Is there some way I can accomplish this?"

Understanding Your Child, Yourself, and the Situation

Hobbies are one of the ways both adults and children can achieve balance in their lives. Discovering and nurturing your children's special interests takes time and openness. If you believe your child should collect stamps but he is interested in playing video games instead, you may be working at cross-purposes. Hobbies need to reflect the current interests of your children. Finding a suitable hobby requires trial and error and the willingness to let go when your child tires of an activity. Hobbies can also be a wonderful way for parents and children to spend quality time together. It is worth nurturing hobbies with children—the more interests they have, the less likely they are to indulge in unhealthy activities.

Suggestions

1. Notice your children's interests and be willing to encourage them. For example, if they love collecting baseball cards, don't forbid them to buy packages of gum with cards inside. If they enjoy skateboarding, don't tell them that they are wasting their time on a stupid activity. If they ask you to drive them to a comic book convention, try to accommodate them. Don't criticize your children's interests.

2. Let your kids have a say. For example, if you think they would enjoy cross-country skiing but all their friends like downhill skiing, be open to trying both. Ask your children if they would be willing to go cross-country with you if you go downhill with them. If you're not a skier, arrange for them to go with a friend or a group.

3. Enroll in activities you can do together, such as dog obedience classes, crafts or cooking courses, or the YMCA Indian Princess program, to name just a few. The possibilities are endless.

4. If your child tires of a hobby, don't berate him or force him to continue—even if you paid for the equipment. It is important for children to know they have the right to change their minds.

5. If your child wants to play a team sport, talk to him in advance about the commitment one makes to a team and how it hurts a team if someone misses practices or drops out halfway through.

6. Many children in 4-H raise animals for a hobby. Offer to help so they can take an occasional break from the daily responsibility.

Planning Ahead to Prevent Future Problems

1. Set an example by having hobbies of your own. Invite your children to join you in them if they express an interest.

2. Make sure you aren't more invested in your children's hobbies than they are. Are you the only one putting the train set together, or are you nagging about piano practice? Children may think they will enjoy something but feel differently after they try it for a while. Don't go overboard spending money until you know this is something they will stick with.

Life Skills Children Can Learn

Children can learn that they are unique people and that everyone has a lot of different interests. They don't have to be the best at everything they do. It's okay just to have fun—and to stop when it's not fun anymore. It doesn't mean that they are quitters if they change their minds. There are some activities that require a big commitment, such as team sports and raising pets, and it's important for them to think that through before they decide to proceed.

Parenting Pointers

1. Hobbies are a great way to spend special time with each child. Don't insist that all of your children have the same interests. Through hobbies, children can express who they are and you can enjoy their uniqueness. See these special interests as a way each of your children enriches the family.

2. One of the greatest joys we have as parents is to see the world through our

Booster Thoughts

Steve Glenn tells the following story:

"When my son Mike decided to take up golf, the first problem appeared when I came home and found my golf clubs on the lawn. My first reaction was, 'I'll kill him!' (I was raised by a man who could not see past the disarray of his tools to the little guy trying to be like him.) But then it occurred to me that if I could encourage his interest in golf, I might have a little buddy to play with. So I went to Mike and said, 'What else can I do to help you disturb my stuff?'

"I talked to my neighbor and we decided, in self-defense, to get the boys their own starter sets for Christmas. The boys were thrilled with their new clubs. Two days after Christmas, we took the boys out to the golf course.

"My neighbor and his son, Andy, reached the first tee ahead of us. Andy grabbed a club at random from his set and leapt joyfully from the golf cart. His dad yelled at him to come back, jerked the club out of his hands, and handed him the driver, saying, 'That's not the one you use here!' The little guy still had some enthusiasm left, so he put down a ball and started to swing. His dad stopped him and said, 'Hold the club this way, bend your knees this way, keep your head down like this, and swing it this way.'

"By the time he was finished, Andy was totally confused. On the next hole, he grabbed the wrong club again. His dad said, as he jerked the club out of his hand, 'Do it right or don't do it at all!' That's all the boy needed. Andy refused to get off the cart for the rest of the day and has expressed no further interest in golf.

"Knowing a bit more about kids, I watched Mike take out the club of his choice and make several attempts to drive the ball. Finally, somewhat breathlessly, he asked, 'Dad, how do I get the ball from here to there?' I said, 'Son, that question has brought presidents of the United States to their knees. In your case, why don't we drive down near the hole. You can throw your ball and we will call it one, and then you can chase it into the hole with your putting iron.' As a result, I have this passionate young golfer who is getting better and better as we share our special time together."

children's eyes. If they are interested in baseball, we can go with them to the ball game. If they like rock music, we can help them find the perfect rock poster and learn about the different drummers and guitar players. If they take dance classes, we can accompany them to local dance performances. Our children feel good about themselves if they know that they are unique and that we appreciate that uniqueness.

Holidays

"The kids are getting excited about Santa Claus, the trip to Grandma's, and all the presents they think they'll get. I'm wondering where we'll have Christmas this year, how we can afford it, what I'll do with the kids home from school for two weeks while I have to work, if I'll be able to deal with the constant messes, and if I can manage a long trip without strangling the kids."

Understanding Your Child, Yourself, and the Situation

With some reasonable expectations and a little advance planning, holiday hassles can be turned into holiday happiness. It's okay to expect vacation time to be fun for the adults as well as the kids. Holiday routines, although different from everyday routines, are still important. Kids can be expected to behave on trips. Families don't have to spend beyond their means. It's okay to start new traditions, even if it means skipping some of the old ones.

Suggestions

1. Use the family meeting to discuss holiday routines with the kids. Get their ideas about wake-up time, chore time, mealtime, bedtime, and special plans. Use limited choices for younger kids: "Now that you're on vacation, would you like to go to bed at your regular time or a half hour later?"

2. Plan some time to do something special with each of your kids.

3. Limit television viewing and don't use the television as a baby-sitter. Make arrangements for child care by hiring sitters, trading with someone, or asking a friend or relative to help out.

4. If you have to leave the kids with a sitter, make sure the sitter knows what routines everyone has agreed upon.

Planning Ahead to Prevent Future Problems

1. For long trips, create a special bag for each kid filled with surprises to play with

on the plane or in the car. Plan to play some games while traveling. Take along a tape recorder and play "talk show" or "make up a story." Stop at roadside areas where kids can stretch and play.

2. Be clear with yourself and your mate about how much money you want to spend on gifts and where you would like to spend the holiday. Give the kids only choices that you are willing to fulfill. If they are too materialistic or self-centered, shop and make things for others. Plan "gifts of love" from your family that you can all work on together. Some families have a "cookie-thon" and bake cookies for gifts. Others may decide to make gifts out of wood or collages out of things found around the house.

3. Everyone has a different picture of how the holiday should be celebrated. Share your pictures and be curious instead of insisting there is only one right way.

4. Give up your need for perfection and be willing to concentrate on having fun together instead of producing fabulous decorations, gifts, and cards. These are great opportunities for all family members to contribute.

5. Don't let alcohol ruin your holidays. In some families, a holiday celebration becomes a reason to drink excessively. Re-

Booster Thoughts

Lisa and Phil's Christmas holidays together were disasters. When Lisa was growing up, everyone in her family received one very nice, expensive present for Christmas. In Phil's family, everyone enjoyed the fun of opening a lot of inexpensive presents. So Lisa would buy Phil one nice, expensive present and Phil would buy Lisa a lot of inexpensive presents. Every Christmas, they felt disappointed and misunderstood, each thinking the other was too dense to know how to *really* enjoy Christmas.[27]

How sad that Phil and Lisa could not see how simply they could solve their problems by learning about their separate realities and respecting their differences instead of holding grudges because the other spouse isn't the same.

27. From Jane Nelsen, *Understanding: Eliminating Stress and Finding Serenity in Life and Relationships* (Rocklin, CA: Prima Publishing, 1997), 46.

member spiced cider, hot chocolate, and sodas when making your holiday shopping list. Plan activities the entire family can enjoy that don't involve drinking. If alcohol is part of your celebration, stop drinking early and end the day with coffee, tea, or other nonalcoholic drinks, so that those who travel can drive home safely.

Life Skills Children Can Learn

Children can learn that they can make the holidays enjoyable for others by giving a gift of love instead of just spending money. Holidays are a time all family members plan together and chip in to help each other. They learn what give and take is all about, because their parents help them find opportunities to experience both.

Parenting Pointers

1. The more you plan in advance and involve the kids in helping, the smoother the holidays will go.

2. Be flexible and keep the true meaning of the holidays in mind. They can be a time for closeness, fun, and caring.

Homework

"Every night there's a battle over homework at our house. Our son is behind at school, and his teacher says if he doesn't start catching up on his homework he may have to stay back a grade. How can we get him to do his homework?"

Understanding Your Child, Yourself, and the Situation

The more you make homework your job, the less your children make it theirs. Kids who think homework is more important to their parents than it is to them don't take the responsibility. Out of fear and frustration, adults will keep trying what isn't working in spite of overwhelming proof that their methods are failing. If forcing kids to do homework was effective, we would not have so many discouraged kids dropping out of high school or so many kids who feel their worth depends on their success or failure (who then go through life as approval junkies looking for someone to please). If it worked, we would not have so many kids who resist being told what to do in order to salvage some sense of themselves. If it worked, we would not have so many parents who feel discouraged, guilty, and like failures if they can't accomplish what the teachers can't accomplish.

Suggestions

1. Much of what you can do to be effective requires advance planning. Read the "Planning Ahead to Prevent Future Problems" and then refer to it often.

2. If the teacher sends you a note or calls, ask the child if it is a problem for him, and if so, what he intends to do about it. Put him on the phone with the teacher instead of thinking you have to handle the problem, or ask the teacher to set up a conference for all of you: teacher, parent(s), and child.

3. When your child waits until the last minute to accomplish an assignment, listen empathetically, but do not rescue. Also avoid the temptation to say, "Too bad you didn't take advantage of my consultation period." (See "Planning Ahead to Prevent Future Problems," item 3.) Lectures of this kind are very disrespectful. They require the assumption that your child is stupid and didn't understand the conditions you set forth. Your child will learn much more from kind and firm follow-through than from lectures.

4. Another possibility when your child complains about beginning an assignment late is to listen empathetically. You might say, "This must be very upsetting for you." Again, avoid the temptation to lecture or to rescue. You might add, "I wonder what happened." Your child may or may not tell you his excuses. Whatever he says, keep listening empathetically.

5. You can also do joint problem-solving with your child. Listen to and understand the child's issues as well as express your own, and then brainstorm together until you find a solution that works for you both. Do not ask for progress reports from the teacher unless you and your child have agreed to this in advance as a way of solving the problem. If your child thinks this will help, then by all means support her by asking for progress reports, but only under these circumstances.

6. Use emotional honesty to tell your children what you think, feel, and want, without demanding that they think, feel, or want the same. This may sound like, "Education is important to me, and I feel scared when it doesn't seem important to you. I really hope you will explore the value of good study habits. If you want my help, please let me know."

Planning Ahead to Prevent Future Problems

1. It is appropriate to set up a routine at your home with a time of day set aside for quiet work without the TV or radio on and everyone involved in some form of learning. Your child may or may not choose to do homework at this time, but it is still important to create the space for contemplation.

2. Before you jump in with any solutions, sit back and watch to see what your child

Booster Thoughts

Sixteen-year-old Frank had to attend summer school one year because of deficiencies in credits toward graduation. His parents didn't shame him or rush around doing makeup work for him. Instead, they planned a nice summer and proceeded without him. Partway through the summer, they discussed what Frank thought about the value of being prepared and doing his homework on time in the future. He said, "I don't like it that I had to miss so much this summer. I don't want that to happen again, so I plan to keep up next year."

Since that summer, Frank has stuck to his plan. His parents never mention homework to him except to ask if he needs help so he knows they are interested.

Although this may sound strange, several parents of preteens found a solution to getting homework done by offering to do their children's homework for them. One father explained how it worked. "I told my daughter that I noticed she never did any of her homework and that I was concerned about it and was willing to volunteer to do her homework for her. She looked at me as if I were crazy, and then grinned and said, 'Sure. No problem.' I told her that she needed to sit me down each day at 5:30 to go over the assignments with me and show me what I was supposed to do, and then sit and keep me company if I had any questions. On the first night, we did this and I did most of the work and had very few questions. The next night, I had to ask her regularly where certain information might be found, or if her teacher had explained how to do a certain math computation so that I could complete the work properly. Before she knew it, she was doing most of the work herself, and I was helping in places where I could clearly see she didn't have the concepts. And we were having fun."

does about homework for at least a week. Then sit down with your child and tell him or her what you noticed, what you wish, and what you will do to help. For example, "I noticed that you didn't start working on your homework until bedtime each night this last week. I wish you would start earlier in the day. I'd be happy to help you look at your schedule to see when a better time would be or even sit down and read my book or work on the computer while you do your homework, if you'd like some company. I'm also available to help between 6:30 and 8:30 P.M., but after that, it's too late for me to focus."

3. Tell your children you will no longer nag or remind them about schoolwork and then follow through by keeping your mouth shut. Let them experience the consequence at school of what happens if their work is undone. Call the teachers and let them know that you are doing this and why.

4. Let your children's teachers know that you believe school is your children's job. If there is a problem, you will be happy to sit down with them and the children to help work it out—if the children want help. There are times a child may need your help to deal with an unreasonable teacher by sitting down with your child and the teacher to make sure everyone is listening to each other.

5. Let your children know you are willing to help if they ask, but only if you can help without taking over or getting into a battle—and only during times you have scheduled in advance. For example, you might say, "I'm available for homework consultation on Tuesdays and Thursdays from 7:00 to 7:30 P.M."

6. Schedule special needs in advance, like trips to the library or to buy materials. Let your children know it is their responsibility to inform you ahead of time about their needs.

7. Do not compare your children. Rather than motivating slower children, this discourages them.

8. Some kids will never like school and are better suited for more individualized programs. Do not buy into the myth that the only way to be successful is to get a college degree. Also know that some children are "late bloomers." They may drop out of school and then decide later that they want a college degree. Let children know that they are not failures if they don't do well in school and that some day they might be motivated to try again.

9. Allow for different styles of learning. Some children study with the radio and television on; others need complete silence. Some kids don't have to study at all and have a knack for understanding the material.

10. Find ways to support your children's schools and the educational process without interfering in their schoolwork—volunteer at school if you have time, take classes, join the PTA, and read books.

11. Be aware of the fact that your child may need extra help. If your child fights your assistance, get a tutor or a friend to help.

12. Involve your child in planning the time of day that is best for him to do his homework and where he wants to do it,

such as at a desk in his room or at the dining room table.

Life Skills Children Can Learn

Children can learn that they can think for themselves and take responsibility for the consequences of their choices. They can discover that mistakes are wonderful opportunities to learn, know how to solve problems, feel good about themselves, and have the courage and confidence to handle situations that life presents. Their parents support them when they take responsibility to ask for their help.

Parenting Pointers

1. Watch out for taking responsibility for your child's work and then living under the illusion that the child is being responsible because the work gets done.

2. Show faith in your children to learn great things through failure instead of shaming, punishing, or humiliating them for it.

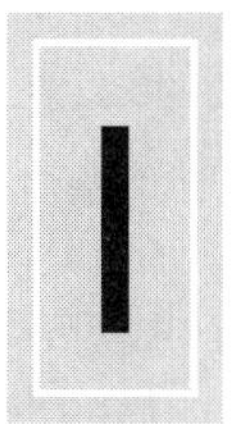

Interrupting

"I can't get on the phone or talk to a visiting friend without constant interruptions from my three-year-old."

Understanding Your Child, Yourself, and the Situation

Children often come to the mistaken conclusion that their belonging and significance are threatened when their parents focus on something or someone else. It helps to understand that this is normal and to deal with the threat in respectful ways instead of increasing the threat through anger or punishment.

Suggestions

1. For children aged two to five, say, "Would you like to get a book or toy so you can sit close to me and look at the book or play with your toy while I'm on the phone?"

2. When a friend comes over, say to your child, "I would like to spend five minutes with you without any interruptions from my friend. Then I would like some uninterrupted time with my friend. You first,

Booster Thoughts

During one of our Teaching Parenting the Positive Discipline Way workshops, we were role-playing effective ways to help children with the mistaken goal of undue attention. The group who planned the role playing chose the behavior of interrupting while Mom is on the phone. In scene one, the person playing Mom portrayed ineffective ways to handle this situation. She scolded the person role-playing her three-year-old daughter. In the second scene, Mom portrayed an effective method, as follows: Mom said "excuse me" to the person she was talking to on the phone. Then she took her watch off her wrist and handed it to her "daughter," saying, "Honey, please take my watch and tell me when the second hand (she showed her which one) goes all the way around and reaches the twelve at the top two times." Then she started talking again. The person pretending to be her little girl watched the wristwatch intently. When her mother hung up the phone, her little girl said, "Mommy, Mommy, you had more time."

This role play portrayed an excellent way to redirect the child and to show her how to get attention in a helpful way.

then my friend." Let your friend know in advance what you would like to do and why—to help your child feel loved and to learn to respect your time, too.

3. Have a phone with a long cord or a portable phone. Take the phone outside a sliding glass door where your child can still see you but can't interrupt.

4. For children aged five to eight, say, "I want some time on the phone or with my friend. What ideas do you have to keep yourself busy for ten to fifteen minutes so you won't need to interrupt me?"

5. Tell the child, "It is a problem for me when I'm interrupted while talking on the phone or visiting with a friend. Would you be willing to write this problem on the family-meeting agenda for me, or should I?"

Planning Ahead to Prevent Future Problems

1. Wait until small children are sleeping to make phone calls.

2. For children aged three to four, let the child help you put some favorite toys in a

box. Label this the "phone box." Plan ahead with your child to keep herself busy with the phone box while you are on the phone.

3. Have a junk drawer near the phone. There are all kinds of interesting throw-away things you can put in a junk drawer. Let your child explore the junk drawer when you are on the phone.

4. When you have planned special time with your child, say, "This is my special time on the phone (or with my friend or with a sibling). I'm looking forward to *our* special time at 5:15."

5. Discuss the problem at a family meeting and get everyone's ideas on how to solve the problem.

6. Set up a special time each day to visit with your spouse without children interrupting. Tell the children in advance that this is adult time. Brainstorm with them places they can play safely and activities they can do. Let them know how important it is to you to have quality time with another adult (or yourself, for that matter) and that you appreciate their help in giving you the time you need. Set a timer or show your child when your time is up on the clock and then follow through by firmly, kindly, and silently removing your child if he or she interrupts you.

Life Skills Children Can Learn

Children can learn that they are loved and important. They can take care of themselves while respecting their parents' desires to pay attention to other people or things.

Parenting Pointers

1. It is difficult for children to take care of themselves until they know they are important and loved by their parents.

2. Anytime you have a recurring problem, you will be most effective if you deal with the belief behind the behavior (help the child feel belonging and significance) and take time for training.

3. You do a real service to your children if you help them correct their mistaken notion that they only count when they are the center of attention. If you do this while your children are growing up, you can save them years of rejection and isolation as adults.

Kidnapping

"I'm so scared that my child will be kidnapped that I'm afraid to let her out of my sight. I know it isn't healthy to be overprotective. How can I protect my child from kidnapping without making her paranoid or afraid of life?"

Understanding Your Child, Yourself, and the Situation

Kidnapping is a real and present danger. It is important to educate children about this threat. Many parents worry about finding a balance between awareness and preparation that still leaves children with the courage to take appropriate risks in life.

Suggestions

1. Don't tell your children to never talk to strangers. Instead, teach them how to tell the difference between healthy strangers and harmful strangers.

2. Tell your children, "Most people in the world are nice people, but there are people in the world who hurt children. I want to teach you some skills so you can protect yourself."

3. If you are concerned about an ex-spouse kidnapping your children, make sure the children know which parent is scheduled to pick them up and that they are not to get into the car with their other parent. Practice this with role playing. (See the "Booster Thoughts" below for more information.)

Booster Thoughts

One of the saddest experiences in life occurs when parents use their children as objects in their struggle with a former mate or other family members. The needs of the child for security, stability, and contact with those who love them are totally ignored by a parent who kidnaps a child or by a parent who tries to prevent an ex-spouse from seeing the children.

Sometimes this is exacerbated by an adversarial procedure for solving domestic problems. Whenever possible, we recommend that parents working out custody arrangements use the services of a mediator who will advocate the child's interest first and foremost (see also *Divorce*).

Planning Ahead to Prevent Future Problems

1. Decide on a family password. Tell your children that if anyone comes to their school or stops them anywhere and says, "Your Mom (or Dad) sent me to pick you up," they can ask the person for the password. If the person doesn't know the password, they should yell for help or run for help as fast as they can.

2. When your children want to go someplace new—like the mall, a park, or a place kids are hanging out—check it out yourself first. Give your kids information about possible dangers and where they can get help if they need it.

3. Encourage your children to go places in pairs or groups. When you are in a public place, have them find a partner (or take them yourself) to go to the rest room.

4. Children see pictures of missing children on milk cartons and posted in public places. Encourage them to express their feelings about this danger in the world. Invite them to brainstorm their ideas about how to protect themselves.

Life Skills Children Can Learn

Children can learn to look for the difference between people with good motives and with bad motives. They also can become assertive in protecting themselves or asking for help.

Parenting Pointers

1. Don't let your fears of scaring your children keep you from giving them the information they need.

2. Teach your children to trust their instincts and that it is okay to say no with firmness when they feel that is the right thing to do.

L

Laundry

"I'm sick and tired of nagging my kids to throw their dirty clothes into the laundry basket. If I didn't go into their room and take out all their dirty clothes, they would have nothing to wear."

Understanding Your Child, Yourself, and the Situation

Some people still make traditional assumptions about female roles that don't fit very well with two parents working full-time or

Booster Thoughts

One of Gina's more important learning experiences came as a result of a family meeting to resolve the problem of laundry. The family members developed a system of individual hampers and a couple of general bathroom hampers and discussed what taking responsibility for one's own clothing involved. Subsequently, a new dress intended for the all-important eighth-grade dance was thoughtlessly thrown into the general bathroom hamper, where it was discovered only hours before the great event. It had been stained irreparably.

Gina went to the dance in something less new and exciting. Later, she and her mother discussed what was learned about taking responsibility and thinking ahead.

single-parent families. There is also a popular notion that children won't do things right or that it is easier for adults to do it themselves rather than take the time to teach the kids. Many parents feel sorry for children if they have to help with chores, thinking it robs them of a childhood. This thinking negates the fact that children want to belong and to make a contribution.

Suggestions

1. With young children, put a dirty clothes hamper in their room. If your children forget to put their clothes in the hamper, you can simply hand them an item and ask, "Do you remember where this goes? I forgot!" Young kids love this game and rush to put the items in the hamper.

2. As the kids get older, let them put their clothes away themselves. They probably won't fold anything, but that's not important. Show gratitude for their help rather than criticizing their lack of perfection.

3. When the kids can push a chair up to the washer, show them how to use the dials and have them be your assistant on laundry day. When they're ready, let them put the clothes in the washer and dryer by themselves.

4. To teach your child about separating colors, put an old white item of clothing into a bucket and then add something bright with colors that run. Ask your child, "What do you think will happen when we add water to this?"

5. By the time the kids are in elementary school, set up a schedule of laundry days so they can wash their own clothing on their day. Some families prefer to have everyone pitch in to help do all the laundry on the same laundry day.

6. If laundry is done at the laundromat, bring the kids along and give each a job to help you. Play games or read books with your children while waiting for the machines to finish.

Planning Ahead to Prevent Future Problems

1. Let the kids know that you don't wash clothes that aren't in the hamper. Make sure each child has his own hamper or laundry basket and that it is his job to put his clothes in the hamper and carry them to the washer.

2. Let your kids know when you will do the laundry. Refuse to give special service by washing out that favorite pair of jeans or gym outfit at the last minute. Children learn to plan ahead when their parents don't rescue them. Do not piggyback criticism or lectures on top of the discomfort your child feels when learning from consequences.

3. Use the family meeting to let the kids come up with a plan for taking care of the laundry. Encourage cooperation, give and take, and helping each other.

Life Skills Children Can Learn

Children can learn that they can be responsible, manage their time, plan ahead, and decide what their priorities are. They can learn how to cooperate and help their family. They can learn from their mistakes and try again.

Parenting Pointers

1. If you are working outside the home, let your children know that you don't want to be hassled when you come home by having a second job. If the kids decide not to help with chores such as laundry, you can say that you will have to hire it out and the family will have less money for fun and special purchases.

2. Remember that building skills can fail if you demand too much too soon. Celebrate the small steps and focus on progress, not perfection. For example, when a child runs the washer for just one pair of jeans, don't scold him for being wasteful but thank him for pitching in. Then discuss how he could add other items to make washing more cost-effective in the future.

Listen, Refuses to

"My two-year-old doesn't listen to me. I know she understands the word no, but she defies me anyway. When I tell her, 'Wait, please!' she laughs and runs away from me. I don't want to spank her, but I don't know what else to do."

Understanding Your Child, Yourself, and the Situation

Younger children don't understand "no" or "wait, please!" in the way you think they do. This is an abstract concept that is in direct opposition to their need to explore their world and to develop their sense of autonomy. As children get older, many parents unintentionally teach them to be "parent-deaf." This disease strikes many of our children early in life—especially when parents scream, yell, or lecture. Don't worry, it's not terminal. Hope is in sight if you learn to act more and talk less. If your child doesn't hear anything you say or if you find yourself repeating things over and over, she may already have tuned you out. Instead of looking for the causes of this problem or deciding it's just a stage, it is more effective to look at your behavior for what you may unconsciously be doing to create the problem.

Suggestions

1. The best way to help your child listen is to say what you mean and then act instead of talk. The fewer words the better. So if your little nine-month-old is climbing the stairs, and it is not okay with you, put a barrier in front of the stairs instead of saying, "No, no, no!" If it is okay with you, but you are concerned about her safety, sit on the stairs close enough to catch her if she falls.

2. If you are screaming, yelling, spanking, or lecturing, stop. All punitive methods are disrespectful and encourage doubt, shame, and guilt—in the future.

3. Instead of telling your child what to do, find ways to involve him in the decision so he gets a sense of personal power and autonomy: "What are we supposed to do next?" For preverbal children say, "Next, we ______," while kindly and firmly showing them instead of telling them.

4. Give her some warning. "We need to leave in a minute. What is the last thing you want to do on the jungle gym?" When a minute is up, leave, even if you have to pick up your child and walk away with a screaming kid.

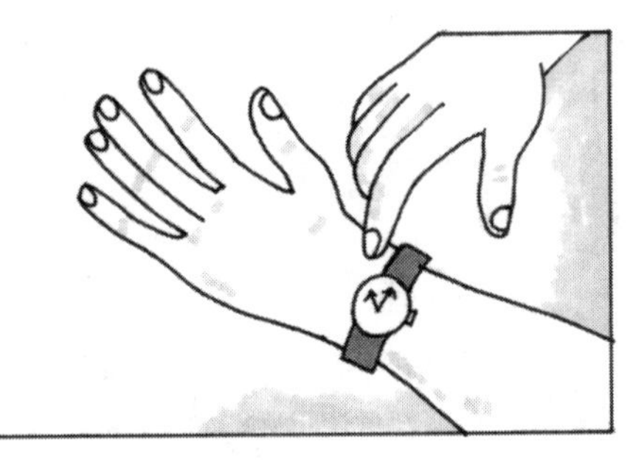

5. Carry a small timer around with you. Let her help you set it to one or two minutes. Then let her put the timer in her pocket so she can be ready to go when the timer goes off.

6. Give him a choice that requires his help. "It will be time to go when I count to twenty. Do you want to carry my purse to the car, or do you want to carry the keys and help me start the car?" "What is the first thing we should do when we get home, put the groceries away or read a story?"

7. Preverbal children might need plain ol' supervision, distraction, and redirection. In other words, as Dreikurs used to say, "Shut your mouth, and act." Quietly take your child by the hand and lead her to

where she needs to go. Show her what she can do instead of what she can't do.

8. Use your sense of humor: "Here comes the tickle monster to get children who don't listen."

9. Be empathetic when your child cries (or has a temper tantrum) out of frustration with his lack of abilities. Empathy does not mean rescuing. It does mean understanding. Give your child a hug and say, "You're really upset right now. I know you want to stay, but it's time to leave." Then hold your child and let him cry and have his feelings before you move on to the next activity.

10. Try using one word to communicate what needs to be done for better listening: "Lawn." "Dishes." "Bathroom." "Laundry." Be sure you have eye contact and a firm and loving expression on your face. Or use ten words or less. "It's time to learn to do your own laundry."

11. Use nonverbal signals: point at what needs to be done. Smile, but don't say a word.

12. Writing a note for a child who can read may get his attention better than talking.

13. Children listen carefully when you whisper (they have to really listen to hear you). Try it.

14. Ask older children to tell you what they just heard you say. Then wait while they paraphrase.

Booster Thoughts

Mrs. Foster was wondering why she ever got into the parenting business. It felt to her that both she and her child were out of control. She did not like it that he would not "mind her," and she did not like it that she was yelling and using punitive methods that didn't work.

She attended a parenting class for parents of preschoolers and learned about age-appropriate behavior. When she changed her expectations about the perfect child who obeyed her every command, she began to enjoy her child's experimentation with autonomy and initiative. Instead of trying to control him, she started guiding him away from inappropriate behavior by showing him what he could do.

She was most amazed at how much her child seemed to calm down when she calmed down. Frustrating episodes occurred less often and were solved more quickly because of her new understanding.

Planning Ahead to Prevent Future Problems

1. Your job is to think of yourself as a coach and help your child succeed and learn how to do things. You're also an observer, working on learning who your child is as a unique human being. Never underestimate the ability of a young child, but on the other hand watch carefully as you introduce new opportunities and activities and see what your child is interested in, what your child can do, and what your child needs help learning from you.

2. Safety is a big issue, and your job is to keep your child safe without letting your fears discourage him or her. For this reason, supervision is an important parenting tool along with kindness and firmness while redirecting your child.

3. Children know when you mean it and when you don't. Don't say anything unless you mean it and can say it respectfully. Do not use baby talk with young children. Speak to them with the same voice you would use if talking to a friend. Then follow through (see Part 1) with dignity and respect—and usually without words.

4. Create routines (see Part 1) for every event that happens over and over: morning, bedtime, dinner, shopping, and so on. The books *Chores Without Wars* and *Positive Discipline for Preschoolers* are excellent resources for learning to create routines for any child. Then ask your child, "What do we need to do next on our routine chart?" For children who are younger, say, "Now it's time for us to _____."

5. Be respectful when you make requests. Don't expect children to do something "right now" when you are interrupting something they are doing. Ask, "Will it work for you to do this in five minutes or in ten minutes?" Even if you don't think a younger child understands completely what you are saying, you are training yourself to be respectful to the child by giving choices instead of commands.

6. You may need to teach your child many things over and over before she understands. Be patient. Minimize your words and maximize your actions. Don't take your child's behavior personally and think your child is mad at you or bad or defiant. Remain the adult in the situation and do what needs to be done without guilt and shame.

7. Ask your children if they are willing to listen before you give them information. "I have some important information about that. Would you like to hear it?" They feel respected because they have a choice. If they agree to listen, they usually will. If they don't agree and you lecture anyway, you might as well be talking to the wall.

Life Skills Children Can Learn

Children can learn that they will be treated kindly and firmly through their age-appropriate behavior. They can learn to stay within respectful limits through the respectful model they experience from their parents.

Parenting Pointers

1. When you understand that children don't really understand "no" the way you think they should, it makes more sense to use distraction, redirection, or any of the respectful Positive Discipline methods.

2. Learn all you can about child development and age-appropriate behavior. The books *Positive Discipline: The First Three Years* and *Positive Discipline for Preschoolers* [28] include information on both of these topics and how they relate to parenting.

3. Don't give up on your children because you think they are too young to learn something. If you are following Positive Discipline methods, by practicing repetition and patience and watching your child carefully to see what she can do as a unique human, you may be surprised at what can be accomplished.

4. It is especially easy to baby and overprotect the youngest child because this child looks so small compared to her larger siblings. Each child needs your time and energy as a teacher/coach to help her learn. Even though younger children watch and copy older siblings, be sure you spend one-on-one time with each child to help structure his or her learning.

Lying

(See also *Fabricating*)

"I don't know how to get my child to stop lying. We have tried very hard to teach high moral standards. The more I punish him, the more he lies. I'm really worried."

Understanding Your Child, Yourself, and the Situation

We have searched and searched and can't find a single adult who never told a lie as a child. Actually, we can't find many adults who never lie now. Isn't it interesting how upset parents get when children have not mastered a virtue they have not mastered themselves? We do not make this point to justify lying but to show that children who lie are not defective or immoral. We need to deal with the reasons children lie before we can help them give up their need to lie. Usually children lie for the same reasons adults do—they feel trapped, are scared of punishment or rejection, feel threatened, or just think lying will make things easier for

28. Jane Nelsen, Cheryl Erwin, and Roslyn Duffy, *Positive Discipline: The First Three Years* (Rocklin, CA: Prima Publishing, 1998) and Jane Nelsen, Cheryl Erwin, and Roslyn Duffy, *Positive Discipline for Preschoolers* (Rocklin, CA: Prima Publishing, 1998).

everyone. Often lying is a sign of low self-esteem. People think they need to make themselves look better because they don't know they are good enough as they are.

Suggestions

1. Stop asking setup questions that invite lying. A setup question is one to which you already know the answer. Instead of saying, "Did you clean your room?" say, "I notice you didn't clean your room. What is your plan for cleaning it?"

2. A slight variation of saying what you notice is to say what you think. "That sounds like a good story. You have such a good imagination. Tell me more about it."

3. Be honest yourself. Say, "That doesn't sound like the truth to me. Most of us don't tell the truth when we are feeling trapped, scared, or threatened in some way. Why don't we take some time off from this right now? Later, I'll be available if you would like to share with me what is going on for you."

4. Focus on solutions to problems instead of blame. "What should we do about getting the chores done?" instead of "Did you do your chores?"

5. Deal with the problem. Suppose your child tells you he hasn't eaten when you know he has. Why would he say he hasn't eaten? Is he still hungry? If he is still hungry, what does it matter if he has eaten or not? Work with him on a solution to deal with his hunger. Does he want attention? Deal with his need for attention by working together to find some time you can spend with each other. Does he want to tell a story? Let him tell a story. Identify it for what it is: "That sounds like a good story. Tell me more."

Booster Thoughts

In hopes of avoiding the crying fits that usually resulted when Micah's mother questioned his stories, she thought she'd try something new. When the eight-year-old said, "I saw an elephant on my way home from school," his mom said, "Wow, I wonder if it was the same one I saw at the grocery store? What color was the one you saw?"

"Mine was green," Micah said.

"Nope," his mom said, "mine was blue and pink."

Micah looked suspiciously at his mom and said, "I think I'll go play in my room now. See you later." His mom smiled to herself, and Micah ran to his room.

6. Another possibility is to ignore the "lie" and help your child explore cause and effect through "what" and "how" questions. If he says he hasn't eaten all day, ask, "What happened? What caused that to happen? How do you feel about it? What have you learned from this? What ideas do you have to solve the problem?" These questions can be effective only if you are truly curious about the child's point of view. Do not use these questions to "catch" him in a lie. If at any time you think it is a fabrication, go back to suggestion 2 above.

7. Respect your children's privacy when they don't want to share with you. This eliminates their need to lie to protect their privacy.

Planning Ahead to Prevent Future Problems

1. Help children believe that mistakes are opportunities to learn so they won't believe they are bad and need to cover up their mistakes.

2. Set an example in telling the truth. Share with your children times when it was difficult for you to tell the truth but you decided it was more important to experience the consequences and keep your self-respect. Be sure this is honest sharing instead of a lecture.

3. Let children know they are unconditionally loved. Many children lie because they are afraid the truth will disappoint their parents.

4. Show appreciation. "Thank you for telling me the truth. I know that was difficult. I admire the way you are willing to face the consequences, and I know you can handle them and learn from them."

5. Stop trying to control children. Many children lie so they can find out who they are and do what they want to do. At the same time, they are trying to please their parents by making them think they are doing what they are supposed to do.

Life Skills Children Can Learn

Children can learn that it is safe to tell the truth in their family. Even when they forget that, they are reminded with gentleness and love. They can learn that their parents care about their fears and mistaken beliefs and will help them overcome them.

Parenting Pointers

1. Most of us would lie to protect ourselves from punishment or disapproval. Parents who punish or lecture increase the chances that their children will lie as a defense mechanism. All of the above suggestions are designed to create a nonthreatening environment in which children can feel safe to tell the truth.

2. Many children lie to protect themselves from judgment and criticism because they

believe it when adults say they are bad. Of course they want to avoid this kind of pain.

3. Remember that who your child is now is not who your child will be forever. If your child tells a lie, don't overreact to the behavior by calling your child a liar.

4. Focus on building closeness and trust in the relationship instead of on the behavior problem. This is usually the quickest way to diminish the behavior that you find objectionable.

Manipulation

(See also *Disagreements Between Parents*)

"My child manipulates her father, and he doesn't even see he's being used. If she wants something, she goes directly to him because she knows he'll say yes. If she asks me first and I say no, she runs to her father and says I've been mean to her. Then he gives her what she wants and criticizes me in front of her. What really worries me is that she has started manipulating her friends and teachers."

Understanding Your Child, Yourself, and the Situation

Manipulation is a learned behavior. Many parents don't realize how they teach manipulation in the name of "love." They do this when they think they are doing their children a favor by giving in to their demands for one more story or buying a toy in response to pleading or a temper tantrum. It doesn't take long for children to adopt the belief that "I belong only when I get my own way" or "Love means getting other people to do what I want." Some children may try manipulation because they feel powerless and don't know how else to get their needs met—or they may feel hurt and try manipulation as a revenge tactic.

Children would not use manipulative behavior if it was not effective. Children who use manipulation are discouraged because they have not learned that they are capable of dealing with disappointment or working for win/win solutions with other people. Discouraged children need encouragement from the adults in their lives. That encouragement needs to take a unique form, as described in the following suggestions.

Suggestions

1. Sometimes children manipulate because they know that if they bug their parent

long enough, a no really means yes. Stop allowing your children to have their way through pleading and/or temper tantrums. Don't say no unless you mean it, and then kindly and firmly stick to your decision.

2. Teach children that it is okay to ask directly for what they want without having to play games. Let them know that you are willing to work with them to help accomplish their goals by helping them figure out ways to succeed instead of giving them everything they want.

3. When your child pleads for one more story, don't say a word. Give your child a kiss and leave the room. If she comes pleading after you, kindly and firmly (with lips closed) take her by the hand and return her to her room as many times as it takes.

4. When your child pleads for a toy at the store, ask, "Do you have enough money saved from your allowance?" If the child says no, say, "Let's go home and figure out

Booster Thoughts

When Tim and Shirley were seven and five years old, they would go to the store on allowance day to spend their money. Tim always bought a comic book and Shirley bought candy. Tim would manipulate until Shirley would share her candy or give it to Tim.

As Mom listened in, it was tempting to interfere and rescue "poor" Shirley from being taken advantage of. Tim would tell her he'd be her best friend if she gave him some candy and then ignore her after he ate the candy. Shirley never seemed to mind or stop sharing.

One day, Mom asked Shirley, "Does it bother you when your brother eats your candy on allowance day?"

Shirley replied, "I don't mind. I like to share and I don't want to get cavities. And someday Tim is going to let me read all his comics."

Even though Mom knew this probably never would happen, the two children were quite content with the plan and it worked for them.

how long it will take for you to save for this toy" (see also *Allowances*).

5. When children tell you that your spouse said they could do something even if you say they can't, say, "Mom (or Dad) and I will discuss this in private and then give you an answer." Then take the time to get together with your spouse so children don't learn to play one against the other. You can also let your children know that they need two yes votes (one from each parent) before a decision can be made.

Planning Ahead to Prevent Future Problems

1. At a family meeting, mention that you are aware of manipulating behavior and that you would like to brainstorm other ways for people to get their needs met or to find respectful solutions.

2. Apologize for your part in teaching manipulation skills. You might say, "I made a mistake. I thought I was showing love for you when I let you have your own way. I was not teaching you that I have faith in you to handle disappointment, to create a plan to get what you need, or to find solutions that are respectful to everyone. It may not be easy for us to change, but it will be more loving for both of us.

3. If you think your child is manipulating because she is hurt and wants to hurt back, ask her what she is upset about. Guess if she doesn't know or can't say. For example, "Could it be that you feel the baby is getting more attention than you get?" or "Could it be that you feel other people boss you around too much and this is your way to feel powerful?"

4. If you notice a child manipulating her sibling or friend, do not intervene during the conflict. Later, ask the sibling or friend if he would like some help in figuring out how to deal with the manipulator.

5. Get your children to help you create bedtime and morning routine charts, and then let the chart be the boss. When children try to manipulate, ask, "What is next on our routine chart?"

6. Are you too quick to say no or "We'll talk about this later"? Sometimes children become manipulative because they get nowhere when they try to deal honestly and openly with a parent.

Life Skills Children Can Learn

Children can learn that their needs and feelings are important and that parents will help them figure out how to get their needs met without manipulating. They can learn that sometimes they can't have what they want and that they can deal with the disappointment. They can also learn that they can't manipulate their way out of important routines, such as going to bed at appropriate times.

Parenting Pointers

1. Sometimes the best approach is to mind your own business and stay out of your child's relationships with others. Others will either figure out what is going on and deal with it, or they will be willing to give in to a child for reasons of their own.

2. Are you setting an example of manipulating to get your way? If so, be more direct about your own needs.

Masturbation

"This is so embarrassing. My three-year-old plays with herself while she is watching TV. She doesn't seem to mind that everyone can see what she is doing. How do I get her to stop?"

Understanding Your Child, Yourself, and the Situation

Parents think it is so cute when their babies discover their toes and their fingers. However, many think their children may be sexual deviants when they discover their genitals. Some form of masturbation (often, children are merely exploring their genitals) is normal for children from six months to six years of age. Most children lose interest in their genitals between the ages of six to ten. Somewhere around the age of eleven interest returns, and throughout adolescence most boys and some girls experiment with masturbation.

Suggestions

1. For children aged two to six, ignore it; most likely, interest will pass, just as interest in other body parts will decline. Making an issue of masturbation could make it worse. If you tell your kids it is bad to play with their toes, they will probably become fixated on their toes.

2. If ignoring is too hard for you (the messages you received as a child may be difficult to overcome), offer a choice. "I'd like you to turn off the TV and go to your room for privacy or stop fondling your genitals while you are around other people." (They usually prefer company at this age.)

3. Another possibility is to teach social appropriateness. When your child plays with herself in public, say, "It is not appropriate to fondle your genitals in public."

4. Don't tell your children that hair will grow on the palms of their hands if they touch themselves in "dirty ways."

5. Usually children aged six to ten are not interested in masturbation, so don't create problems that don't exist by making threats or using scare techniques. If you have strong religious views on this subject, remember that guilt, shame, and scare tactics

Booster Thoughts

In his book, *The Inside Story: Psychiatry and Everyday Life,*[29] Dr. Fritz Redlich of Yale University gives the following possible arguments for ignoring masturbation when it does occur:

"First, there is no danger that your child will suffer physical harm from a limited amount of masturbation. The old wives' tales about its causing blindness, insanity, bad complexion . . . have been scientifically disproved. Secondly, there is some danger that an emotionally charged parental forbidding of the child's touching himself may result in such repression of the child's sexual urge that when grown up he may not be able to function normally in this respect. Thirdly, there is comparable danger that the child may develop terrible self-loathing and lack of confidence when he finds he cannot (when half-asleep) completely keep himself from doing what he has been so forcefully told is unnatural and vile. . . . If we have never frightened our child about masturbation, he may feel free to tell us when and if little school friends make physical advances (which little school friends sometimes do), thus enabling us to protect him."

29. Fritz Redlich and June Bingham, *The Inside Story: Psychiatry and Everyday Life* (New York: Alfred A. Knopf, 1953), 145.

are more likely to produce negative long-term results than positive. You will do better with openness and honesty. Use "I feel _____ because _____ and I wish _____" statements to share your thoughts and feelings (see "Emotional Honesty" in Part 1).

6. For children aged ten to eighteen, allow your kids to have privacy in their own rooms. Do not go into their rooms at night to see if they are sleeping with their hands outside the covers.

7. Teach children to use the washer and dryer and let them be in charge of washing their own sheets and making their own beds.

Planning Ahead to Prevent Future Problems

1. Make sure lack of cleanliness is not a problem that is creating irritation and itchiness.

2. Help your child develop interesting activities. Masturbation often takes place when children are bored.

3. If you are worried that your child's interest in masturbation seems excessive after reading this section, you may wish to consult a therapist. In some cases, excessive masturbation may be a sign of possible sexual abuse.

Life Skills Children Can Learn

Children can learn that they have the right to figure out what is best for them sexually as long as they are not hurting anyone else. They are not bad or evil for normal exploration and stimulation of their bodies.

Parenting Pointers

1. Avoid overconcern.

2. Research shows that 98 percent of men admit that they masturbate. We wonder if the other 2 percent are lying.

3. Trying to force your religious or moral convictions on your children may create open rebellion or sneakiness. It is not helpful to teach children that they are bad for doing something that appears to be a normal human behavior.

Materialism

"I'm concerned about my children's materialism. They can't seem to live without brand-name clothes, sunglasses, expensive cars, and more junk food than my family could ever afford when I was growing up."

Understanding Your Child, Yourself, and the Situation

Our children live in a consumer age in which the media portrays a world of new, exciting, wonderful—and usually expensive—things. It is easy for children to get the idea that they are deprived if they don't have these things. Parents often give their children too much because of the mistaken notion that their children should not have to do without—and because they are materialistic themselves. Parents can fall for the argument of "All my friends have it" and give in to peer pressure of their own, not wanting to be different from other parents. We deprive children of the opportunity to learn essential skills when we provide things for them that they could earn (or at least partially earn) for themselves.

Suggestions

1. If you can afford it, don't say you can't afford it. Be truthful. Say, "I'm not willing to spend my money that way. When you earn your own money, you can decide how you want to spend it."

2. Don't accept promises; require that the work or savings be accomplished before obtaining the desired item. This will teach patience and deferred gratification.

3. Children should not be allowed open choices. For children aged three to five, choose two pairs of shoes that fit your budget and practicality and give your child a choice of which she would like.

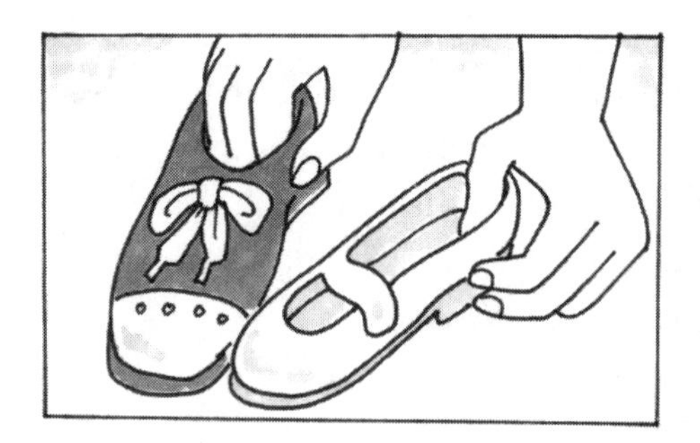

4. For children aged five to eight, tell the child what your budget is. "Let's go to the store and you can choose a pair of shoes within our budget."

5. Ask, "What is it that you need and how is that different from what you want?" (The child may need new shoes but want an expensive brand name.) For children aged eight to twelve, say, "I'm willing to provide the best quality for the most reasonable price for items you need. If you want something more than that, then I need to know what you will do to contribute to the difference." (Some ideas are: working more on Saturday, saving his allowance, or taking a paper route.)

6. For children aged twelve to sixteen, teach budgeting through regular discussions with them concerning their present and future needs. Provide an agreed-upon clothing budget (see *Allowances*). Allow children to learn from their mistakes by being nonjudgmental and not rescuing them.

7. For teenagers aged sixteen to eighteen, start the weaning process. Discuss what you have been providing and your desire to provide less now that they are capable of doing more.

Planning Ahead to Prevent Future Problems

1. Help children develop an attitude of gratitude. Allow time during family meetings or at dinner time for family members to share things for which they are grateful.

2. Avoid the temptation to give your children everything they want. This may lead to decisions on their part that "Love means getting material things from others."

3. Help older children plan for the future by discussing their needs for such things as cars, gas, dating, and savings and what they can do to meet these needs. For young children, it might be saving for the ice cream truck or a desired toy. Then leave it up to them as much as possible (resist your urge to rescue).

4. When children make mistakes, ask, "What happened? What choices or decisions on your part led to what happened? How will you use what you have learned from this to do better in the future?"

Booster Thoughts

We foster materialism by teaching kids they can have just about anything they want if they hassle us enough. We do this by setting limits we don't respect and threatening children with things that we don't deliver. We often say things we don't mean, like, "I can't afford it." What does "I can't afford it" mean to children who have never had to do without and have found that most of the things that they want come without a struggle?

When a child says she wants a new bicycle, and her father says he can't afford it, she wonders, "What on earth could Daddy be saying to me?" She reflects on her experience and remembers, "The last three times Daddy said that he couldn't afford it, I hassled him until I got what I wanted. So he must mean that I haven't hassled him enough for him to make this a priority."

Father says, "I can't afford it."

And she says, "Hassle, hassle."

He reassures her, "No, dear, I really can't afford it this time."

And she says, "Hassle, hassle, hassle."

Finally he says, "Look, the only way I can consider it is on my credit card, and it is full."

She thinks, "Now we're making progress. He's considering ways to get it for me. I'm very close." So she continues to hassle.

Father's last weapon is to say, "If I get this for you, you have to give up your allowance for three years."

She thinks to herself, "Well, last time I gave it up for two years and still haven't gone without a nickel for one day in my life, so that's no big deal."

She proceeds with hassle, hassle, hassle, and finally Father gives in.

What is her perception of how you get what you want? Wish for it, hassle for it long enough, and you can even overcome "I can't afford it."[30]

---

30. From H. Stephen Glenn and Jane Nelsen, *Raising Self-Reliant Children in a Self-Indulgent World* (Rocklin, CA: Prima Publishing, 1989), 127–128.

5. Encourage your children to serve others unselfishly through charitable work, such as providing child care, helping the homeless, buying toys at holiday time for needy children, and visiting nursing homes.

6. Watch for examples in life, the media, and books where service to others holds a higher value than materialism. Emphasize these stories through personal appreciation and discussion with your children.

7. Resist parent peer pressure by ignoring "How will I look in the eyes of other parents?" Ask yourself instead, "How can I best teach my children the life skills they need?"

8. Watch TV and read ads with your children and discuss how advertisers work to create wants in us for things we don't really want or need.

9. Don't be afraid to live simply. Your children will learn a lot from what you do and not just from what you say.

10. Involve your children in recycling projects, Earth Day celebrations, and environmental issues.

Life Skills Children Can Learn

Children can learn to understand the difference between wants and needs and have confidence in their ability to fulfill some of those wants and needs through their own efforts (sometimes with help from their parents). Children can learn that happiness and fulfillment don't come from how much you buy or own.

Parenting Pointers

1. Throughout history, parents have tried to make abundant for their children that which was least abundant for them as they grew up. When they succeed, they generally end up criticizing their children for not appreciating "all the things we provide for you." Appreciation comes from hard work, not from handouts.

2. Children learn their values by watching what we do more than by listening to what we say. If you live a materialistic lifestyle, don't be too surprised if your children follow suit.

Mealtime Hassles

"My kids' table manners are atrocious. They get up and down during the meal, grab food across the table, and complain about my cooking. Any ideas?"

Understanding Your Child, Yourself, and the Situation

Mealtime should nourish both the body and the soul. Too many families forget this and turn mealtime into a nightmare of corrections, nagging, threats, fighting, and individual grandstanding. Parental concern for healthy children can become out of proportion around the subject of food, especially since many of us have our own hang-ups about weight, looks, and diet. We try to be good parents by making sure our children eat properly. Quite often, instead of providing healthy choices and trusting our kids to eat when they are hungry and stop when they are not, we interfere in this natural process. Without knowing it, we can plant the seeds for eating disorders. We are most effective when we encourage children to listen to their bodies' clues and trust themselves to eat appropriately.

Suggestions

1. If kids know it's okay to eat what they eat and leave what they leave, they are less apt to complain. Do not insist on children eating everything on their plates or tasting every food. Avoid potential eating disorders by turning eating over to the child.

2. It is normal for young children to play with their food, spill their milk, and drop food on the floor. Behavior appropriate for their ages is not misbehavior. Clean up spills, let kids finger paint in their food, and get a dog to eat what drops. If you don't have a dog, put a plastic sheet under a young child's place.

3. Some families allow children to make themselves a sandwich if they don't like the meal. Do not cook special dishes for each child.

4. Let your kids serve themselves and do not discuss what they eat or don't eat. Simply clear their plates at the end of the meal (ten to fifteen minutes is plenty of time).

5. If kids complain about your cooking, tell them it's okay not to eat what they don't like, but it hurts the chef when people complain. With a young child, if he says, "I don't like this," remove his plate and say, "Okay, you don't have to eat it." That usually ends the complaining very quickly.

6. Do not eat in front of the television. Adults should sit down and eat with the kids. Set the table with flowers, candles, or place mats, or eat in the dining room to create a special experience for the family.

7. If you think your children's behavior has become too obnoxious, you might try deciding what you will do instead of trying to control your children. Pick up your plate and go to another room to eat.

8. Another possibility is to ignore the behavior. Many children stop obnoxious behavior when it doesn't get a rise out of their parents.

9. If your child decides to become a vegetarian or wants to try out any other health-conscious new way of eating, ask your child how you can be supportive. Don't make fun of your child or insist he or she

eat the way you do or treat the new habit as an eating disorder. Many vegetarians made the decision to change their eating as very young children. If you are a vegetarian and your child insists on eating meat, the same advice applies. Do not force your way of eating on your children.

Planning Ahead to Prevent Future Problems

1. One of the best ways to prevent or stop a potentially damaging pattern is to avoid interfering with your children's eating. That includes putting them on diets, nag-

Booster Thoughts

Bonnie married a widower with six children. The oldest was eight years old, and the youngest were two-year-old twins. The mother of these children had died in childbirth when the twins were born. You can imagine how difficult it was to find a baby-sitter for six children, including baby twins. Even those who were desperate for a job did not stay long, so the children had not had the stability of consistent discipline before Bonnie became their new mother. This was especially evident during mealtime, which was a terrible ordeal because the children would fight, argue, and throw food at each other.

Bonnie had taught Adlerian/Dreikursian principles before she had a chance to practice them. Now she had her chance.

The first thing Bonnie did was hold a family meeting. She did not even discuss their mealtime behavior. She simply asked them to decide how much time they needed to eat their food after it was on the table. They talked it over and decided fifteen minutes was plenty of time. (They forgot to consider how much time it takes to fight, argue, and throw food.)

They all willingly agreed to a family rule that dinner would be served at 6 P.M. and the table cleared at 6:15.

The next evening, Bonnie and her husband ignored the fighting while they ate their food. (I know how difficult this is for parents to do.) At 6:15, Bonnie cleared the table. The children protested that they were still hungry and were not through eating. Bonnie kindly and firmly replied, "I am just following the rule we agreed on. I am

ging, criticizing, or taking them to clinics and doctors without their agreement.

2. Look at your own attitudes about weight, food, and eating patterns and what they may be suggesting to your children. Are you saying things like "Finish everything on your plate" and then later getting upset because your child is overweight? Do you tell your kids they can't eat between meals, which may encourage them to binge at mealtimes? Consider other ways in which you are unconsciously trying to control your child's food intake.

sure you can make it until breakfast." She then sat in front of the refrigerator with a novel and earplugs for the rest of the evening.

The next night was a repeat of the previous night, as the children tested to see if their new mother was for real. By the third night, they knew she was, and they were so busy eating that they did not have time to fight, argue, or throw food.

There is a lovely sequel to this story. Six years later, I had the opportunity to stay with these children while their parents took a weekend vacation. They were so responsible and capable that I did not lift a finger the whole weekend.

The children prepared all the meals and did their chores without any interference from me. They showed me their meal and chore plan. They planned all their menus for a month during the first family meeting of the month. They all had a night to cook, except Mom (who did all the shopping) and the oldest boy (who had football practice).

I asked them if things always ran so smoothly. One of the girls told me that they used to have a rule that whoever cooked did not clean the kitchen. This caused problems because those who had the cleanup chore always complained about the messy cooks. They decided to change the rule so that the cook also cleaned the kitchen. This solved the complaints and gave everyone a longer break before it was their turn again.[31]

---

31. From Jane Nelsen, *Positive Discipline* (New York: Ballantine, 1996), 192.

3. When children complain about the food, it may be time to involve them in choosing what they eat, at least one night a week. Let each child cook dinner one night a week. Even small kids can cook hot dogs, open a can of beans, and make a simple salad.

4. Plan with kids what they can do to contribute. Talk about the different jobs that need to be done, such as setting the table, cooking dinner, washing the dishes, and feeding the pets.

5. Stress that mealtime is a time to share stories about the day, visit with each other, and share the good feelings of being together as a family.

6. Practice good table manners at a time other than mealtime. Kids love to role-play. Pretend you are having a party and invite your children and all their stuffed animals. Set the table with a snack. Ask the kids for their ideas as to what constitutes bad table manners. Give a limited choice of what will happen when bad table manners occur: either the stuffed animal's plate is removed or the animal is removed from the table and can eat again at the next snack party. Demonstrate follow-through with the stuffed animals so the children can see ahead of time what will happen.

7. Choose one night a week to practice table manners. Make it fun. Invite everyone to exaggerate, saying, "Pleeeeease pass the butter." Make a game of getting points for catching others with their elbows on the table, talking with their mouths full, interrupting others, complaining, or reaching across the table. The one with the most points gets to choose the after-dinner game.

8. Schedule your meals and don't make children wait until they are overly hungry to eat. If you have snacks in the family, limit snacks to certain times of day or keep fresh fruit and vegetables cut up in the fridge for those who like to eat less more often.

9. During a family meeting, get the whole family involved in planning ways to make mealtime enjoyable for everyone.

Life Skills Children Can Learn

Children can learn that they are not going to get in trouble at the table, so they don't have to sidetrack their parents with bad manners. The table is a fun place to be, and there are many positive ways to get attention by joining in and being part of the family.

Parenting Pointers

1. If parents worry less about manners and more about creating a positive experience for family members, kids will quickly learn

that meals are times when everyone wants to be together, and table manners will take care of themselves.

2. You can help your child learn to listen to his or her feelings and body wisdom instead of training the child to be an overeater to please you or a picky eater to defeat you. Think of how many overweight adults were members of the "Clean Plate Club" as children and have completely lost touch with the meaning of the word "hungry."

3. If you see mealtime as a time to make kids eat and to lecture about manners, the kids will probably pay you back with bad manners. If your attitude is that meals are one of the special times that families can share together, the kids will probably reflect that thinking.

Morning Hassles

"By the time my kids leave for school every morning, my nerves are frazzled and I'm practically in tears from fighting with them to get ready. Then when they're finally out the door, I'm faced with a big mess to clean up and a rush to get myself off to work. Is there an alternative to this situation?"

Understanding Your Child, Yourself, and the Situation

The family atmosphere is established by the parents, and the tone for the day is set in the morning. Many children and parents start each day with a struggle because they don't take the time to establish a morning routine that works for everyone. Children need adults to supervise setting up a routine. Once children learn how to plan their time in the morning, they feel better and the day goes more smoothly for everyone.

Suggestions

1. Set a deadline for morning chores. In many families, the deadline is breakfast. You can establish a nonverbal reminder to show that a child still has unfinished work. As a family, agree what this nonverbal signal should be.

2. Spend your time taking care of your chores and do not nag or remind the kids about what they need to do. Let them experience the consequences of forgetting. If a child comes to the table with unfinished duties, turn her plate upside down and let her finish her work before she joins the rest of the family for breakfast. This signal needs to be agreed upon with your child in advance.

3. If it is difficult for you to refrain from nagging, take a long shower while your children get ready for school.

4. Establish an agreement that the television doesn't go on in the morning until the

Booster Thoughts

Mrs. Farnsworth had been taking the responsibility to get Dan, her thirteen-year-old son, out of bed on Tuesday mornings for an early-morning class. She would wake him up; he would go back to sleep. This scenario would continue, with increasing anger on both sides, until Mrs. Farnsworth would yank the covers off. Dan would then stumble out of bed, saying, "Get off my back," and finally leave about half an hour late.

Mrs. Farnsworth received a letter from the teacher saying that if Dan missed one more time he would fail the class.

One morning after Mrs. Farnsworth decided to "let go," she went into Dan's room and respectfully asked, "Do you want to go to class this morning, or do you want to miss it and fail the class?" Dan was quiet for a few seconds before saying,

chores are done. If your children are watching television and their work is incomplete, simply turn off the set.

5. Let the morning routine chart (see "Planning Ahead to Prevent Future Problems," item 1 below) be the boss. Instead of nagging, ask your children, "What is next on our morning routine chart?"

Planning Ahead to Prevent Future Problems

1. Create a morning routine chart. Sit down with your children at a time when you feel calm and help them brainstorm a list of things they need to do to be ready for school each day. Help them make a chart to help them remember the things on their list. Kids enjoy cutting out pictures from magazines or drawing pictures to paste next to each task on the chart. The chart should be used as a reminder and not as a way to reward children for doing what needs to be done.

2. Get alarm clocks for the kids as soon as they start school and teach them how to use them.

3. You might want to have all the children include a small job that helps the family as part of their list: setting the table, making toast, pouring juice, scrambling eggs, or starting a load of laundry.

4. Let your kids decide how much time they need to accomplish everything on their lists and then figure out the time they

"I guess I'll go." Then his mother said, "Do you want me to help you get up, or do you want me to leave you alone?" He said, "Leave me alone." She left, and he called out, "Thanks, Mom." (Quite a difference from "get off my back.") Five minutes later, he was in the shower and left on time. Mom guessed he could feel the difference in her manner and tone of voice and sensed that she would not argue with him.

Mrs. Farnsworth told her parent study group, "It may have been better for me to stay out of it completely and let him experience the consequence of failing the class, but I wasn't quite ready for that. I *was* ready to accept negative answers to my questions. I *was* ready to have him consciously choose to sleep in and fail the class."[32]

32. From Jane Nelsen and Lynn Lott, *Positive Discipline for Teenagers* (Rocklin, CA: Prima Publishing, 1994), 203.

need to set on their alarm clocks. Allow them to learn from mistakes.

5. Take time for training and have fun by role-playing how the morning will go from the time the alarm goes off.

6. Avoid rescuing kids who need a little time to learn that they can be responsible. Contact their teachers and explain your plan for helping your kids learn to be responsible for getting themselves up and off to school in the mornings. Ask the teachers if they would be willing to allow the kids to experience the consequences of being late to school. It usually takes one or two tardies to change a person's slow morning habits. They might stay in at recess or after school to make up the work they miss.

7. As part of your children's bedtime routine, include preparation for the morning, such as deciding what they want to wear and putting their homework by the front door. Many morning hassles can be prevented by evening preparation.

8. Don't forget to discuss morning hassles during a family meeting, and ask everyone to brainstorm for ideas to make mornings a positive experience.

Life Skills Children Can Learn

Children can learn how to plan their time and contribute to the family. They can learn that they have control over their time and can feel as rushed or calm as they choose. They are capable and do not have to be babied to get things done.

Parenting Pointers

1. Never do for children what they can do for themselves. Empower your children through teaching instead of being a slave to them.

2. With a routine firmly in place, morning can be a delightful and special time with your children. They go off to their day feeling happy, and so do you.

3. Some parents sleep in while their children get ready. Instead of seeing this as neglectful, we notice that the children are often very responsible. If this plan works for you, be sure to find special times to spend with your children later in the day.

Motivation, Lack of

"My child does as little as he can to "get by" in school. He doesn't do his chores around the house. We have offered rewards and taken away privileges. Nothing seems to work. He just doesn't seem to have any motivation. What should we do?"

Understanding Your Child, Yourself, and the Situation

When a child lacks motivation, it is helpful to get into his world to discover the purpose of his behavior. Perhaps your child is trying to tell you, "You can't make me," in order to win a power struggle. Perhaps he feels hurt by your high expectations and the perception that your love is conditional and wants to hurt back by not trying. Perhaps your child believes he is incapable and has given up because it is easier to avoid trying than to face failure. Your child may be comparing himself to a sibling and trying to find belonging and significance in the family by being different. Whatever the reason, a child who lacks motivation presents one of the most challenging and discouraging situations a parent faces. Typical responses are for parents to do things for him, to push him harder, or to make him feel bad in the hope that he will change his ways. Other responses are to try to embarrass him or simply to avoid him. All these responses make the situation worse. The challenge is for parents to stop doing things that don't work and take time to find ways to encourage both themselves and their children.

Suggestions

1. Take a look at your own behavior. Are you not giving your child enough quality time, which may invite her to seek atten-

tion, even if it is negative attention? Are you so controlling that you invite power struggles and rebellion? Are your expectations so high that your child feels she can't live up to your expectations and feels hurt by your conditional love? Are you doing too much for your child, which may invite her to believe she is incapable? If so, stop any of these behaviors and choose any of the following suggestions to create a more respectful relationship.

2. Instead of expecting your child to be perfect and to follow through, you be the one to follow through (see Part 1) with kindness, firmness, dignity, and respect. Use one word to communicate what your child needs to do: "Homework." "Chores." Make eye contact, and try to have a firm yet kind expression. If you still get resistance, keep your mouth shut, give him a knowing smile, a wink, or a hug, and point to what needs to be done. These methods are much more motivating than words that invite a power struggle.

3. Act. Take a young child by the hand and lead her kindly and firmly to the task that she needs to do.

4. Offer your honest emotions: "I feel upset because you spend time on everything but your schoolwork, and I wish it was more of a priority for you."

5. Let the consequences be the teacher. (Consequences are what happen as a result of a child's choices, not something you impose.) If a child is not doing his homework, this will be reflected in poor grades and in missed opportunities. Show empathy for the child when he experiences the consequences of his inactivity. Don't display an I-told-you-so attitude.

6. Follow up with "what" and "how" questions to help him explore and understand the cause and effect, and use this information to form a plan for success. "How do you feel about what happened?" "What is important to you?" "What are the benefits to you now or in the future if you do this?" "How will you be affected if you choose not to do this?" "How would you be contributing to others if you did this?" (If he says, "I don't know," say, "Why don't you think about it and get back to me later because I know you are a good problem solver.")

7. Engage in joint problem solving. Decide together what the problem is and what some possible solutions are. Begin by sharing your perspective: "I notice that you aren't making any effort to do your schoolwork or to help around the house." Then invite your child to share his picture of what's happening. This is effective only if he feels you will listen without judgment. Then brainstorm together for solutions and pick the one that works for both of you.

8. Discuss all the things that are going well, giving your child a chance to speak first. Then ask for her opinion of what

needs improvement. Brainstorm with her what she could do and what you could do that would be the most encouraging and helpful to her.

9. Let go and allow your child to work out the problem. There's a difference between letting go and giving up. When you let go, you can stay connected while handing the responsibility for the problem back to your child. When you give up, you cut all ties and send the message that you are no longer available.

10. Assure your child that you know he is capable of doing whatever he needs to do to be successful.

Planning Ahead to Prevent Future Problems

1. Explore your child's lack of motivation through the four mistaken goals of behavior (see Part 1). Find productive ways for her to get attention, to feel like she's in charge, to deal with hurt feelings, or to get help when she feels like giving up.

2. Notice when a child who usually participates abruptly stops. This may be an indication that something is happening at school or at home, such as a divorce or serious illness. Or the child could be having problems with peer relationships.

3. Have regular family meetings and joint problem-solving sessions. Keep two things in mind. First, when children are involved in making decisions, they are motivated to adhere to the decisions. Second, children participate more when they understand the relevance of what they're doing.

4. Consider different styles of dealing with stress. A child who is afraid may withdraw and do nothing. What you can do for this child is to honor his pace, help him identify what he fears, look for a small first step, and require movement—however gradual—toward a goal.

5. Build on strengths. If a child is doing well in any area, encourage her to spend more time in this area. (Don't forbid her to spend time on a subject in which she does well until she does better in another subject.) A child needs to feel encouraged in her areas of strength. Teach her to manage her weaknesses, and let her know that barely passing or dropping a class once in a while is okay as long as she is doing well in areas where she has strength.

6. Avoid lectures and show empathy when your child experiences failures. Teach that mistakes are wonderful opportunities to learn.

Booster Thoughts

In the eighth grade, Stuart lost interest in school. His mother would coax and then yell at him to get up in the morning and to go to school. Stuart would finally get up but would act angry and sullen. He refused to work hard in school and skipped classes, and his grades were slipping.

Finally, his mother decided to stop engaging in the power struggles. Instead she asked Stuart to sit down with her in the family room. She then asked, in a friendly manner, a series of "what" and "how" questions. "What do you think will happen in your life if you don't get a good education?" she asked. Stuart replied sullenly, "There are lots of millionaires who don't have a good education." Mom acknowledged, "That is true. How many people do you know who have dropped out of school?" "A few," Stuart said. Mom asked, "How are they doing?" Stuart looked a little sheepish as he said, "One is in jail. Another one is working at McDonald's."

Mom avoided the temptation to say, "Well, is that how you want to end up?" Instead, she continued to invite Stuart to explore possibilities. She asked, "What kind of jobs do you think you will be able to get if you don't have an education?" Stuart said, "Well, I could be a contractor." Mom said, "I'm sure you could. What kind of jobs will you not be able to get without an education?" Stuart thought about it. "Well, I couldn't be an engineer or a pilot." Mom then asked, "What do you want to do about your education?" Stuart replied, "Well, I'm going to get one, but I'm not going to like it." Mom said, "Sounds like you have come to the conclusion of many successful people—to do something even if you don't like it because you see the long-range benefits."

7. Have faith in your child, even when he has a setback. Instead of trying to control him, say, "I have faith in you to work this out and to learn what you need to learn from whatever mistakes you make."

8. Provide tutoring if your child agrees that this would be helpful.

9. Be a cheerleader to your child. Appreciate effort as well as finished products.

10. Teach your children to be "good finders." During family meetings, provide time for each family member to verbalize positive things they have seen or experienced during the week. This can go beyond the compliment time (as described in Part 1) and include positive things in the community or world. Give each member of the family a "gratitude journal." Share items from the journals at mealtimes.

Life Skills Children Can Learn

Children can learn that it is okay for everyone to be different and unique and that what is important to one person may not be important to another. Children can learn that it is natural to have periods of being unmotivated and that there are ways to get back in the swing of life. Children can learn that others are there to help them feel successful but ultimately success or failure depends on the effort one exerts on one's own behalf.

Parenting Pointers

1. Stress to yourself and your children that the problem isn't failing but what one does after failing. Your job is to help your children find and maintain their courage.

2. Be careful that you aren't trying to make your children into little clones of yourself and your value system. Children need room to be themselves and to be respected and loved for their individuality.

3. If your home has no routine and your life is chaotic, it may be difficult for your children to feel motivated. If they are struggling to cope with situations that are overwhelming, like abuse, divorce, or death, they may be sad and discouraged rather than unmotivated.

Moving

"We have to move to another state. My eight-year-old is devastated. Will he survive?"

Understanding Your Child, Yourself, and the Situation

Moving can be a devastating experience for children—but they do survive. It can be difficult to give up familiar places and people. You may also be dealing with your own loss and therefore have a more difficult time as you try to help your child. The grieving process for a move can be similar to that of a loss through death. Understand this and allow the process to take its course. On the other hand, there are families that move regularly, and the children think of this as life, they are quite used to it, and they don't see it as a disadvantage. It is best not to make assumptions. Moving could be hard for you and easy for your child or vice versa, so make sure you check out how a family member feels without assuming that you know.

Suggestions

1. Share your grief without being morbid. Also share your plans to deal with your grief.

2. Listen to your child without trying to talk him out of his feelings. Just listen.

3. Have faith that your child will be okay. The experience will pass. You don't need to fix things for your child. Trust the process and the healing powers of time.

4. Avoid getting so focused on the move that you neglect your children. The more you involve them, the less neglected they will feel. Take time to be aware of their feelings and to listen and help them process their feelings. Just listening is often enough.

5. Include your children in the packing and allow them to take their important treasures. This is not a time to argue with them about things they want to keep. Save spring housecleaning for another time.

6. When you arrive at the new destination, help your children explore the new area. Take them to the library to get library cards. Go for bike rides to explore the neighborhood. Find the closest parks and recreation centers to see if special classes are offered. Visit the Chamber of Commerce to learn about special features of the new area. Take your children to the closest shopping center and movies. (It won't be long before they will have friends and your teenagers won't want to be seen in these areas with you.)

Planning Ahead to Prevent Future Problems

1. During a family meeting, have a brainstorming session in which everyone can come up with suggestions for making the adjustment easier. We call this making lemonade out of lemons.

2. Help your children decide on ways to stay connected to the old location. Plant a memorial tree. Plan return visits. Give friends ten self-addressed, stamped envelopes to encourage writing. Plan a small phone budget. Let your children have their own e-mail address. These plans provide a bridge until children make new friends and lose some interest in their former home.

3. Continue to discuss your kids' experiences with change, such as beginning a new year at school, making a new friend, or going someplace new for vacation. Emphasize what was gained through the experience. Then explore what they may gain through moving.

4. If possible, include the children in looking for a new house or apartment. Let them help decorate their new rooms.

Life Skills Children Can Learn

Children can learn that it is okay to feel sad about loss and change. Plans help them through transition periods. Time does help, even though they may not like hearing that at the time. Children also learn the old wisdom: Nothing ventured, nothing gained.

Parenting Pointers

1. Avoid being overly responsible for the child's struggle and feelings. Show acceptance and understanding, but avoid rescuing him.

2. Share with your children some of the transitions you have experienced in which you faced fear and uncertainty but grew through the process. Make it a personal sharing rather than a lecture.

3. Avoid bribes and blackmail as ways to resolve conflict, so that you demonstrate acceptance and cooperation rather than manipulation.

Booster Thoughts

There was a time when it was assumed that "military brats" would have problems because their families constantly moved. Today, in a mobile society, they are among the more secure. In general, their parents anticipate moving and prepare children through their positive attitudes and family discussions. When there is a move, there are still uniforms, bases, post exchanges, and rituals that are the same from place to place.

Family meetings, rituals, and traditions provide a portable structure that helps with transitions. Religious practices that persist from place to place are helpful. Traveling on vacation and experiencing new and different aspects of life help people resolve the fear of moving. Virtually all migrant societies cope with movement by maintaining rituals and structures from place to place. Perhaps this could be stated as a principle: "When changing venue, don't change the menu!"[33]

---

33. From H. Stephen Glenn, *The Greatest Human Need* (Orem, UT: Empowering People Books, Tapes, and Videos, 1989), videocassette.

Naps

(See also *Bedtime Hassles*)

"My child refuses to take a nap, but she gets so tired and cranky by 5:00 that everyone is miserable. Sometimes she falls asleep by 5:30 or so and then wakes up raring to go around 8:00. Then bedtime becomes a nightmare. How do I get her to take a nap when I know she needs one?"

Understanding Your Child, Yourself, and the Situation

Children resist sleep, not because they don't need it but because they don't want to miss out on anything as they explore their exciting world. It is important to treat their need for autonomy with dignity and respect while helping them learn to make choices and follow rules that make life more enjoyable for themselves and others.

Suggestions

1. Don't tell your child she is tired (even though you think she is). Admit another truth—that *you* are tired and need a break.

2. Tell your child she doesn't have to sleep but that she has to stay in her bed for one hour doing something quiet, such as looking at books or listening to soft music.

3. Give her a limited choice: "Do you want to start your nap at 1:00 or at 1:15?"

4. Follow through with kindness and firmness. Every time your child gets up before nap time is over, gently take her by the hand and lead her back to bed. You may have to repeat this twenty or more times for several days until she knows you mean what you say.

Planning Ahead to Prevent Future Problems

1. Establish a routine and stick to it. Nap time can be preceded by five minutes of special time to read a story or play a game.

2. Children enjoy routines and should be involved in setting them up. Use questions and limited choices to find out what your child thinks will work.

3. While planning a nap time routine, be sure it follows quiet activities instead of activities that are stimulating.

4. Try making nap time different from bedtime. Allow your child to choose a special nap time stuffed animal, a different bed, or a different blanket.

5. Teach your child to use a simple cassette player. Let him choose from a collection of

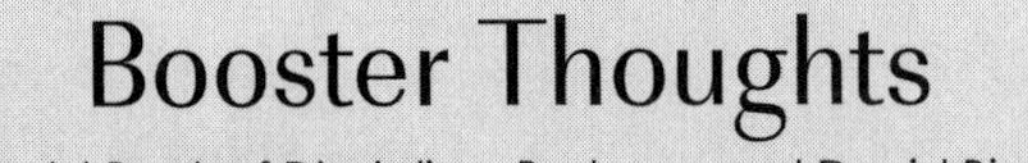

In their book, *Parents' Book of Discipline,* Barbara and David Bjorklund give the following examples:

One mother we know lets her preschooler take his nap in his older brother's room, as long as he . . . goes to sleep nicely. Another grandmother we know keeps a Mickey Mouse sleeping bag in her closet that belonged to the kids' uncle. They can pick any room in the house for a nap and use the sleeping bag to "camp out" if they go right to sleep. (These kids never nap at home, but always take two- or three-hour naps at Grandma's.)[34]

34. Barbara R. and David F. Bjorklund, *Parents' Book of Discipline* (New York: Ballantine Books, 1990), 211.

nap time music and start the cassette player himself.

Life Skills Children Can Learn

Children can learn that their resistance will be treated with dignity and respect. They can learn that, while they have some choices, they also need to follow routines that are respectful to everyone.

Parenting Pointers

1. All children do not need the same amount of sleep. Quiet time may work better for some children than nap time. Some are through with napping by two or two and a half years old. Others need naps until they start kindergarten.

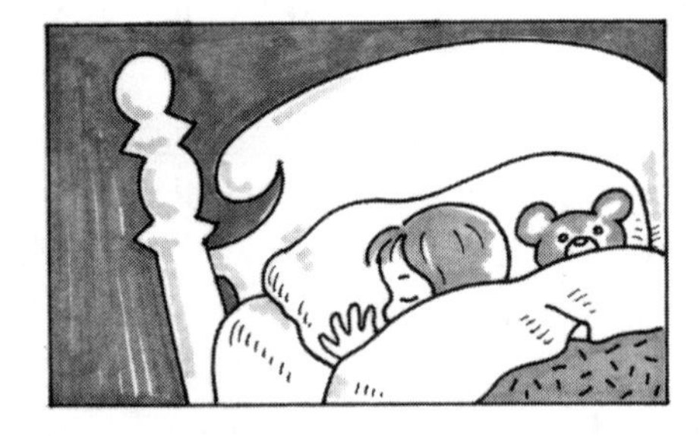

2. It does not hurt your child's self-esteem to demonstrate his frustration by "crying it out." It is damaging to self-esteem for a child to develop beliefs that "I'm not capable to handle disappointment," "I don't have to follow any limits," or "I can manipulate others to give me my way."

Negative Child

"I am so worried and irritated with my son that I don't know what to do. Nothing is ever right or enough for him. We just had his birthday party, which he planned. He rented a game, had a friend over, and at the end of the party, when I asked him if he had a good time, he said, 'Well, sort of.' I would fall over if he ever sounded positive. All he can think of is what he doesn't have or didn't do."

Understanding Your Child, Yourself, and the Situation

Children who never seem satisfied by what they have are difficult to be with and hard to like. If they feel cheated and compare themselves to their friends, insisting all their friends have something they don't, they may be stuck in trying to keep up with a standard that doesn't fit your pocketbook or your value system. You probably want your children to be happy and positive, because it would be nice for them and nicer for you and everyone else to live with them. When your children are unhappy, you may think it is a reflection on you and that you must have done something wrong. Perhaps you feel disappointed because you have made every effort to create an enjoyable situation, trying to make your child's world nice. Yet in spite of your efforts, for your child things are never quite right.

Children need to learn that they are part of their universe and world and not the center of it. They need to learn to entertain themselves, express gratitude and appreciation for what is given to them, and have an ability to roll with the ups and downs life brings.

Suggestions

1. Don't ask questions like "Did you have a good time?" or "Are you happy?" to a negative child, as you are asking for a cloud to rain on your parade. A sense of humor might work better. Try working with a rating system: "On a scale of one to ten, how bad was your day?" or "Show me with your hands how much you hate your new outfit."

2. Be accepting of your child as he is. It's okay to acknowledge that your child sees the glass half empty or that Oscar the Grouch is going to get a run for his money.

3. Tell your child you are willing to hear about the disappointments but would also like to hear about the positives.

4. When your child complains, listen without talking or fixing. You don't have to make her world better every time she complains.

5. Don't compare your children to each other or to other kids. Each child is unique. Find what is special about your child and tell him.

6. When your child blames everyone else for her problems, listen respectfully and then say, "That's her part. What do you think caused that to happen? What might your part have been? Do you want help problem solving this situation, or were you simply wanting to tell me how you feel and what happened?"

7. Ask others (siblings, relatives, and other parents) to avoid labeling the child.

Planning Ahead to Prevent Future Problems

1. Help your child learn how to create successes for himself. Show the child how to

Booster Thoughts

Ian was convinced that his mother liked his brother more than him and that his brother always got his way. No amount of explaining and coaxing could get him to change his mind. He drew a picture of the family. His brother had a halo over his head and Ian had horns. His mother was worried about Ian's attitude but also weary of his constant complaining.

One day, she took Ian out for lunch and told him she had a serious problem she wanted to talk over with him and get his help on. Ian figured he was in trouble again and grumbled all the way to the restaurant. Once they were seated in the booth, Mom began.

"Ian, I just don't know what to do about your brother. He's such a goody-two-shoes that he's driving me crazy. I'm sick and tired of his constant volunteering to help with everything. He's like an octopus, and no one else ever gets a chance when he's around. Do you have any ideas of what I might do?"

Ian's jaw hung down to the table and he sat in shock, unable to say a word. Finally he said, "I don't know what you can do, because he makes me mad, too. I thought he was your favorite."

"Well, Ian, I guess we'll both have to give this more thought. Thanks for listening to me. Now what should we have for dessert?"

When they went home, Ian seemed lighter. Even though this didn't completely change Ian's negativity, he seemed to have more positive moments and could be seen winking at his mother every time his brother offered to do one more nice thing.

set up a savings account for toys and items important to the child or how to earn extra money by doing extra work at home or in the neighborhood, or create a list *with* your child of things he can do when bored and hang it on the fridge.

2. Teach your child how to express feelings, using the "I feel _____ because _____ and I wish _____" formula (see Part 1).

3. Spend special time each day with your child so that she can get attention by doing something with you other than complaining.

4. Really listen to your child. Perhaps he has a legitimate problem and you aren't taking the child seriously.

5. If you have another child who is positive, realize that a lot of what you are dealing with is sibling rivalry. See *Sibling Rivalry* for more tips on how to deal with that.

Life Skills Children Can Learn

Children can learn that life has ups and downs, that they are able and responsible to make their worlds more interesting and rewarding, and that the universe doesn't revolve around them.

Parenting Pointers

1. The more you empower instead of fix or scold your child, the happier you all will be.

2. Create your own schedule, get a life, and be clear about what you are willing to do for and with your child. Make sure your child knows that you have important things to do for yourself and others. If this bothers your child, that is okay. Let the child have his feelings without trying to fix or change them.

No, Saying

(See also *Listen, Refuses to*)

"My toddler is always saying no. It doesn't matter if I ask him to do something nicely or yell, he says no. He even says no when I ask him to pick out a storybook. I've heard of the 'terrible twos,' but this is ridiculous."

Understanding Your Child, Yourself, and the Situation

Your child is going through a normal individuation process—he is taking steps to separate himself as an individual from his parents. This is an ongoing process of child development that seems to intensify at ages two, six, eight, and during the teen years.

Erik Erikson identified the developmental period from one to two years of age as the stage of autonomy versus doubt and shame. During this time, if children are hindered through excessive control or punishment when they try to assert their autonomy, they develop a sense of doubt and shame about themselves. It is possible for parents to nurture and support the individuation process so that it does not turn into a power struggle.

The use of the word "no" is not only a developmental process. Children also say no because the word is fun and easy to say. Your child may not even mean "no." You could be turning the word into a power struggle by taking it too literally. Some toddlers use the word for everything, so listen carefully and be sure to put the word in context.

Suggestions

1. Limit your own use of "no." It is amazing how many times parents say no and then act surprised when children follow their lead.

2. Once you have stopped saying no, ignore it when your child says the word. When possible, simply leave the scene. If action is required, act with your mouth shut. For example, if your child needs to go to bed, take her by the hand and lead her to the bedroom.

3. Give choices that can't be answered by a yes or no. "Do you want to wear your yellow pajamas or your blue pajamas?" "Do you want a long story or a short story?"

4. Give your children power by asking for their help and inviting them to make decisions. "I need some help cleaning up this mess. Which part do you want to do, and which part do you want me to do?"

5. Celebrate. "Hooray! You are starting to think for yourself and deciding what is important to you." A two-year-old may not understand what you are saying, but it will help you remember how important it is for your child to establish himself as an individual.

Planning Ahead to Prevent Future Problems

1. Learn about age-appropriate behavior[35] so you won't expect your child to do things (or to avoid things) that are not developmentally appropriate. With this knowledge, you will understand the importance of using Positive Discipline methods that teach life skills and invite cooperation instead of rebellion.

---

35. Refer to Jane Nelsen, Cheryl Erwin, and Roslyn Duffy, *Positive Discipline: The First Three Years* (Rocklin, CA: Prima Publishing, 1989) and Jane Nelsen, Cheryl Erwin, and Roslyn Duffy, *Positive Discipline for Preschoolers* (Rocklin, CA: Prima Publishing, 1989).

Booster Thoughts

Mrs. Knight was relieved to learn about the individuation process. She had been engaged in a heavy-duty power struggle with her son. She thought it was her duty to make him mind her and do what she told him to do. The more she said, "Yes, you will," the more her son said, "No, I won't."

She started to use humor. The next time he said no, she grabbed him in a big hug and said, "What do you mean, no? I'm going to tickle you until I hear a yes." Soon they were laughing, and the power struggle was forgotten.

Other times, when her son would say no, she would say, "Actually that is what I meant." Then she would sing, "No, no, a thousand times no." Again, the power struggle was diffused and she would gently lead him to what needed to be done.

2. Give your child many opportunities to make decisions and choices that foster a sense of power and importance.

3. Do not say no when your child wants to explore and touch. Remove things or distract your child: "You can't touch this, but you can touch this" (see also *Touching Things*).

4. Never say "bad boy" or "naughty girl." Children may do unacceptable things, but they are never bad.

5. Don't underestimate how much your children really understand. Talk to your children and explain things and then wait and see if they get the concept. For instance, you could say, "The stereo might break if you play with the knobs. If you want to play music, come get me and we'll turn it on together."

Life Skills Children Can Learn

Children can learn that their parents respect them as individuals and will help them have as much autonomy as they can handle. They can learn that parents will not insist on total control but will be there for support and guidance.

Parenting Pointers

1. Think of your children as cute and adorable as they seek autonomy. This will help you avoid reacting and provoking a power struggle.

2. Children who do not accomplish this process of separating themselves successfully may become adults who are approval junkies.

Obedience

"My child is disobedient. I'm worried that if I spare the rod I will spoil the child, but the more I punish him to get him to obey, the more disobedient he becomes."

Understanding Your Child, Yourself, and the Situation

Teaching children to be obedient is dangerous in today's society. Rebellious children are often the result for parents who try to force obedience. Children who learn obedience may be obedient to whomever wants to exercise control over them—first family, then peer groups, gangs, cults, and perhaps autocratic spouses. It is better to teach children cooperation, problem-solving skills, and respect for themselves and others. Biblical scholars tell us that the rod was not used to hit or punish but to guide. Children need guidance, not punishment.

Suggestions

1. For children aged two to four, use the many parenting tools suggested throughout this book: follow-through; asking "what," "how," and "why" questions; positive time-out; taking time for training; and age-appropriate chores to teach responsibility, cooperation, and the value of making a contribution.

2. For children aged four to eighteen, use the above parenting tools plus family meetings to teach problem-solving skills, emotional honesty, and letting go to teach children mutual respect and life skills.

Planning Ahead to Prevent Future Problems

1. Help your children learn to deal with arbitrary rules they might encounter in the outside world. Teach them to accept what is appropriate and beneficial and to respectfully try to change what is inappropriate and disrespectful. This can be done at dinnertime or through family-meeting discussions in which you explore the possibilities and consequences of following, defying, or changing rules.

2. Not teaching blind obedience, however, does not mean permissiveness. There are times when it is appropriate to work out solutions together, and there are times

when action is more important than discussion. Decide in advance what you will do and follow through with dignity and respect. If your children run into the street, grab their hands and hang on. Say, "I'll let go when you are ready to stay by my side." If they run around at the grocery store, say, "I'm not willing to take you this time because you ran around the store last time. We'll discuss how to behave later and you can try again next time."

Life Skills Children Can Learn

Children can learn self-discipline, responsibility, cooperation, problem solving, and respect for themselves and others.

Booster Thoughts

In the so-called good old days, there were many models of submission. Even Dad obeyed the boss so he wouldn't lose his job. Remember when Mom obediently did whatever Dad said—or at least gave the impression she did—because it was the culturally acceptable thing to do? Remember when minority groups accepted a submissive (obedient) role? Children had many models of submissiveness.

It is difficult these days to find models of submissiveness for children. Today, minority groups are actively claiming their rights to full equality, dignity, and respect. Many women want a marriage of partnership instead of submissiveness. Many men want a mate who contributes financially instead of someone who needs to be taken care of. Men don't want a second-class role any more than women do and have formed many groups to assess their roles and assert their rights.[36]

As Rudolf Dreikurs pointed out, "When Dad lost control of Mom, they both lost control of the children." Children are simply following the examples all around them.

Psychiatrist Rollo May once said, "What America should ultimately do is erect a statue of responsibility in San Francisco Harbor to offset the Statue of Liberty in New York Harbor to remind us constantly that without one we cannot have the other."[37]

---

36. Jane Nelsen, *Positive Discipline* (New York: Ballantine, 1996), 4.

37. Rollo May, *Love and Will* (New York: Norton, 1969), 630.

Parenting Pointers

1. Obedience may have been an important characteristic necessary to survive in society many years ago. To be successful, happy, contributing members of society today, individuals need inner control and the life skills taught through Positive Discipline methods.

2. When parents use punishment and reward with the intention of teaching children to be obedient, what they actually teach is that children need to be obedient only when the parents are around. It becomes the parents' responsibility to catch kids being good and give them rewards and catch them being bad to punish them. What happens when the parents are not around?

3. Parents are often fooled when they use punishment, because the behavior stops for the moment and they think they have achieved obedience. They might be surprised if they check out what the child is really learning. Children usually make one of five decisions when they are punished:

- Resentment: "This is unfair. I can't trust adults."
- Revenge: "They are winning now, but I'll get even."
- Rebellion: "I'll do just the opposite to prove I don't have to do it their way."
- Sneakiness: "I just won't get caught next time."
- Reduced self-esteem: "I am a bad person and can't think for myself. Unless I do as I'm told, I won't be loved or have worth."

Pampering

"I know I pamper my son too much, but I don't know how to stop. He seems so helpless and is so clingy. It feels cruel to push him away."

Understanding Your Child, Yourself, and the Situation

Pushing away is not the only alternative to pampering. Pampering creates clinging and helplessness. Pampering helps children decide that "Love means having someone else take care of me. I'm okay only if I can charm and manipulate other people into my service." It is cruel not to help children learn to feel capable and confident to live a life separate from their parents.

Booster Thoughts

Since pampering is so damaging to children, why do parents do it? Many parents really think it is the best way to show love to their children. I have heard some argue that children have plenty of time to adjust to the cold, cruel world, so why not let them have it easy and pleasurable for as long as possible? These parents are not aware of how difficult it is to change habits and characteristics once they are established. Other reasons parents might pamper are because it is easier, it fills their needs to be needed, they think that is what "good" parents are supposed to do, they want to be sure their children do not experience the difficult childhood they feel they had, or they feel pressure from friends and family.[38]

38. Jane Nelsen, *Positive Discipline* (New York: Ballantine, 1996), 43.

Suggestions

1. For preschool children, make arrangements for your child to spend time away from you. Trade child care hours with a friend or relative, or find a good preschool (see *Preschool* and *Baby-Sitters and Child Care*).

2. Give children chores appropriate for their ages[39] (see *Chores, Age-Appropriate*) so they can develop appreciation for making a meaningful contribution.

3. Have faith in your child. When she says, "I can't" and you know she can, say, "I'm sure you can handle it." When your child says "I can," but you think she can't, stand back close enough to lend a helping hand but far enough to let her try and learn from her mistakes.

4. Be careful that you don't overprotect your youngest child and think he is incapable just because of looking younger and smaller than other family members.

39. For many suggestions on how to involve family members in helping with chores, read Lynn Lott and Riki Intner, *Chores Without Wars* (Rocklin, CA: Prima Publishing, 1997.

Youngest children often lose out because they are kept as babies in the family.

Planning Ahead to Prevent Future Problems

1. Be willing to suffer now to prevent greater suffering later. Your children's crying and pleading for special service probably hurts you more than them. When you are confident that it is not helpful to your children to pamper them, it will be easier for you to kindly and firmly avoid pampering.

2. Spend special time with your children (see Part 1) to reassure them that you love them, so they won't fear abandonment.

3. Take time for training to make sure your child develops self-confidence based on skills.

4. Avoid feeling sorry for your children. They feel this attitude in your energy and often adopt it themselves. They will also feel the energy of your confidence in them.

Life Skills Children Can Learn

Children can learn that they are capable. Children can learn they belong by being part of a group instead of the center of the universe.

Parenting Pointers

1. Have you ever heard people complain about how incapable their grown children are? You can avoid this problem years from now by not doing everything for your child now. Rudolf Dreikurs said, "Never do for children what they can do for themselves."[40] Doing favors is an exception, but when it becomes the rule you are robbing your children of self-respect and self-confidence.

2. Mrs. Redbird loved her child so much she could not stand to push him out of the nest. In the name of love, her child never learned to fly.

Pest

"My child is so annoying. She is constantly interrupting me, insisting I spend all my time playing with her or answering her questions. I can't spend time with my husband or any of the other children without her bugging me. Even her teacher complains about how rude she is, constantly interrupting in class."

Understanding Your Child, Yourself, and the Situation

Pesty children give everyone the opportunity to learn about mutual respect. Chil-

40. Rudolf Dreikurs with Vicki Soltz, *Children: The Challenge* (New York: Plume Books, 1990),193.

dren learn at a very early age how good it feels to have attention, but sometimes they have the mistaken belief that they don't count unless they are the center of attention at all times. The more they demand, the more parents—and teachers—give them attention, be it positive or negative. No amount of attention can fill the hole for children who believe they do not belong unless they have constant attention. It is important for parents to give them opportunities to find belonging through cooperation and contribution. It is also important that parents respect themselves as well as their children. It is okay for parents to have time to themselves and let their children figure out how to entertain themselves. They won't die from lack of attention. In fact, pesty children often receive too *much* attention, not too little.

Suggestions

1. If your child has been waiting all day to play with you, when you come home from work ignore the chores and spend fifteen minutes having fun with her or ask her to work with you.

2. Spend time with your spouse and other adults while your children are around. This lets them know that they will get some of your time, but not all of it. If they interrupt, move to another room where you can put a door between you and them or ask them to play somewhere else.

3. Let your children know that you hear them interrupting but you choose not to respond when you are busy doing other things. One way to do this is to put your hand on their shoulder gently while ignoring their demands. This lets them know you care about them even though you won't respond to constant demands.

4. You can also use nonverbal signals to show that you are aware of your child's desire for attention but you are not willing to give any at the present time. Stroking his arm, holding your hand out in the stop position, or putting your finger to your lips all work well. You might also leave the room without saying a word.

5. If your children tattle or bug you to do things they could do for themselves, say, "I'm sure you can work that out yourself. I have faith in you."

Planning Ahead to Prevent Future Problems

1. If your child is being a pest, plan special time with her in which she has you all alone. When she bugs you, say, "This isn't our time to play. I'm looking forward to our special time at two o'clock."

2. Set up places where your children can play safely and entertain themselves. Let your children know that you still love them when you are busy with another child but it is not time for you to be with them. If

they can't handle that, ask them to play in their rooms and try again later.

3. Let your children know when you are available for certain activities, such as, "I'm free from seven o'clock to nine o'clock to help with homework." "I will be happy to make library runs on Monday and Thursday after school." "I'd like to read the paper first and then spend time hearing about your day." Then act like you mean it. Keep control of your schedule.

Life Skills Children Can Learn

Children can learn that parents also have rights. They can learn respect and courtesy as well as how to entertain themselves. Most important, they feel better when satisfaction comes from within instead of constantly searching for recognition from others.

Parenting Pointers

1. Children who demand constant attention are discouraged and are acting out their

Booster Thoughts

Sometimes children work as a team to keep parents busy with them. They have learned the skill of group pestering. Mrs. Latimer found that out when her three nephews were dropped off to spend an afternoon with her children. Mrs. Latimer had noticed how pesty her nephews were around their mother, but she was surprised when they started behaving the same with her. She had spent several hours playing with the children and was ready for a break. She told the kids she'd be in the next room reading a book and taking some time for herself.

No sooner had she sat down than a nephew came running in to say that his older brother wouldn't let him watch his favorite television show. "I'm sure you can work it out," she said and returned to her book. Her nephew persisted for several more minutes. When he didn't get more attention, he stomped out of the room. Several minutes later another child came to tattle. Mrs. Latimer repeated her same phrase, and she got the same response.

As she sat quietly reading, Mrs. Latimer overheard the boys arguing in the next room. One of the boys said, "I'm going to tell Auntie on you." Another voice chimed in and said, "I wouldn't bother if I were you. She'll just say, 'You can work it out,' so why don't we?" Mrs. Latimer chuckled to herself and continued her reading.

discouragement by being pests. They have decided that they are unloved unless they are getting constant attention. Let your children know you love them and that they can amuse themselves or play with other children as well as spend time with you.

2. If you feel worried and anxious about your child's need for attention, those feelings are clues that your child thinks she counts only when she is noticed.

Pets

"How do I get my child to keep her promises about taking care of her pets?"

Understanding Your Child, Yourself, and the Situation

All children want pets, and all children soon forget the promises they made to take care of them. It would be hard to find a child who remembers to take care of pets all the time. Likewise, it would be hard to find a parent who isn't upset by this. It helps to see the problem as normal and then use it as an opportunity for the continuing process of teaching responsibility. (The key words are "continuing process.")

Suggestions

1. Accept the fact that your children won't remember to take care of their pets. Accept the possibility that you will need to remind them (this is not a time to allow children to learn from the natural consequences by allowing the pets to go hungry) and do it kindly and firmly. You might even ask your children what kind of reminder will work best for them. They might choose a reminder through charades, a finger pointing to what needs to be done, or by asking them what needs to be done. Acceptance is the key to saving yourself from upset and anger.

2. You can make it your pet and responsibility—which you allow your children to share.

3. Keep your expectations realistic. Create a schedule that is easy to check on, such as "Feed the dog before we sit down to eat." If the dog dish is empty and the dog looks hungry, use follow-through and ask whose job it is to feed the dog before sitting down to eat.

Booster Thoughts

So often what seems to have been a miserable failure is really a big learning experience to share and cherish. My son Noah's first pet, Rose, helped teach him that mistakes are great ways to learn. He also learned that we, his parents, mean what we say—follow-through can be counted on.

There comes a time in most families when you hear the familiar request: "I really want a dog! Please . . . I promise to feed it and walk it and clean up all the messes." Here's how it happened at our house:

Noah was only five and we were well aware of the need to "take time for training," so we researched and conferred and agreed upon a turtle. The pet store informed us that turtles carried diseases and were a bad choice, and wouldn't we like a rat? They love to be held and never bite. All they need is food, water, a clean cage, and lots of love. It was a perfect match. Noah agreed to feed her daily, clean her cage, and play with her each day. He paid two dollars for Rose. We paid thirty dollars for Rose's necessities and the training began. We worked diligently at teaching Noah how to feed Rose and love her. At first we did it together, then Noah did it with us observing. Soon he knew all the steps and was confidently caring for his pet.

Then the novelty wore off. Our family-meeting agenda always seemed to have Rose on it. We devised signals and hung pictures to remind Noah to feed her. We broke it all down into small steps again. We reminded and coaxed and discussed. Almost a year passed. Finally it was time to state the consequences that would be forthcoming. If Rose was to stay, Noah was to take responsibility for her by the end of one month. The first week we worked on feeding, then we added love and attention, followed by cleaning without complaining. He started out fine but, the second week, feeding seemed to be less consistent. My husband and I agonized as the deadline drew nearer. What had we done wrong? Maybe the consequences were too harsh, our training time insufficient. Perhaps we hadn't given him enough time, or had given him too many things to remember. We really wanted Noah to succeed.

The meeting arrived and we reviewed the consequences. Rose was to go to a new home. Tears flowed. Noah wanted another chance. He told us how he loved Rose, how she was his pet and he would never give her up. I experienced the pain of following through on a consequence that seemed to be breaking my child's heart. In the weeks that followed, we struggled with Noah's resistance to finding Rose a home. No one was quite right and the deadline was approaching. Then, a friend's twelve-year-old agreed to adopt Rose. Noah agreed to the adoption.

On the day of Rose's departure, Noah darkened his room, drew the curtains, hid, and cried. He also took a little revenge—he hid my shoes! Rose left with her happy new family. We talked about the feelings and, most importantly, we talked about mistakes. Noah cried, "I'm only a little boy and my life is very busy. I don't have time to take care of her!" We agreed and said that it was okay, that he was too busy and Rose needed to be somewhere where she could get good care. He now knew that it wasn't the right time for him to have a pet.

A great part of the experience for our family was acknowledging that mistakes are part of life and are opportunities for big learning. As parents, we were reminded that consequences are sometimes hard to administer. If we were "doing *it* right," wouldn't he have taken better care of her, learned to avoid the consequence? No; he made choices. Our job was to honor those choices and follow through on our word. It was a hard lesson for us.

Noah bounced back quickly. He likes to visit Rose—about every six months or so. He hasn't said he misses her in some time. We all agree that we are not ready for a dog or a bird or even a fish right now, but some other time we could try again.

We didn't fail at all. We learned a lot and self-acceptance grew in each of us.[41]

---

41. Laurie Stolmaker, "The Truth About Consequences: A Boy and His Pet Rat," *Family Education Centers Newsletter* (fall 1992).

4. Appreciate the ways children do contribute to having a pet. Don't discount petting, playing with, talking to, and walking the pet.

5. Some parents may want to give a choice. "We can take care of the pet or we can find a new home for the pet where people will care for it." Follow through even though it is difficult with all the tears. Don't be vindictive. Simply say, "I know this is hard. I will miss our pet, too. Maybe we'll be ready to try again in a few years." (See the "Booster Thoughts" on previous page).

4. Avoid blame, guilt, and shame, and work on solutions on a continuing basis. Although it helps to accept that children may always need to be reminded, you can still use the problem as an opportunity to keep working on solutions.

Planning Ahead to Prevent Future Problems

1. Involve the children in discussing the joys and responsibilities that go along with pet ownership before getting the pet. Make lists of responsibilities.

2. If the pet will cost money, let your children earn money and contribute to a pet fund before it is purchased. Let the children contribute (even if it is only ten cents to one dollar) to a fund for food, supplies, and veterinarian bills.

3. Discuss the problem in weekly family meetings. Get your children involved in solutions and agreements. At the next meeting, discuss solutions that did not work and create new ones.

Life Skills Children Can Learn

Children can learn that even though they aren't consistently responsible, they will be held accountable consistently and with dignity and respect. Opportunity and responsibility go hand in hand.

Parenting Pointers

1. We can save ourselves so much grief by accepting the fact that children are normal—not defective or bad—when they shirk responsibility. They have other priorities in life, but they still need to learn responsibility.

2. If you want a pet, don't use your children as an excuse. Get one and take care of it.

Poor Sport

"My child can't stand to lose. It breaks my heart to see him get so upset. He usually drops out of competitive sports as soon as he starts losing. I let him beat me when we play games, but I don't know how to protect him from losing when he plays with others."

Understanding Your Child, Yourself, and the Situation

We might guess that this child is an oldest or only child who has adopted the belief that "I feel that I belong and am important only if I am first or best."[42] This belief is prevalent in a society focused on competition where the prize or praise goes to the winner, where children are compared to others, or where parents are competitive with each other and fight over issues of right and wrong. This belief is dispelled in an atmosphere of cooperation where effort and enjoyment are more important than winning, where children are valued unconditionally and uniqueness is appreciated, and where parents practice cooperation and problem solving.

Suggestions

1. Stop overprotecting your child and allow him to experience disappointment without interference. This helps him learn that disappointment is a part of life that he can handle. Do listen and validate his feelings without fixing the situation.

2. When you purposefully lose all the time, you give your child the false illusion that she can always win. When you win some of the time, she can experience losing in a safe environment. Make the environment safe by showing both empathy for her disappointment and your joy in the game (not in the win).

3. After your child has calmed down from losing, ask "what" and "how" questions. "What did you enjoy about the game? How did you feel about your participation? How do you think others would feel about playing with you if they always lost? What can you do to enjoy the game whether you lose or win?" Asking "what" and "how" questions, in a friendly manner, eliminates the defensiveness created by lectures.

4. Avoid giving conditional approval ("I'm proud of you for ___"). Instead, give encouragement with thoughtful feedback: "What I appreciated most about ___ is ___."

Planning Ahead to Prevent Future Problems

1. Discuss sportsmanship. "What do you think it means to be a good sport? How do

42. See Jane Nelsen, *Positive Discipline* (New York: Ballantine, 1996), Chapter 3 for exceptions to this rule and for more information on birth-order beliefs.

you feel about bad sports? What do you think is the most important thing a bad sport could do to become a good sport?" Look at your own competitiveness at work, play, with your spouse, or with other parents, and be willing to admit to your child that you are also working on this issue.

2. Don't demand immediate change. Show faith in your child to learn how to experience disappointment with grace.

3. Share your successful handling of disappointments with your children. Tell them what you learned from the experience and how you think that will help you in life.

4. Play cooperative games with your children that don't involve winning and losing. There are many books at your local bookstore with noncompetitive activities.

5. Watch the Olympics or other sporting events together and pay special attention to the attitude of those who compete but do not win.

Life Skills Children Can Learn

Children can learn that it's not whether they win or lose that is important but being involved and how they play the game.

Parenting Pointers

1. Show gratitude and joy in participating in games for the fun of it.

2. Some coaches and teams are more destructive than beneficial for your children. Don't hesitate to remove your children from such an experience if that is what they want.

Booster Thoughts

Mark is an oldest child who, by age eight, could not stand to lose at games. Dad was contributing to Mark's attitude by always letting him win at chess because he didn't like to see Mark get upset and cry. After learning about birth order, Dad realized it was important to allow Mark some experience with losing, so he started winning at least half the games. Mark was upset at first but soon began to win and lose with more grace. Dad felt a milestone had been reached one day when he was playing catch with Mark and threw a bad ball. Instead of getting upset about missing the ball or blaming his dad for the bad throw, Mark used his sense of humor by commenting, "Nice throw, Dad. Lousy catch, Mark."

Pouting and Complaining

"My child pouts or complains when she doesn't get her own way. It is most annoying when I have been doing so much for her all day and all she can do is complain and pout about how awful her life is and how she 'never gets to do what she wants.' When I get angry and remind her of all the good things she does have in her life, she gets more sullen and moody and pouts and whines until I threaten her with taking away something she really likes if she doesn't stop immediately."

Understanding Your Child, Yourself, and the Situation

A pouting, whining, negative child usually has a controlling or easily manipulated parent. The child has learned an unhealthy way to have some power over her life and to get her needs met. We all get frustrated when we don't get what we want. It is worse when we don't seem to have any control over the situation. However, we all need to learn healthy methods for control and healthy ways to deal with our feelings when we don't get our way.

Pampered children often pout because they get their way most of the time and don't know how to handle it when they don't. Controlled children don't learn to say what they want or feel. They may believe the only way they can get what they want is to pout, whine, or complain, which gives them some sense of power. Scolding, threatening, shaming, or punishing a pouting child only deals with the symptom and is disrespectful. We need to use nonpunitive methods that allow children to experience their feelings and still deal with the situation without diminishing their self-esteem.

Suggestions

1. Do not scold, threaten, punish, or shame your child by calling her names or using guilt.

2. Take a look at your own behavior. If you demand compliance without giving your child a voice, learn methods to invite cooperation respectfully by trying one of the following:

- "Now that you have identified the problem, what are you prepared to do to solve it?"
- "I notice you are complaining a lot. Do you want me to listen or to help you out?"
- "I'm willing to listen to complaints if they are accompanied by something positive."
- "How much longer will you be complaining? Do you need three more minutes or five?"

3. If your child pouts, maintain your routine and have faith in him to work it out.

Ignore the pouting and proceed as planned. For example, go to the car, saying, "I'll be waiting in the car. I know you are disappointed but I have faith in you to work it out." When you handle your child and the situation with dignity and respect, often it doesn't take more than a few minutes for him to realize pouting isn't effective.

4. Verbalize the feelings. "I know you are disappointed and upset. I feel that way too when things don't work out the way I wish

Booster Thoughts

Mrs. Maxwell became exasperated with seven-year-old Jenny's increasing pouting. She decided to try discussing the problem at a family meeting. When Mrs. Maxwell brought up the subject of pouting, Jenny said, "Well, I don't like it when you are so bossy."

Mrs. Maxwell felt defensive for a minute, but then she thought about it and said, "I think you are right. Let's put that on our list of possible solutions—for me to stop being bossy. What other solutions can you think of?"

Since Mrs. Maxwell was willing to admit she was bossy, Jenny said, "Well, I could stop being so mad at you when you ask me to do something."

Mrs. Maxwell said, "Wow, are we ever making progress. What other ideas can we think of to help me not be so bossy and you not be so mad?"

They discussed the possibilities of planning ahead, allowing people to feel disappointed and then have a few minutes to adjust to change, and verbalizing their feelings respectfully. They decided to try all of these plans. They also decided to use nonverbal signals to let each other know when they were "misbehaving." When Jenny thought her mother was getting too bossy, she would put her hands on her hips and wink at her mom. When Mom thought Jenny was getting too mad and pouty, she would put her hands over her heart and wink at Jenny.

They had created such a sense of fun around the problem that they could hardly wait for the other to boss or pout. They would then give their signal and both start laughing. The good feelings they created made it easy to work together and solve the problem.

they would." Then use action instead of words.

5. Say, kindly and firmly, "I know you feel upset. I don't blame you, but we still need to _____." Then offer a limited choice: "Do you want to get your things, or do you want me to?" "Do you need three minutes or five minutes to adjust to the idea of leaving?"

6. Present the following motto to your family: "We are not interested in blame. We are interested in solutions." Avoid blaming yourself and help your children focus on solutions.

Planning Ahead to Prevent Future Problems

1. Practice methods that allow children to have healthy power over their lives, including choices, family meetings, joint problem solving, and planning ahead with the children's help.

2. When you are planning an outing, discuss it before you go. Talk about the time you will be leaving. Ask your children to help you come up with a plan that will make leaving easier for them.

3. During a family meeting, discuss the issue of being disappointed when things don't turn out the way one hopes. Invite everyone to brainstorm on ways to deal with this and how to support each other.

4. Another subject to discuss during a family meeting is the matter of feelings (see *Upset Child*). Remind everyone that sometimes it takes time to experience feelings before deciding what action to take.

5. Do not pamper your child or be a permissive parent. Children who are pampered often develop the belief that "Love means getting others to let me have my way." When permissiveness is used, children develop avoidance skills instead of cooperation skills.

6. Do not use excessive control with your children. Children who are overly controlled often become either pleasers or rebels. Pouting could be a mild rebellion on the part of your child if you are using too much control instead of advance planning and problem solving *with* your child.

7. Speak to your child in a respectful tone instead of yelling at her. If your child yells at you, ask her to use her "quiet voice."

Life Skills Children Can Learn

Children can learn that things don't always work out the way they want but they can handle that. They can learn that their feelings are acceptable but don't need to dictate their actions. They can learn that their parents support them in adjusting to situations with firmness and kindness.

Parenting Pointers

1. It is important to help our children develop and maintain healthy self-esteem

while being firm about what needs to be done.

2. We need to have self-discipline when our children are out of control. Use empathy and understanding along with Positive Discipline methods.

3. We ask of children what we often don't have ourselves: control and self-discipline. We have control when instead of reacting to provocation we act thoughtfully with long-range goals in mind. We have self-discipline when we see the big picture: the importance of helping our children develop and maintain healthy self-esteem no matter what the situation.

Practicing (Piano, Dance, Sports, and Other Activities)

"My child wanted to take piano lessons, but now she won't practice until I threaten to take away some privileges. I wish my mother had made me practice so I could play the piano today. I don't want my child to say that about me when she gets older. I hate the battles, but I think it is important for her to practice."

Understanding Your Child, Yourself, and the Situation

It is normal for children to think they want to do something and then change their minds—either because it is harder than they thought it would be or because they don't like it as much as they thought they would. Parents often want their children to accomplish the things they didn't accomplish. Some parents think it is a character defect to start something and not finish it; others may be upset about spending a lot of money to help a child take up an interest and see the money as being wasted if the child changes his or her mind.

Suggestions

1. If you have regrets from your childhood, take music lessons yourself and practice until you can play as well as you would like. Then you can stop blaming your mother.

2. Take lessons with your child and practice with her.

3. Be willing to spend the practice time sitting with your child or at least be in the same room.

4. Get into your child's world and explore what is really important to her. Ask "what" and "how" questions, such as, "How do you feel about playing the piano? How do you plan to accomplish what you want?

What are some of the problems you have with practicing? What ideas do you have to solve some of these problems? How long do you think it will take to get over the hard part so it becomes more enjoyable? How do you think you might feel as an adult if you don't take the time to practice now? What help do you need from me?"

5. Share your own childhood feelings about practicing. Be honest about your agenda—trying to encourage your child to avoid mistakes you think you made. Be sure this doesn't sound whiny or preachy and it is heartfelt sharing. Respect the possibility that your child may not be impressed.

6. Help your child have realistic expectations by telling stories of how it takes time to learn something new. Set up an agreement that your child can't quit an activity

Booster Thoughts

At a parenting class, a group of parents were talking about practicing and how long to expect a child to stick with a new hobby or sport. One of the parents was power-struggling with her child about practicing the flute. She insisted her child continue with the flute and practice daily, because she didn't think her child was old enough to know what was best. She asked the group what they thought.

One of the parents said, "There are times when, as parents, we see the value of music lessons and our kids don't. Making a deal with our kids often motivates them to get started. Since certain physical skills and eye-hand coordination are more effectively learned in childhood, we want them to take music or dance lessons. We worked out a system with our kids where they agreed to take lessons until they reached a certain level of skill (for example, being able to play a piece of music at a given level), and this seems to be satisfactory for all of us."

Another parent said, "With our children, sometimes the agreement is to try out a class or instructor for three to ten lessons. If at that time our child remains disinterested, she can drop the class. We know of children with great talent who have learned to hate music or dance through being forced to fulfill someone else's dreams, and we don't want our children to end up angry and resentful at being forced to practice or perform."

until she has tried it out for a month or four times or however long you both decide on.

Planning Ahead to Prevent Future Problems

1. Make an appointment with a professional musician, dancer, or athlete, and let your child talk to this person about his or her experience with practicing.

2. Take your children to concerts (including rock music concerts) or other events featuring their interests and then let them follow their own inspiration about what to do.

3. Work together on a practice schedule. Make an agreement that feels good for both of you. Then don't get upset when your child doesn't keep his agreement, because this is normal. Simply use follow-through (see Part 1).

4. Get an agreement from your children that when they grow up they promise not to blame you for not making them practice.

5. Be willing to let your children try out many different activities to help them find their interest areas.

6. Don't compare children to each other. One child may love music, another sports. On the other hand, if your child wants to do something because a sibling did it, that's okay too.

Life Skills Children Can Learn

Children can learn that their parents care about what is important to them. Parents help them figure out what they want and what they need to do to accomplish it. Children can figure out ways to conquer the hard parts of what they want to do. They can change their minds and still experience unconditional love.

Parenting Pointers

1. Practice time could be an opportunity to spend special time with your children. Feeling your love and interest in taking the time with them might motivate them to look forward to this time.

2. A primary key to motivation is positive involvement.

3. Be supportive and unconditionally loving when your child changes his mind.

Preschool

"I have been thinking about sending my child to preschool, but I don't know if it will be good for her or not. How can I know if my child is ready for preschool, and how do I find a good one?"

Understanding Your Child, Yourself, and the Situation

Some parents do not have the option to stay home with their children and must find all-day child care. Even if you do stay home, preschools can be beneficial for both children and parents, depending on the age of the child and the quality of the preschool. Children as young as two years old can benefit from spending a few hours away from Mom and Dad. In a good preschool, children spend time with other kids in a child-oriented environment and start learning self-reliance in small steps. It can be healthy for Mom and Dad to have a few hours away from the children to pursue interests of their own and to learn that their children can survive without them.

Suggestions

1. Have confidence in your decision. Children absorb the energy of your attitudes and react to them. If you feel fearful, so will your child. If you feel guilty, your child may find an opportunity to use manipulation. Reputable university studies have proven (even though many political groups do not like these studies) that children do very well at a "good" preschool.[43] This knowledge may help you feel confident about your decision to have your child attend a good preschool.

2. You may want to consider sending your child to a parent cooperative preschool. At a co-op, you can share the school experience with your child, save money, and be involved in parent education classes. However, if you have an extremely possessive child who does not want to share you with other children, a co-op could be a stressful experience.

3. Allow five to ten minutes for transition when you take your child to preschool and when you pick her up. When arriving, let her show you some of her favorite things and/or introduce you to her friends. At departure time, let her show you things she has done during the day.

Planning Ahead to Prevent Future Problems

1. The following list will help you find a good preschool.

---

43. NICHD Early Child Care Research Network, "Characteristics of Infant Child Care: Factors Contributing to Positive Care-Giving," *Early Childhood Research Quarterly* 11 (1996): 267–306.

• Check the credentials of the people supervising and working in the preschool. The minimum requirement should be a two-year degree in an early childhood education program.

• Interview the preschool staff members regarding their discipline policies. Make sure they do not advocate corporal punishment or any kind of punishment that is humiliating or disrespectful to children.

• When you find a preschool that seems good to you, ask if you and your child can spend at least three hours at the school so you can observe the school in action and how your child responds to it. This also gives you an opportunity to find out if what the staff members say is what they do. If this is against school policy, find another school where observation is welcome.

2. For children aged two to three years, two to three mornings a week is ample time for a good preschool experience. However, if you require full-time child care, know that your child will be fine if you have taken the time to find a good preschool.

3. Most children aged three to five do fine extending their preschool time to five mornings or three days a week. Use your judgment about what works for you and your child.

4. Prepare your child for separation. Take time for training through role playing. Pretend you are going to the door of the preschool and ask your child if he will give you a big hug before he goes to school. Show him the clock (even though he can't tell time yet) and tell him you will be back in three hours. Have him pretend that he is clinging to your leg. Role-play removing him to play with the other children. Be aware that your child may not understand the abstract concepts you are trying to teach. Even so, this "time for training" may have some effect.

Life Skills Children Can Learn

Children can learn that they feel safe and loved by their parents and are capable of enjoying themselves when apart. Their parents care about them but don't let them be manipulative. Their parents like to spend some time away from them, but that doesn't mean the parents don't love them.

Parenting Pointers

1. In the name of love, many parents rob their children of the opportunity to develop courage, self-confidence, and self-reliance. They overprotect their children instead of letting them experience a little discomfort and learn that they are capable of handling it.

2. Kids pick up the vibrations of your faith or lack of faith in them and in yourself. If you treat them as helpless and get hooked by their crying or other kinds of

Booster Thoughts

A young mother chose two preschools that sounded perfect for her son. Observing one of the schools, she realized that the school personnel didn't practice their stated philosophy. They expected two-year-olds to sit on chairs for longer periods of time than is appropriate for that age and then treated the children as though they were misbehaving when they didn't comply.

She was delighted with the second school after spending three hours there with her son. They had many routines to help the children feel capable. After shopping for groceries, the school director backed her station wagon into the yard and let the children each carry one item at a time into the kitchen.

The children took turns helping the cook prepare a hot lunch. They were allowed to dish up their own food. When they finished eating, each child scraped off his or her dishes. When it was time to go, her son did not want to leave. He obviously enjoyed the many opportunities to be involved and feel self-reliant.

Once he starts school, home is no longer the sole focus of the child's interests. He has, in a way, a life of his own. With the young child who has "his" school, things that may go wrong at home are of less importance.

Thus, if the nursery school is well run and the child's adjustment favorable, not only will he have a good time at school, but it can be for him a definitely maturing experience. It can help him to adapt to his home life with increased effectiveness. Thus we do not maintain that all preschoolers should go to nursery school, but in our opinion the majority not only can adapt, but do definitely benefit from a nursery school experience.[44]

---

44. Frances L. Ilg and Louise Bates Ames, *The Gesell Institute's Child Behavior from Birth to Ten* (New York: Harper & Row, 1955), 257–258.

manipulation, they will act helpless and manipulative. This does not mean you should not listen to their concerns during calm times. If your child cries when you start to leave, give her a hug, say, "I'll be back in three hours," and leave.

Procrastinating

"I can count on my son to say 'later' or 'in a minute' to any request I make. I would fall over if he ever did anything immediately. His father procrastinates all the time, too, and it drives me crazy. Is this genetic?"

Understanding Your Child, Yourself, and the Situation

Procrastination is not genetic, but it can drive others crazy. Even the procrastinator gets irritated by his or her own behavior. Procrastination is a socially acceptable way of saying, "I don't want to and you can't make me." When children are slow or forgetful, they aren't in as much trouble as if they look a parent in the eye and say, "No, I don't think I'll do my homework" or "No, I don't really care to help with chores around the house." Procrastination is a way of looking good while doing bad—in this case, doing exactly what they want instead of what the parent wants. Another name for procrastination is passive power. If left unchecked, it can become a lifelong habit. Procrastination can also be an unconscious way of getting recognition, revenge, or avoiding tasks that seem too hard. People who procrastinate are probably unaware of the purpose behind their behavior.

Suggestions

1. Allow your children to experience the consequences of their procrastination without bailing them out or reminding them.

2. If your child forgets to do something on time or procrastinates and then is upset at the deadline or with the consequence, listen with empathy but don't fix the situation. Many children only learn when they experience the consequences themselves instead of being told what might happen.

3. Assess who owns the problem. If it's your child's problem, mind your own business and let him work out the consequences. Don't accept excuses. Say, "These are excuses, and they won't get the job done any faster. How about doing the job and talking to me about your successes instead."

4. Don't ask questions that can be answered with yes or no unless you are willing to take no for an answer. Offering a choice is one way of sharing power: "Do

Booster Thoughts

Hal and his son, David, are great procrastinators. One day, they decided to have some fun with their unique style and think up businesses and business cards that would be perfect for a procrastinator. Their business would be called Procrastinator and Son, and their logo would be "No job too small to put off." Their phone number was the best: Dial NO-LATER. Sometimes a sense of humor is the only answer to living with procrastination.

you want to do this in five minutes or in ten minutes?"

5. If you say something, mean it—if you mean it, follow through. If you make a request and your child says, "Later," say, "That isn't one of the choices. Do it now. Call me when you're done, so I can check your work." Then wait until she starts moving.

Planning Ahead to Prevent Future Problems

1. Look for areas where you are bossing your children and expecting them to do as you say instead of setting up opportunities for their input or for them to have a choice. Children are more willing to do things when they have advance warning—and especially when they have been respectfully included in the creation of the plan.

2. Get agreements ahead of time from your children and let them be part of the planning process (see "Routines" in Part 1 and *Chores, Age-Appropriate*).

3. Don't leave lists of jobs for children to do while you are at work and expect them to be done before you get home. It is better to create deadlines that you are around to enforce (see "Follow-Through" in Part 1).

4. Ask your children if procrastination is a problem for them and if they would like help with it. If they do, help them think through a project, starting backward from the deadline and planning a timeline for all the steps that need to be done.

5. Create situations where your children can make mistakes and you help them learn from the consequences. For instance, if your child said he would complete a project before leaving to play with a friend and the project isn't done, don't remind him. When it is time to go, tell the child he needs to call his friend and say he will be late because he has a project to finish first.

Life Skills Children Can Learn

Children can learn what will happen if they put things off. They can develop skills in planning and organizing so they get things done. They can also learn that their actions are much more impressive than their excuses.

Parenting Pointers

1. If you think your child is putting something off because the project seems too overwhelming, help her find small steps to get started. Let her know that mistakes are wonderful opportunities to learn and grow and that she doesn't have to be perfect.

2. Respect your child's style. Some people work better under pressure. What seems like procrastination to you may just be a child waiting for the edge of anxiety to help her finish a project.

Property Destruction

"My daughter threw a ball through her window in a fit of rage. What should I do?"

Understanding Your Child, Yourself, and the Situation

Children are going to break things and damage property in the course of their growing up. Most times, this will happen by accident. Sometimes children damage property (such as drawing on a wall) just because it seems like a lot of fun at the time. Occasionally, children may seek revenge or express their anger by damaging property. In any case, it is up to parents to help their children repair or replace the damaged property without piggybacking (see "Logical Consequences" in Part 1) additional punishment or protecting their children from the consequences of their acts.

Suggestions

1. Avoid overreacting and yelling at your children or calling them names like clumsy or stupid.

2. Even if it takes more time, involve your children in the cleanup. Work with them to repaint a wall, use soap and water to take off pencil marks, or scrub a floor. Children don't have to suffer to learn. Don't punish them for making a mistake—show them how to rectify it.

3. If it costs money to repair damaged property, you could advance the money and collect payments on a weekly basis from her allowance in amounts your child can afford. You may wish to cover part of the cost and let her cover the rest. Keep track with her in a payment book. Perhaps she can do extra chores or work for you to help pay off the debt. She can choose how to pay—not whether to pay.

Planning Ahead to Prevent Future Problems

1. Are you too fussy about your home and forget that children are children? Do you have a special place where the kids can play and where if they spill or drop things it won't destroy valuable property? If not, create one.

2. Reach agreements with the kids about where they can ride bikes, play ball, roughhouse, paint, or do other activities that have the potential to cause damage. If you have a basement, it's a great place to set up a recreation room for the children.

3. Put up large sheets of paper that children can draw on, so they don't need to draw on walls. Have young children paint or color at the kitchen table with newspapers underneath to avoid dirtying the floor or carpet. As soon as they are old enough, include them in the preparation so they learn about protecting property.

4. Let your children help decorate their rooms, picking colors, themes, bedspreads, pictures, and room arrangements. Use materials that are age-appropriate so you don't have to worry about spills and marks from toys and shoes.

Life Skills Children Can Learn

Children can learn that it is okay to make mistakes and that they can fix their mistakes without suffering pain or humiliation. Children can also learn that they are responsible for their actions and that others will not experience the consequences instead of them. They can learn social skills and manners about where it is appropriate to participate in different activities.

Parenting Pointers

1. Be aware of the goals of your children's behavior and look for the beliefs behind the behavior (see Part 1).

Booster Thoughts

Bill complained that his thirteen-year-old son Marcus was extremely destructive and constantly threatening others that he would break their toys, hurt them, or damage their property. One day, Bill got a call from the police saying Marcus had been involved in an act of vandalism by dropping a gopher gas bomb down a chimney at the local park. The chimney caught on fire, and the fire department had to come to put out the fire. There was very little damage due to the fire department's quick response. The police let Marcus go with a warning.

Bill was concerned about Marcus not learning from the consequences of his behavior, so he told him to call the fire department and make an appointment to talk to the firefighters. Bill said he would accompany him and be there as support, but it was up to Marcus to let the firefighters know he had made a mistake and was sorry and would be willing to do what he could to help repay the damages and their expenses.

Marcus was scared to face the firefighters, but with Bill's help he went to the station and told them about his mistake. They explained what could have happened if they hadn't responded so quickly and asked him if he had learned anything from the experience. They assured Marcus that he didn't have to pay for damages, but they appreciated his honesty and his taking the time to come talk to them.

As they left the fire department, Bill put his arm around Marcus and said, "I know that was hard, and I'm proud of you." Marcus responded with a hug back, saying, "I don't think that will happen again."

2. Don't let your children find they can push your buttons by drawing on the wall or other destructive acts. Children love watching their parents fly out of control and may find it worth destroying property to get a rise.

3. If your children are feeling hurt and destroying property to hurt you back, give them lots of hugs along with the cleanup time. Do not perpetuate a revenge cycle. Let them talk about their feelings and what might be hurting them.

Reverence

"How do I get my child to be quiet in church or other places where quiet is needed?"

Understanding Your Child, Yourself, and the Situation

You need to take into account the age and individual characteristics of the child when considering this question. It is unrealistic to expect young children to be quiet for long (and sometimes short) periods of time. Individual characteristics refer to the fact that each child is different. It is unrealistic to set one standard for all children.

Suggestions

1. Examine your motivations for wanting your children to be quiet in a place of worship. Are you worried about what others might think? Do you think you are a bad parent or that your children are bad if they won't be reverent? Relax. Consider the age and the unique characteristics of your children. Then use your common sense.

2. Children are naturally reverent and spiritual in the true sense of the words. Their curiosity and joy for life are reverent. Their loving natures are spiritual. Virtually all world religions have philosophies concerning children and their inherent innocence and worth. Children express reverence and spirituality differently than adults, and sitting quietly is not a sign of these values for them.

3. Be a model for the kind of love and spirituality you expect from your children. Don't try to teach respect by being disrespectful. Spanking is very disrespectful.

4. If your child is restless and noisy in church, take her by the hand and quietly and firmly walk outside. Ask her if she thinks the behavior is appropriate for the situation. Don't lecture. Give her a choice of going back in and trying again, going home, or going to an available child care program. Let her know it is okay to try again later or, if more appropriate, the following week.

5. If your child strongly objects to Sunday School or church or insists that he has a different religious view than the rest of the family, take him seriously and listen to his thoughts and feelings. You might tell him that you are willing to allow him to take a break for a while or let your child know that it is okay to feel differently but that church and Sunday School are mandatory until age ten to twelve (or until confirmation or whatever time you feel comfortable with).

6. If you don't attend church and your child would like to, be supportive of his need for a spiritual connection and help drive or make arrangements for him.

Planning Ahead to Prevent Future Problems

1. Children can learn to be quiet for short periods of time appropriate for their age. Take time for training. Discuss the reasons for being quiet in church through "what," "why," and "how" questions: "Why do you think it's important to be quiet in a place of worship? What ideas do you have about what you could do to make church a good experience for both you and others?" Let your children practice holding a service with their dolls and stuffed animals.

2. There are many products on the market to help children be quiet, such as quiet books that have snaps, zippers, and buttons; drawing toys; and the old standbys, crayons and coloring books. Help your children pack a bag of things to do while they are being quiet.

3. Your children may be able to attend a nursery school or religious class while you are in the service. If your church doesn't have such classes, start a committee to organize them. Some churches put together a children's bulletin that has religious word games and other activities for the kids to do during services.

4. Sit where the children can see during a service instead of looking at the back of someone's head for an hour. If you sit toward the back but at the end of a row, your child can move out into the aisle a bit to see better when the congregation stands.

5. Let your child know why it is important to you that the family attend church together.

Life Skills Children Can Learn

Children can learn that they can show reverence in an atmosphere of mutual respect because their parents show reverence for them and their age-appropriate level.

Booster Thoughts

A six-year-old was asked why she liked one church Sunday School better than another. She said, "Because we do fun things. In the other church it was sit, sit, sit, listen, listen, listen."

Parenting Pointers

1. Many children grow to hate spiritual events because they are expected to behave in ways that are unrealistic for their age levels. For many families, a day of worship becomes a day of turmoil instead of a day of spiritual love and growth.

2. When your expectations are appropriate for your children's ages, you stand a better chance of leaving them with a good feeling about reverence instead of a rebellious feeling.

Rooms, Messy

"My children refuse to clean their rooms. They have dirty clothes under the bed, dirty dishes and spoiled food on their dressers, and toys strewn everywhere. No matter how much I nag and complain, we don't seem to make any progress on their rooms."

Understanding Your Child, Yourself, and the Situation

Messy rooms and unfinished homework are the two biggest complaints we hear from parents of children of all ages. These issues become a real battleground in many families. Often children share rooms, and this becomes another reason for fighting. Some families are comfortable letting the children keep their rooms the way they like them; however, it is possible to have a semblance of order in your children's rooms if that is important to you. Helping your children organize and clean their rooms can be worth the effort, as children learn many transferable skills through this process. To succeed, however, requires commitment to time for training and ongoing supervision on your part.

Suggestions

1. With young children, it is important to clean with them, as the mess overwhelms them. Sit in the middle of the room and pick up a toy, saying, "I wonder where this goes? Can you show me?" Wait until the child puts the toy away and then start over. Do this at least once a week.

2. Many preschool children collect scraps of paper, rocks, string, and other treasures. It is okay to remove these objects when your child is out. If he objects, let him help sort the items, but usually young children don't miss the clutter and just start collecting again. When children get old enough to notice and care, be respectful of their treasures and leave them alone.

3. You may be part of the problem if you buy your children too many toys. That is easily corrected. Suggest that they choose some to put on a shelf and take down later. You might also suggest that your children clear out toys they no longer play with and give them to a charitable organization for other kids to enjoy.

4. Do not bribe or reward children for doing what needs to be done. Caring for their rooms is their job to help the family, and they don't need a prize to do it. Don't say, "If you promise to take care of your room, I'll buy you a new outfit." Do not make purchases conditional on promises. By the same token, do not threaten to take away your children's possessions if they don't take care of them. Set up ways for them to be responsible about their things instead.[45]

5. Some parents choose to ignore messy rooms. They allow children to keep their rooms any way they want but get them involved in solutions to keep common rooms clean.

6. Another possibility is to give your child a choice: "Do you want to clean your room or do you want me to?" It is understood that if you clean it you get to throw things away that seem worthless. Another choice could be, "Do you want to clean your room or pay a housekeeper out of your allowance?" Your tone of voice will determine whether or not the choice is received respectfully or as an invitation for a power struggle.

7. For children who argue over sharing a room, suggest they work it out together or at a family meeting.

Planning Ahead to Prevent Future Problems

1. Let your children have a say in how their rooms are decorated. Children have distinct taste in colors and decor, and it is important that their rooms be theirs and not yours. Make sure they have plenty of containers and shelf space for their toys and possessions.

2. With children aged two to ten, it often works to say, "Here is how your room needs to be kept. You may play with your toys or move things around, but put them back the way the room is set up when you are done." Some children are perfectly happy to comply with your wishes when stated unemo-

45. For more information on getting children involved in family work, read Lynn Lott and Riki Intner, *Chores Without Wars* (Rocklin, CA: Prima Publishing, 1998).

tionally. If your children want more say, follow the other suggestions.

3. At a family meeting, set up a routine with your children for cleaning rooms. With school-age children, one that works well is to have the room cleaned before breakfast. If the child forgets, simply turn her plate upside down as a nonverbal reminder to go clean her room before joining the family for breakfast. If the children take part in making the plan, they will cooperate in following through with it. Be realistic about what you consider clean. If children push things under the bed or pull the covers up over wrinkled sheets, let it go.

4. As children get older, it works better to have one day a week when they clean their rooms. They need to return dirty dishes to the kitchen, put their laundry in the laundry basket, vacuum, dust, and change their sheets. Having a deadline that you enforce works best. For instance, the room must be cleaned before dinner on Saturday. If you aren't around to enforce the deadline, don't expect your children to clean their rooms.

Booster Thoughts

Krista and her brother, Tom, loved to decorate their rooms. Every two or three years, their taste would change completely—from circus themes and kittens to baseball players and ballerinas to rock stars and movie heartthrobs. There were times when posters covered every square inch of wall and ceiling space and times when the walls were painted hot pink or black. The rooms reflected their unique personalities, interests, and tastes.

Tom and Krista helped paint each other's rooms and pick out fabrics for drapes and bedspreads. The posters they wanted would be at the top of their birthday or Christmas wish lists. On occasion, they could be found moving their furniture around into some new arrangement. Some years the rooms were orderly and clean; other years they collected chaos and confusion. Each room usually boasted at least one sign on the door: "Come In," "Keep Out," or "Beware."

These two children were encouraged to be themselves and express the ways in which they are unique. They loved the opportunity to express their individuality, and their parents enjoyed watching each new aspect of their personalities develop. We wish this for you and your children.

5. Twice a year, go through your child's clothing with him to remove clothing that no longer fits. It's less confusing for the child if you put away clothing that is out of season.

6. You may wish to have a discussion about your minimum standards for a room, especially as your children get older. You might say, for instance, "I'm not happy with the situation, but I'm willing to live with your room the way you like it as long as my minimum standards are met. They are that the dirty dishes be returned to the kitchen once a week, that the floors get vacuumed once a week, and that the sheets are changed on weekends."

Life Skills Children Can Learn

Children can learn how to maintain a routine, contribute to the family, organize and care for their possessions, and cooperate. They can also explore their own taste and express their uniqueness in the decoration and organization of their rooms.

Parenting Pointers

1. A clean room may be high on your priority list but very low on your child's. If you choose to make this a battleground, your child may keep a messy room just to win the battle. Many "neat" adults were once "messy" children.

2. Don't worry that your friends will look at your children's rooms and wonder about your housekeeping. Your friends can tell the difference between your standards and your children's.

School Problems

(See also *Homework*)

"My child was caught cheating at school. Now I have to go to a parent-teacher conference. I feel intimidated and embarrassed that I am failing as a mother. How can I make my child behave at school? He is fine at home."

Understanding Your Child, Yourself, and the Situation

School problems indicate another area where we may need to deal with the belief behind the behavior as well as the behavior. There are so many different reasons for misbehaving at school. They usually are related to wanting power or revenge, although some kids who are failing in school decide they can get recognition as troublemakers or decide not to try at all for fear of not being perfect.

Too often we assume children are at fault, when it could be that the school environment encourages competition, does not provide opportunities for children to be respectfully involved in learning problem-solving skills, and does not honor different learning styles. Your child may be treated disrespectfully by a teacher who is punitive and shaming. Some children are unable to function in an environment of disrespect and need a parent who is an advocate to help them find a safe place to learn. Perhaps your child is afraid to go to school because of a bully or gang situation.

Suggestions

1. Spend some time getting into your child's world to discover the belief behind the behavior. Sometimes this just takes hanging out and listening. Sometimes it is effective to ask "what" and "how" questions. Be sure to listen to your child's side of the story.

2. Approach the situation in a positive way. "It must be very important to you to do well in school if you are willing to cheat to achieve that goal. How does that help you or hurt you in the long run?"

3. Engage in joint problem solving. Together decide what is the problem and what are some possible solutions.

4. Tell the teacher that you prefer a parent-teacher-child conference. Since the conference concerns your child, it will be more effective if he is present to help with understanding the problem and working with you on solutions. Suggest that the tone of the conference be "We are not looking for blame. We are looking for solutions." Let the child give his perceptions of the problem and possible solutions before the teacher and you do. Children usually know what is going on, and they feel more accountable when they tell instead of being told. Be sure to also discuss all the things that are going well, again starting with the child.

5. Discussion may be enough. Too often we focus on consequences or solutions and undervalue the power of understanding that may be gained by a friendly discussion. When children feel listened to, taken seriously, and loved, they may change the belief that motivated the misbehavior.

6. With some children, switching teachers or finding a new school may be the road to school improvement. Don't hesitate to help your child make those changes if you and your child feel they will help.

Planning Ahead to Prevent Future Problems

1. Take the time to visit the school. Sit in classrooms and see what it feels like. Are the teachers encouraging or discouraging?

Booster Thoughts

Sixteen-year-old Diane started sleeping in every morning. Her mother became involved in a battle to get Diane out of bed and off to school on time. A full-fledged power struggle evolved with Mom yelling, lecturing, and even trying to pull Diane out of bed. Diane would yell just as loud and finally shouted one morning, "Leave me alone. I hate you."

Mom was stunned, but fortunately that comment reminded her of some concepts she had learned in a parenting class the previous year. She remembered that sometimes the most important thing is to create a relationship of closeness and trust instead of distance and hostility. She decided to stop trying to control Diane and to support her daughter in her decisions with unconditional love.

The next morning, Mom did not try to wake Diane up and allowed her to sleep in. When Diane finally woke up, Mom sat on the side of her bed and said, "Honey, since you don't want to go to school, why don't you just drop out and get a job?"

Diane was surprised by this change of attitude and support from her mother. The power struggle dissipated and Diane started sharing with her mom.

Diane: I don't want to drop out. It's just that I've gotten so far behind that I can never catch up, so I figure why bother. It doesn't seem to matter what I do; my

Do they treat children as passive objects or recipients, or do they get children actively involved in the learning process? Do teachers use class meetings? If not, are they open to this possibility?

2. Give information, not lectures, about why you think a good education is important. Use emotional honesty to share your values: "I feel _____ because _____ and I wish _____."

3. Create closeness and trust. Lectures and punishment create distance and hostility. Getting into the child's world and actually listening create closeness and trust. A foundation of closeness and trust is vital for positive parenting tools to be effective.

4. Take responsibility for your part in creating the problem. Taking responsibility does not mean to feel guilt but to gain insight and awareness of what you create. Is

teachers just keep penalizing me. It's hopeless. I wish I could go into continuation school, where they let you work at your own pace.

Mom: I will support you if that is the way you want to deal with it.

Diane: Everyone thinks you're a loser if you go to continuation school.

Mom: What do you think?

Diane: Well, I am losing now. If I went to continuation school, I know I could catch up. The problem is you have to get kicked out of regular school before you can go to continuation school.

Mom: Why don't you go see your counselor and see what you can work out? I'll be happy to go with you if you need my support.

They went to see the counselor, and he suggested individual study for a semester instead of continuation school. Diane was excited about this plan and worked very hard to catch up so she could go back to her regular school for her junior year. Her counselor told her he had never seen a student do so well in individual study and commended her self-discipline.

Diane appreciated the unconditional love and respect she received from her mother and the encouragement from her counselor. When they worked *with* her instead of against her, Diane was motivated to end her downward spiral and pursue a productive plan.

your child feeling conditional love ("I'm loved only if I do well in school")? Is she feeling too much pressure to perform up to your expectations? If children see us taking responsibility, they may be willing to take responsibility for their part.

5. Decide what you will do and let your child know in advance. "I have faith in you to work out your problems at school. When the teacher calls, I will hand the phone to you. I will not lie for you when you skip school. I will listen, and I will offer suggestions only when you ask me to."

6. Some children do poorly in school because their parents are too controlling and try to manage their schoolwork and school experience. Try backing up and watching to see what your child will do without your constant nagging. Wait a week, observe,

and then discuss what you have noticed with your child.

Life Skills Children Can Learn

Children can learn that they are accountable for their choices. Their parents help them think through what happened, why it happened, and what they can do if they want different results. Most important, they can realize that they are loved unconditionally and can learn from their mistakes without guilt and shame. Children also learn that their parents care enough to look at both sides of the story.

Parenting Pointers

1. It can be difficult for parents to face teachers who seem to be blaming them for their children's behavior. It helps to make a conscious decision to be more interested in your child than in your ego.

2. Teachers can feel defensive and intimidated too. When you set up a positive parent-teacher-child conference, show compassion for the teacher instead of defensiveness. Someone needs to break the chain of defensiveness and create a chain of mutual concern for everyone involved.

Self-Esteem

"My child is convinced she is ugly. She has such a poor opinion of herself. How can I help raise her self-esteem?"

Understanding Your Child, Yourself, and the Situation

Self-esteem—the collection of pictures children carry around of who they are and how they fit in—is formed early in life. Even though children make these decisions internally, parents have a tremendous influence on the unconscious decisions children form. The way parents communicate, both with words and actions, helps children form healthy or unhealthy decisions about themselves. Children usually form healthy self-esteem decisions when parents demonstrate that they believe their children are capable by giving them opportunities to experience their capability. They thrive when parents create an environment where children are allowed to contribute and when parents let children influence what happens to them by participating in decision making. Children usually make unhealthy self-esteem decisions when they think they have to change to be good enough or when parents do too much for them so they don't experience their capability. As a parent, you may think your children are great just the way they are, but what is more critical is what your children decide is true.

Suggestions

1. Avoid any kind of name calling. Do not call your children stupid, lazy, irresponsible, or any disrespectful put-down. Focus on solutions instead of blame.

2. Separate the deed from the doer. Deal with the behavior, making it clear for example that you love the child but you don't like crayon drawings on the wall. Remember that mistakes are opportunities for your children to learn and grow and are not character defects.

3. Listen to your children and take them seriously. They are forming their ideas and opinions. How they think today may be different from how they think tomorrow, but they still need their parents' ear and support. They need validation that their opinions are important.

4. Stay away from the use of praise. Praise may seem to work when things are going well and the child is succeeding. However, your children may be learning to be approval junkies, which means they believe they are okay only if someone else tells them they are. If you overuse praise, what do you do when your child is failing? That's when she needs encouragement the most—some word or gesture that lets her know "You're all right!" Encouragement is different from praise as it teaches self-evaluation. "I'm so proud of you for getting that A," is praise. "You worked very hard to get that A," is encouragement.

5. Do not compare children to each other. Each child is a different, unique person and is valued and belongs just the way he or she is.

Planning Ahead to Prevent Future Problems

1. Watch out for having overly high expectations for your children or making your love conditional on their behavior.

2. Hold regular family meetings so children have a place to air their opinions and to be reassured that they belong and are significant. Brainstorm for solutions to problems so they learn that mistakes are opportunities to learn. Plan opportunities for them to contribute and experience their capabilities.

3. Spend special time with each child alone, reminding each one of his or her uniqueness and how much you appreciate the child's special qualities.

4. Don't play favorites.

5. Be sensitive to situations where your children are being put down by siblings,

teachers, classmates, friends, and other family members. Talk to your children about their feelings and share yours. Let them know that some of the mean things people say and do are about their own insecurities and have nothing to do with your children.

6. You may choose to remove your child from a classroom if a teacher uses methods that are detrimental to the development of healthy self-esteem. However, there is a fine line between overprotectiveness and alertness to a negative environment.

7. Don't try to make everything even, equal, and fair. That gives your children the idea that something is unfair and usually has the opposite effect from what parents wanted.

8. Don't forget to have fun with your children.

Life Skills Children Can Learn

Children can learn that they don't have to prove themselves to be loved and that they are good enough the way they are. Also, they can learn that they are capable of solving problems and making a contribution.

Booster Thoughts

There are times when staying positive about teenagers can be a real challenge. In the case of sixteen-year-old Jesse, his family members were all having a hard time for various reasons. His mom was angry because he was flunking out of school. His grandmother was worried about him because he had pierced his ear. His father was upset that Jesse didn't follow through on his commitments, and his stepmother was ready to choke him for leaving his laundry in the washer, dryer, hallway, or car.

Thank goodness for Grandpa! Just when he was needed the most, he came to visit. He watched everyone nag, lecture, and avoid Jesse, and in his grandpa way he didn't say a word. But out of nowhere, Jesse started finding notes in the strangest places, and they all said the same thing: "Jesse, you're all right!"

There were times when the family would be sitting around the table and Grandpa would look at Jesse and say, "Jesse, guess what?"

Jesse would grin from ear to ear and say, "I'm all right?"

"Right, and don't forget it."

Parenting Pointers

1. Value the uniqueness of each child. Avoid comparisons and work at finding out who your children are instead of trying to get them to live up to a picture of who you think they should be.

2. Work on your own self-esteem. The better you like and accept yourself with all your mistakes and shortcomings, the better model you give your children about self-acceptance.

Sex Exploration and Sex Education

"I caught the neighbor boy and my five-year-old daughter with their pants down. I don't want to punish her, but I don't want her playing around sexually. I don't know how to teach her propriety regarding sex."

Understanding Your Child, Yourself, and the Situation

It is very difficult to find an adult who didn't engage in some form of sex exploration or curiosity about the sexual organs as a child. The desire to explore sex and the sex organs is normal, not bad (see *Masturbation*). We are not talking about sexual abuse, which is covered as a separate topic. Good sex education can help a child have information about how the body parts work, what is normal and what is not, how babies are made, what it means to be sexual, and confidence to say no to an older child or adult who wants to take advantage of him or her.

Suggestions

1. When you catch your child exploring sex or sex organs with another child of a similar age, this is a clue that your child is ready for sex education. Do not scold, embarrass, humiliate, or shame your children. Let them know it is okay to be curious about sex and all the body parts. Tell them you will answer questions and explain how things work, but you do not want them playing "doctor" or "show and tell" with other children, because the sex organs are a private part of the body.

2. Ask your children what questions they have about sex or the penis, vagina, or breasts (use the correct words). Answer the questions honestly and without embarrassment if you can. Do not give more information than your children have asked for, unless you feel it is needed. Use your common sense to help you know how much your children can understand.

3. Go to the library with your child and check out some good books on sex education, suitable for your child's age level.

Planning Ahead to Prevent Future Problems

1. Find some good sex education books designed for small children and start reading them to your child at two or three years of age. At this age, your child won't understand much of what you are reading but will still enjoy the book. When your child is older and the neighborhood kids try to give him information, he will be able to say, "Oh, I already know all about that."

2. For children aged two to ten, while you are tucking your child into bed at night, occasionally ask, "Do you have any questions about sex or how your body works?" The answer will usually be no, but you are establishing that sex and conversations about how the sex organs work are valid topics of conversation, just like school or toys. You may need to keep answering similar questions over and over as your child becomes older and is able to understand more.

3. Children today see more explicit sexual interaction on television and in movies than their grandparents fantasized in an entire lifetime. Children aged six to eighteen need to talk with adults about what they are seeing. Draw your children out by asking "what" and "how" questions: "What do you think about what you are seeing on television? How do you feel about it? What conclusions are you making? How do you think this will affect your decisions about sex in your own life?"

4. As your children grow older, give them information about why they will benefit from postponing sexual activity until they are adults. As adults, they will have greater emotional maturity and wisdom. Hopefully they will have the self-confidence and self-love to do what feels right for them instead of feeling that they have to please others at their own expense. Kids need to know that if someone says, "If you love me, you will have sex with me" or "If you don't have sex with me, I'll find someone else who will," they should run in the other direction as fast as they can.

5. We should not use the threat of AIDS or other sexually transmitted diseases to instill fear and guilt—that invites kids to rebel. Information about these diseases should be given in a matter-of-fact way that encourages kids to listen and make intelligent decisions.

6. Tell your children you will explain any word they hear that they do not understand and that you want them to ask you questions about their body that they don't understand, like discharges or emissions or menstruation. It is best to let your children know ahead of time about these things and that they are normal, so they don't have to live in fear of being weird or having some life-threatening disease. Be calm no matter what they ask—and don't pass judgment on the friend who said the word. If you need help answering questions, ask the physician to answer what you don't know or find books and other

resources to put your child's mind at ease.

Life Skills Children Can Learn

Children can learn that sex is a wonderful part of them and of life and that their sex organs and their functions are normal and not to be feared or be ashamed of. It is okay to discuss anything with their parents, who will give them honest and helpful information. With the right kind of information, they can make the right decisions for themselves, no matter what anyone else thinks.

Parenting Pointers

1. If you are embarrassed about sex or think it is bad, this is the message your children will receive. They may adopt your attitude or simply decide to hide their feelings, questions, and actions from you. It is not what you say but how you say it that has the greatest influence on your children.

2. Most parents never discuss sex with their children. If you are uncomfortable talking about sex, share that with your child and why. Then talk about it anyway.

Booster Thoughts

A little girl suffered as a child because she could not discuss sex with her parents—they were too embarrassed. When she was six years old, a neighbor boy wanted to show her how to "fuck." He took her to a barn and told her to pull her pants down and squat. He then proceeded to urinate on her bottom. Later the little boy told all the other kids that he had "fucked" the little girl. This information followed her all through elementary and high school. About once a year, she became the topic of ridicule. The kids would chase her around the yard and tease her about having babies in her belly. In junior high, the kids would pass a note about her reputation. When she walked into the room, they would hide the note and start giggling. As she matured, she started getting propositions from other boys, who believed in her bad reputation.

Sex education was so lacking that this little girl did not know she had not had sexual intercourse or that, even if the little boy had known how, it would not have been her fault and she was not bad. The little girl is a woman and can laugh about it now, but sex education or honest communication with her parents could have saved her a great deal of pain.

Sexual Abuse

"I can't pick up a newspaper or magazine without seeing a story about a child being sexually abused. How do I protect my children from having something like that happen to them?"

Understanding Your Child, Yourself, and the Situation

The statistics are overwhelming. The incidence of child sexual assault is growing, or perhaps the number being reported is growing. When a child is sexually abused, the devastating effects may be lifelong. Most children who suffer abuse decide it was their fault and that they are bad. They spend a lot of time hiding because they think they are different and live in fear of others finding that out. In some cases, the memories of the abuse fade, but the feelings and decisions stay. Later in life, they may start having flashbacks of abuse and think they are going crazy. There are many things we can do as parents both to protect our children and to help them if they are abused.

Suggestions

1. Children are people and not sex objects. It is damaging to use a child as a sex partner. If you are doing this, stop and call for help. You are not bad, but what you are doing is wrong. There are agencies and people who are trained to help both you and your child.

2. If you suspect sexual abuse by a spouse or other family member, get help. The worst thing you can do is keep your fears a secret and try to handle this alone or hope it will pass. If you are scared that the abuser will leave or hurt you if you tell, get professional help. Call Child Protective Services, the police, or any agency or public service organization dedicated to helping families dealing with abuse. Professionals deal with these issues daily and are there to stop the abuse and protect you and your children, as well as help the perpetrator.

3. If your child is hinting about being abused or complaining of physical problems in her genital area, take the complaints seriously and get help. Don't assume your family doctor has an understanding about the symptoms of physical abuse—some do and others don't. If you see bruises or cuts or your child has urinary or vaginal infections, she may be a victim of sexual abuse. Reassure your children that they won't get in trouble if they talk to you—that you are there to help and that you will believe them if they say someone is abusing them.

4. Most children who are being abused have been threatened that if they tell anyone, they'll break up the family, or everyone will think they are bad, or someone will get hurt. It takes a tremendous amount of courage for a child to break the silence and share the secret, so take him seriously.

Booster Thoughts

Mrs. Allen was always very protective of her children. She made sure she never left her children in an unsupervised situation or with people she couldn't trust. When she found out that two of her children had been violated by one of her relatives, she was shocked and disbelieving. Her children said that the relative had fondled them and asked them to touch his penis. Mrs. Allen kept saying, "How could this have happened? I was always with you and never left you alone."

Mrs. Allen wasn't trying to be unsupportive of her children, but they interpreted her shocked response as a statement that she thought they were lying. They felt very scared, because they were used to their mother being protective and supportive. They didn't understand that their mother didn't want to face the truth because if she did she would interpret the situation as proof she hadn't done a good job as a parent.

Mrs. Allen's response to the situation wasn't atypical. Fortunately, she was wise enough to seek professional help so a trained person could help her deal with her guilt and shame while at the same time making sure her children got the help they needed.

You cannot reassure a child enough that what happened isn't his fault.

Planning Ahead to Prevent Future Problems

1. Talk to your children openly about the possibility of sexual abuse. Tell them there is a difference between the touch that gives and the touch that takes away. Make sure they know it's okay to say no if they are uncomfortable with the way anyone touches them. Keep the lines of communication open so they feel free to tell you if something is wrong.

2. Tell your children that their bodies belong to them and that no one has the right to hurt them, to put things into their bodies, or to make them perform sexual acts.

3. If your child is acting strangely or acting out in a sexually inappropriate way, talk to your child about secrets and let her know she can trust you, even if someone has told

her to keep it a secret. Get secrets out in the open. If you suspect something is happening, use frank words with your child, for instance: "I'm wondering if when your uncle kisses you he puts his tongue in your mouth." "Has Daddy ever asked you to kiss or suck on his penis?" "Did the babysitter ask you to touch his penis, or did he touch your vagina? It looks red and sore."

4. Watch for revenge cycles between siblings. Sometimes an older sibling will sexually abuse a younger sibling as a way of hurting back if he thinks the younger child receives more love or attention. Teenagers may experiment sexually with their younger siblings. Let them know this is not acceptable behavior. Talk about this in front of all the children at the same time.

Life Skills Children Can Learn

Children can learn that they are people and that they have the right to decide what happens to their bodies. They can learn that there are people who will take them seriously, love them, and help them if someone is sexually abusing them.

Parenting Pointers

1. If you were molested as a child or if you molested someone, you need to get professional help, as it is very difficult to be there for your children when you have unresolved issues about your own sexual abuse.

2. When you allow children to be assertive, take them seriously, and give them opportunities to contribute to the family and discuss their ideas, you are indirectly preventing sexual abuse. Children who have a strong sense of worth, who believe that they have rights and that their feelings are legitimate, and who are given information about the possible dangers are not good candidates to be molested.

Sharing

"My child refuses to share his toys with anyone. When his friends come to play, he grabs toys out of their hands and yells, 'Put that down! Don't touch it! It's mine!' The other day, he hit his sister when she picked up one of his books. She ran screaming to her room while he yelled at her, 'Leave my things alone!' He is so selfish I don't know what to do."

Understanding Your Child, Yourself, and the Situation

Sharing is not an inborn trait. It is learned. Sometimes parents expect sharing before it is developmentally appropriate. If there's more than one child in a house, there will probably be fights about sharing. This is natural, but that doesn't mean parents should ignore it. Too often the parents' solution to this problem is to tell the child, "You should share your toys or no one will like you" or "How can you be so selfish?" It is important to separate what the child does from who he or she is and make sure the message of love gets through. Sharing has to do with ownership and respect. If a toy, item of clothing, bedroom, and so on, belongs to the child, he should not be expected to share unless he wants to. It is easier for children to learn to share when the concept makes sense to them on some level.

Suggestions

1. Don't expect children to share before the age of three without lots of help. You may need to have more than one desirable toy around or use distraction to get small children interested in something else. Even after age three, sharing is not always easy. (Don't you have some things *you* don't want to share?)

2. Teach your children to be respectful by asking first if it is okay to play with or borrow someone else's property or to enter someone else's space. Set an example of respect for private property by saying to kids who want to use something you own, "This is mine, and I don't wish to share it."

3. If your children are being bothered by infants or toddlers who get into their toys, help them find a place to play that is out of reach of little fingers.

4. If kids are fighting over a toy, put it away and let the kids know they can have it back when they've figured out how to share it without fighting. Help them work out a plan by providing a timer and letting the children decide how much time should be set before the other gets a turn.

5. In the case of large equipment like stereos, televisions, and computers, make the item off-limits until the children are ready to share without fighting. You can create a schedule or the children can, but the item can't be used until it is used with respect.

Planning Ahead to Prevent Future Problems

1. Start by letting children know the reason for sharing. If the child is in a school situation, sharing is necessary because the equipment, toys, and other items belong to the school and not to the child. In a family, children may be expected to share certain items that everyone uses because they are too expensive or impractical to buy in duplicates. When friends come to play, a willingness to share can make or break a friendship.

2. It is easier for children to share some things if they don't have to share everything. Help your child find a special shelf

Booster Thoughts

Francesca loved coloring with new crayons. She worked very hard to keep her crayons in the original box without breaking any of them. Her mother, Elena, scolded her for not sharing with her little brother, Raymond, but when Raymond used the crayons, he always broke them or colored so hard that the points wore down. Elena couldn't understand why her daughter cried and stomped off to her room when asked to share. She thought Francesca needed to learn to share or she would grow up to be a selfish person.

Elena didn't understand that she was treating Francesca disrespectfully by not trying to understand Francesca's feelings. It would have been easy to allow Francesca to keep her special box of crayons in a safe place and have a large container of community crayons for Raymond to use as he pleased. In her effort to teach Francesca a lesson, Elena may have inadvertently been encouraging her to be even more possessive of her things.

The Graysons had two boys, a few years apart in age. The boys, Clem and Clark, wore each other's clothes, played with each other's toys, and shared everything. If something was missing from one of the rooms, Clem or Clark would simply go into his brother's room, find the missing item, and take it back. Each boy had a few items the other had no interest in, but for the most part, the boys thought of their property as something that belonged to everyone. Even at Christmas or on birthdays, it wasn't unusual to see one of the boys wearing an item that had just come out of a box destined for the other brother.

This "live and let live" attitude didn't extend to sports, where the boys were extremely competitive. On one occasion during a golf game, one of the boys threw his brother's clubs in the pond when his brother hit a ball farther than he did. The boys may have been willing to share their golf clubs, but they drew the line when it came to sharing the limelight as to who was the better athlete.

or box for those things he doesn't wish to share. Make sure that the family guideline is "We don't go in someone's room or use their things without their permission."

3. A child should not be required to share a toy that belongs to her if she doesn't want to. If your children are having friends over, discuss ahead of time which toys they are willing to share. Suggest that they put away the things they don't want to share.

4. If you do decide to loan out your property, make your expectations clear about how you want it used and returned. Sometimes it helps to get collateral. For instance, children can give you their favorite toy to hold until they return your sewing scissors.

5. Use the family meeting for kids to discuss their feelings about sharing. The family can work out a schedule to rotate popular family toys such as video games. If the kids still can't share them without fighting, it is okay to put the toys off-limits until they or the family come up with a win/win solution.

6. Take time to teach about sharing. Once a month, include a sharing segment in your family meeting. Give all family members an opportunity to give an example of how they shared something, how it made them feel, and how they think it made the other person feel.

7. Teach that sharing includes more than material possessions. It could include sharing time, sharing feelings, or sharing ideas. While tucking your children in bed at night, invite them to share their saddest time of the day and their happiest time. Also share your saddest and happiest moments of the day.

8. As a regular part of your family meetings, plan special time to share together as a family.

Life Skills Children Can Learn

Children can learn that there are times for sharing and times to respect not sharing. They can learn that sharing involves much more than sharing objects.

Parenting Pointers

1. Children need to have privacy and respect for their boundaries. They should not have to share everything with everybody.

2. Do not tell children they are selfish or label them with any other disrespectful term. Instead, make sure you say, "I'm unhappy with the way you fought with your sister over the game."

3. When someone calls another person selfish, could it be that the name-caller is not getting his own way?

Shopping with Children

"I can't afford a baby-sitter when I go to the store, so I have to take my children with me. They run around, hide, and throw tantrums until I buy them a toy or a treat. I see other children with their parents, and they seem so well-behaved. Is something wrong with my kids?"

Understanding Your Child, Yourself, and the Situation

We see as many misbehaving parents at grocery stores and shopping malls as we see misbehaving children. We see parents yelling, spanking, making demands that are inappropriate for their children's ages, giving in to demands, and using bribery. Often children don't look forward to going to the store any more than adults look forward to taking them. However, there are ways to make shopping more enjoyable for those times that the kids have to go with you.

Suggestions

1. Be clear about what behavior you expect, before leaving home. Many children do not know what their parents expect.

2. If there are carts with children's seats or strollers, put young children in them. If they climb out, tell them it is not okay and return them to their seat. Follow through with action and as few words as possible. Children can tell when you mean what you say.

3. Do not leave a child in the car or a store unattended. It is unsafe and very frightening to the child.

4. If you can, give the kids a job to do, such as pushing the cart, finding the item you are looking for, or carrying packages. They won't get bored so easily.

5. If your children run away, go after them and then have them hold your hand or the cart. If you follow through with action instead of yelling orders at them from another aisle or ignoring them, they will know that you mean what you say.

6. Be flexible and be willing to cut the trip short if the kids are too unruly. There are times when you may have to leave your purchases and try again another time. If your child has a temper tantrum in a store, you can wait quietly until he is done, hold him firmly while you finish shopping, or hug him until he calms down. Do not let tears influence you.

Planning Ahead to Prevent Future Problems

1. When children help plan the menus, they are more interested in finding the ingredients at the grocery store.

2. If your child has a clothing allowance, make a date to shop just with her, instead

of trying to combine her trip with your own shopping. Don't rush her.

3. Suggest the kids pick a toy or a book to take along in case they get bored.

4. Do not promise treats or toys as a bribe if the kids will behave, but do follow through on your promise if you say that you'll get them a treat. Take time to stop and browse in stores and areas that interest them.

5. Give your children allowances. If they want special treats, remind them about

Booster Thoughts

Some children love browsing through bookstores and shops, and others hate it. Kids who have had exposure to shopping in short bursts and who have an allowance and control over their money tend to enjoy shopping more than those who get dragged along without consideration for their needs.

One family decided to help their sons, who hated shopping, learn that it can be fun. They planned a day in San Francisco with no other agenda than to have a fun-filled day of shopping. They took the kids out to lunch, let them ride up and down the escalators at a large department store, and stopped in pet stores, comic book stores, and dime stores. They did everything they thought the kids would like—even riding the cable cars.

The boys were crabby, complaining, and sullen the whole day.

Why? Because no one had remembered to ask them if they would like to participate in this activity. It was assumed they would love the experience, but because they weren't part of the planning, they felt forced and reacted accordingly.

If the parents had enlisted the boys' cooperation in advance, they might have experienced a different outcome. The parents could have said, "I know you hate shopping, but sometimes it can be fun. Would you be interested in an experiment? We'd like to take you to San Francisco today. We want to take you out to lunch, ride the cable cars, and browse through some of your favorite stores. At the end of the day, you let us know what parts you enjoyed, what parts you disliked, and any ideas that would make the family outing more fun next time. What do you say?"

their allowances. If they can't afford an item, help them figure out how to save for it instead of advancing them money.

6. If you aren't shopping for them and it is at all possible, you might ask a friend to watch them, have your mate handle their care, or put the kids in child care. Try trading baby-sitting with a friend. That way, you get a break too.

7. Tell the kids that you have no choice but to take them shopping, you understand it may not be a lot of fun for them, and you appreciate their help. Ask if there is anything you could do to make the trip more enjoyable.

Life Skills Children Can Learn

Children can learn about give and take and how to entertain themselves. They can also learn how to find their way around a store, help the family shop, and cooperate.

Parenting Pointers

1. It is humiliating and disrespectful to yell at your children, spank them, or discipline them in public. You can let them know you are angry and will talk about what is bothering you in the car, at home, or at a family meeting.

2. If you keep your shopping trips short, your children are more likely to look forward to going with you.

Shyness

"My child is so shy. Whenever people talk to her, she hides her head and won't answer them. Everyone says how shy she is. Does this mean she has low self-esteem? What can I do to help her with this?"

Understanding Your Child, Yourself, and the Situation

There are some who think that children are born shy. Children may be labeled shy if they act in an introverted way. Children often accept a label that is given to them and then may use it to get undue attention (for passive power), to get revenge when they feel hurt, or as a way to give up when they feel discouraged.

It is important to recognize and appreciate differences—and to understand that introverts have as many strengths as extroverts. Being an introvert has nothing to do with self-esteem. Low self-esteem comes from not accepting ourselves or from not being accepted for who we are. Also, shyness may be a behavior that has an unconscious purpose and creates certain results. In some cases, the child may have an outgoing, sociable sibling and the shy child

Booster Thoughts

Norma and Doreen enjoyed getting together once a week for coffee. Doreen's four-year-old daughter, Vicki, usually accompanied her mother. When Norma said, "Hi, Vicki," Vicki hid behind her mother's leg and Doreen explained, "She's shy."

When Norma asked Vicki, "Would you like some nice juice and a cracker?" Doreen answered for her daughter. "She's too shy to talk, but I'm sure she would love one. Why don't you set it out for her and she'll help herself, won't you, honey?"

When Norma asked Vicki if she would like to play with the other children, Vicki said, "I can't. I'm shy."

Norma invited Doreen to a parenting class where she learned about the four mistaken goals of misbehavior. When discussing the four mistaken goals, the instructor explained that if parents feel annoyed by a behavior it is a sign that the child thinks she belongs only if you are noticing her. Doreen realized she did feel annoyed by Vicki's shyness but kept feeding it by giving her so much undue attention.

Doreen stopped telling other people Vicki was shy and stopped talking for her. She told Vicki, "I notice that there are times when you choose not to answer when people ask you a question. That's okay with me, but it would help if you would tell people you don't want to talk. When you are quiet, I'm going to guess that you don't feel like talking unless you tell me otherwise, and I'll go about my business. I love you whether you talk or not. You let me know if you want something."

Within a short time, Vicki stopped acting shy. Doreen later told Norma, "I don't know for sure when she stopped acting shy. I became so unconcerned about her choice to act that way that I hardly noticed when she did it or when she stopped. I started focusing on her strengths and the fun times we had together. I wonder if that had anything to do with it?"

may have unconsciously decided that she had to find another way to belong in the family. In other cases, without meaning to, parents train a child to be shy by labeling the child's behavior and trying to control or change it. This label can last a lifetime and become a major part of a person's identity.

Suggestions

1. There are times when it makes perfect sense for children to hold back, especially if they are checking out a new situation, if they don't feel like interacting, or if they are being pushed to act according to someone else's standards. They should be allowed to approach those situations with caution without being labeled shy.[46]

2. If your children do hold back, don't speak for them or try to coax them to talk. Simply go on with the conversation and trust that they will enter in if and when they are ready.

3. Don't introduce your child as shy or tell others she is shy when she refuses to talk.

4. Look for ways you may be trying to force your child to act a certain way. You may be in a power struggle, and she is using the passive power of silence to show you that you can't make her do what you want. Back off. Let your child have her own relationship with others without you getting in the middle.

5. Don't let your child's so-called shyness be an excuse to stop her from doing things she needs to do. Tell your child, "It's okay to feel uncomfortable, but you still need to go to school. Are there some ways I could help you feel more comfortable?"

Planning Ahead to Prevent Future Problems

1. Teach your children that introverts have just as many strengths as extroverts. They are just different strengths.

2. Don't overprotect your children. Everyone experiences some pain in life (just be sure you don't add to your children's pain by not accepting them as they are or by overprotecting them). The important thing is for your children to learn that they can cope with disappointments and pain. If they don't like the consequences of their lifestyle choices, it is up to them to change what they want to change. Your children will feel freer to change what they want to change when they feel that an introverted style is a valid choice.

3. Talk with your children and try to get into their worlds to find out if their behavior is a problem for them. Ask if there are ways you can help them feel more comfortable around others.

---

46. See Chapter 7 on temperament in Jane Nelsen, Cheryl Erwin, and Roslyn Duffy, *Positive Discipline for Preschoolers* (Rocklin, CA: Prima Publishing, 1998).

4. Don't try to force your children into situations that they aren't ready for. Help them find small steps they can take to feel more comfortable. Don't try to make them perform (sing songs or play musical instruments) in front of your friends or relatives.

5. Talk about your child's behavior instead of labeling it. For instance, you might say to your child, "I notice that when people say 'hello,' you hide your head behind your hands. Do you do that because you think it's a game, or do you do that because you want them to leave you alone? If you would like them to leave you alone, perhaps you could tell them, 'I don't feel like answering any questions right now.' "

6. Create a safe environment where your children can learn to speak up at home and then allow them to make the choice about whether or not to speak up away from home. One way to do this is through regular family meetings, where children can learn to express feelings, give and receive compliments, and brainstorm for solutions to problems.

Life Skills Children Can Learn

Children can learn that they can behave in ways that feel comfortable without being labeled or pushed to do something they don't want to do. They can also learn to say what they want instead of expecting people to read their minds.

Parenting Pointers

1. Some people choose a quiet, introverted lifestyle. We need to accept and respect different lifestyles. Accepting the label of shyness and going through life as a shy person can have devastating effects, including loneliness, alienation, and a fear of trying new situations.

2. Familiarize yourself with the four mistaken goals of misbehavior (see Part 1) and decide if your child is discouraged and wants attention, power, revenge, or to be left alone. How you encourage a child should be related to the form of discouragement.

Sibling Rivalry

(See also *Fighting, Siblings*)

"We recently took our two boys on a trip with their cousin, who is an only child. The three boys spent the entire trip vying for position and trying to find their special place in the group. Is this normal?"

Understanding Your Child, Yourself, and the Situation

Everyone needs to feel that he or she belongs and is significant. The first place we make decisions about how we belong is in our family of origin. Children are good observers but poor interpreters. When a new baby arrives, the older child often believes,

"Mommy doesn't love me as much as the baby." As children get older, they often mistakenly believe that only one person in a family can have a certain claim to fame. If a child thinks his sibling already has the place of being athletic, for example, he may decide to be studious, musical, or a social butterfly. Children often develop typical characteristics based on their birth order. The oldest child usually tries to be first and boss; the second looks for the injustices and often becomes a rebel or may try hard to catch up with the first; the youngest thinks he is entitled to extra attention; and the only child wants to be special. If adults are trying to control a situation in which kids are trying to find ways in which they are unique, it is wasted effort. The kids will find their own ways to belong and feel significant.[47]

Suggestions

1. Get into your children's world. The oldest usually feels "dethroned," just as you would if your spouse brought home a new lover. The youngest often feels inadequate when comparing herself to the capabilities of the oldest. Understanding how they might feel helps you interact with them with compassion. Never say, "You shouldn't feel that way." Allow children to feel what they feel.

2. Compassion does not mean sympathy. It is not helpful to overprotect your children and try to save them from the many feelings and emotions they will experience in life. Compassion helps you maintain kindness with firmness while applying any of the following suggestions.

3. Avoid victim and bully training. This happens when you assume the oldest is always at fault (the bully) and rescue the youngest (the victim). Often the youngest starts a conflict (that you don't see) just to get you to rescue her. Treat them the same. Verbalize faith in their ability to work things out, or separate them.

4. Make sure that you have one-on-one special time with each child sometime during each day. If a child is jealous of another, let him know that you want to be with each child and his time will come. Tell him that it is okay to feel jealous.

5. If the situation between the kids gets out of hand, see if you can redirect them into activities, such as contests or relays, where cooperation is more important than competition.

Planning Ahead to Prevent Future Problems

1. Give positive messages to every child so each knows how special he or she is. For in-

47. For more information on birth order, see Chapter 3 in Jane Nelsen, *Positive Discipline* (New York: Ballantine, 1996).

stance, with the three boys mentioned above, one was told, "You're really good at organizing activities." Another was told, "You're really good at ignoring group pressure and doing what you like." The youngest was told, "You sure have figured out how to let these big guys think they're the boss, while you get exactly what you want."

2. Find activities that stress group cooperation and teamwork. Help the kids discover that things are more fun when they include people who have different strengths.

3. Make it a point to let the kids know how much you appreciate their special qualities that set them apart from the other kids.

4. Don't compare the kids in a misguided attempt to motivate them to be like another child. This is very discouraging.

5. At family meetings and other activities, stress how great it is that we are all different

Booster Thoughts

Pam's two children tussled on the floor, punching, threatening, teasing, and wrestling with each other. Every time she tried to get them to stop, their behavior got more intense. She was upset about the sibling rivalry and was worried that her children would never be able to get along with each other.

Her friend Rita had been attending a parenting class. She suggested that Pam accompany her to the class and bring up this problem for discussion. Pam did so and was amazed to find that the other parents all had similar situations. Knowing that brought a certain amount of relief, but Pam still wanted guidance on what to do about her fighting children.

The group brainstormed a list of suggestions. The one that Pam decided to try for a week was to think of her children as bear cubs, scuffling together. It was amazing how much less the children's behavior concerned her when she simply changed her attitude. Instead of trying to make the kids stop, she sat back and enjoyed the show. She realized that her kids were really playing with each other and having fun together. She was the only one who had been upset. As she hassled them less about it, they seemed to have less need to wrestle, although they didn't give up their fun "game" completely.

and bring different skills and ideas to the family.

6. It does not help to read stories about new babies to children under three. They cannot understand abstract concepts. They will understand concrete actions if you spend as much time with them as you do with the new baby.

7. Don't gush and make a fuss over the new baby in front of an older sibling. This enhances the belief of the older child that she has been "replaced."

8. Get rid of your "fair button." Kids will push it and use it to manipulate you.

Life Skills Children Can Learn

Children can learn how to be together and realize that each one is unique and special. Children can learn that everyone is different and that is okay. They can learn how to be resourceful and solve their own problems. Most important, they can learn that they are all loved and that love is not conditional on being one certain way.

Parenting Pointers

1. Sibling rivalry is normal and happens in just about every family that has two or more children. It is more intense for children who are born less than three years apart. Rivalry increases when parents are competitive and decreases when parents cooperate respectfully.

2. Problems result when children decide that being loved is conditional. If parents stress competition, which emphasizes comparing and judging, instead of cooperation, which stresses uniqueness and differences, sibling rivalry can get out of hand. Make sure the message of love gets through and that each child is loved for being the unique human he or she is.

3. If there is a change in how one child finds belonging and significance in a family, all the other children have to reevaluate their unique places as well. Often when families get into therapy, the "good" child gets worse while the "problem" child begins to behave better. This is normal until each child sorts out his or her special place in the family.

Sickness

"Sometimes my children get so sick it scares me, and other times I think they're just saying they are sick to get my attention or to get out of going to school. How can I tell the difference?"

Understanding Your Child, Yourself, and the Situation

Getting sick is part of life, and it is the parent's job to help children deal with being sick. It can be frightening to have a sick child and devastating when a child faces a life-threatening illness. However, most times, children will recover. In some families, children have learned that being sick is a way to escape from something unpleasant or a chance to get some special treatment. Claiming false sickness may be a cry for help—or a bid for undue attention. In either case, it is important to deal with the belief behind the behavior as well as the behavior.

Suggestions

1. If you suspect your child is using illness as an excuse to miss school, explore this possibility in a nonthreatening way. "I don't know for sure, but I wonder if you are having some problems at school and you want to be sick so you don't have to go. If that is true, I would like to hear about it and help you work on the problems when you are ready."

2. Encourage your children to say how they feel and then take their feelings seriously. Teach them to say, "I feel scared" (or worried or uncomfortable) when that is what they mean, instead of having to say "I am sick" to get help.

3. Keep a thermometer handy so you can take your child's temperature to help you decide whether or not he is sick. Underarm thermometers are now available for young children. Consider other symptoms, too—a child can be sick without a raised temperature.

4. If your child says he doesn't feel well, take him seriously instead of assuming he is trying to trick you. Listen to him and validate his feelings.

5. Many parents are so in tune with their kids that they can almost tell the minute their child gets sick. Trust your feelings and get outside help to ease your fears. Also trust your feelings when you suspect your child needs help dealing with an overwhelming situation or when you suspect your child is simply avoiding responsibility for a situation he could handle. Act accordingly with confidence.

6. When your child is sick, make sure he knows what is going on and how to take his medicine. Do not force the medicine, but explain why it is needed and ask him for his help and cooperation. Let your child hold the spoon and give himself the medicine.

7. If someone is sick, don't ignore the rest of the family or yourself. Take a break to be with the others and get some rest. Be honest with all family members about what is happening and how you are feeling.

8. Allow your children to have mental health days every now and then so they can take a day off from school without having to get "sick."

Planning Ahead to Prevent Future Problems

1. Teach your children how to listen to their bodies and how to care for themselves with rest and a good diet.

Booster Thoughts

Four children, aged eight through twelve, were left alone in a new house and city while the parents went out for the evening. No one asked them if they were ready to handle this—it was just assumed that they were.

Within minutes of the parents leaving, the eight-year-old got a stomachache. The oldest called a neighbor for help and said, "I don't think she's really sick. I think she's just scared and so am I."

The parents had not told the neighbors that their children would be calling them in case of an emergency. Still, the neighbors took over some soup, soft drinks, and popsicles and tried to offer some comfort.

About an hour after the neighbors left, the twelve-year-old called again. This time, one of the children had a headache, and they couldn't find any children's aspirin in the house. The neighbor ran to the store for some aspirin and decided to stay with the children until the parents came home. The neighbor knew these children had been left with a bigger responsibility than they were ready for.

Children are inventive. If they are treated disrespectfully, they may figure out that being "sick" is a sure way to get a grown-up to take them seriously.

2. Pay attention to your own baggage about illness. Do you think it is best to fuss over sick people or to leave them alone? Do you see illness as a hassle, or are you prepared to take it as it comes? Your beliefs about illness could be coloring how you treat your children and how they feel about being sick.

3. Use nonmedicinal treatments as much as possible so your children don't get the idea there is a pill for everything. TLC goes a long way to help children through illness.

4. Don't suggest that your children will get sick if they don't wear a jacket when it's cold, don't sleep enough, and so on, as you may be programming them to get sick instead of preventing illness.

5. Keep emergency information handy so anyone can get help quickly.

Life Skills Children Can Learn

Children can learn to listen to their bodies, care for themselves, and ask for what they need without having to use "I'm sick" as an excuse.

Parenting Pointers

1. If you get sick, make sure you have family and friends you can call to help supervise the kids and care for you.

2. No matter how many preventive measures you take, children will still get sick, so deal with it instead of blaming yourself or overprotecting them.

Single Parent

"I feel guilty about being a single parent. One reason is that I'm afraid my child will be deprived by not having two parents. The other reason is that I just don't want to spend the time trying to be both mother and father. I want some time for myself. How much will my child suffer because of my inability to do it all?"

Understanding Your Child, Yourself, and the Situation

It is a myth that children are more deprived because they live with a single parent. They could be much worse off if their unhappy parents stayed together and set an example of an unhealthy relationship. Many happy people were raised by a single parent. It is not our circumstances but how we deal with those circumstances that has the greatest impact on what we get out of life.[48]

Suggestions

1. You do not have to make it up to your child for being a single parent—or try to be both mother and father. One healthy parent is enough. Develop a good attitude about being single. "This is how it is, and we are going to benefit from how it is."

2. See the benefits of single parenting. You don't have to fight about which way to parent. It is a myth that it is always easier

48. See also Jane Nelsen, Cheryl Erwin, and Carol Delzer, *Positive Discipline for Single Parents* (Rocklin, CA: Prima Publishing, 1994).

Booster Thoughts

When her children would threaten to go live with the other parent, one mother would say, "Okay, but you can leave once and you can come back once." None of her children took her up on this. They realized that she took them seriously and respected their right to live with the other parent. This made them think about whether that was really what they wanted to do. After giving it some thought, they decided to stay where they were.

for two parents. They often fight about how lenient or how strict they should be, or they criticize each other for not spending enough time with the children. Don't idealize other circumstances. The grass usually is not greener on the other side.

3. Another benefit of single parenting is that children have the opportunity to feel needed. It is very important that you do not pamper your children in an attempt to make it up to them. Have family meetings (even with just one parent and one child) and get the children involved in chore plans, problem solving, and planning fun events. In single-parent families, kids definitely have an opportunity to make meaningful contributions and feel needed, listened to, and taken seriously.

4. If your child threatens to go live with the other parent, ask yourself: Is she just angry and trying to hurt me? Is she trying to get out of doing a chore? Does she really think it would be better at the other parent's house? After a cooling-off period, check out the possibilities with your child. "I wonder if you were angry about _____?" Follow up by working on solutions to the problem.

Planning Ahead to Prevent Future Problems

1. Create a support network of extended family and friends to help with child care, to act as male or female role models, and to have fun with.

2. Join or start a single-parenting class.[49]

3. If you are divorced and your ex-spouse seems irresponsible, decide what you will do instead of wasting time with anger, frus-

49. Call Empowering People Books, Tapes, and Videos, at 800-456-7770, or Lynn Lott, at 707-526-3141, ext. 3#, for information on the *Teaching Parenting the Positive Discipline Way* manual and classes and the *Positive Discipline for Single Parents* supplemental manual. Also, ask about the facilitator training.

tration, and disappointment because the other person won't do what you want.

4. Don't fall for your kids' attempts to manipulate you through comparisons with the other parent. Use emotional honesty to share your feelings and state your position confidently.

5. Help your kids deal with their disappointment about having only one parent or their anger if there has been a divorce. Help them express their feelings and then make plans for what they want to do. (All feelings are acceptable and valuable. What kids do with them is a different matter.) Help them learn emotional honesty to stick up for themselves and share their needs and wants.

6. Find ways to fill your own cup and take care of your needs so you have energy and enthusiasm to enjoy your kids. Don't feel guilty about taking time for yourself. See it as a gift to you and your children.

Life Skills Children Can Learn

Children can learn that life presents all kinds of circumstances, some of which they may not like. They can learn, grow, and benefit from life's challenges. They can't control everything that happens, but they can control how they deal with what happens.

Parenting Pointers

1. Emphasizing the benefits of single parenting does not mean that problems don't exist. It does mean that idealizing a different situation and a negative attitude do not help.

2. Your children will be influenced by your attitude. If you act like a victim, chances are that your children will feel like victims. If you have an optimistic, courageous attitude, chances are that your children will adopt this attitude also.

Stealing

"Money has been disappearing from my purse and from the kids' piggy banks. My twelve-year-old daughter insists she hasn't taken it, but I notice she is buying lipstick, nail polish, and treats for her friends that she couldn't possibly afford from her allowance."

Understanding Your Child, Yourself, and the Situation

Most children will steal something at least once (probably most of us did too, when we were children). When they do, most parents overreact. In their panic, parents often accuse a child of being a thief or a liar.

Booster Thoughts

Rebecca came to a counseling session extremely distraught. She suspected her daughter, Julie, was stealing makeup from her and money from her brother. When the school called and said that food items were missing from a fund-raiser, that was the final straw. Rebecca was ready to send her daughter to jail.

In the past, Rebecca had handled incidents of stealing by confronting her daughter. Julie had responded by insisting she was innocent, even when the money or items were in her room. Then Rebecca would get angry and call her a liar and ground her for a week.

Rebecca decided to handle things differently this time. She told Julie the school called to say she was short on her food deliveries for the fund-raiser. Rebecca said she would be happy to advance Julie the money needed to make up the difference and take it out of her allowance each week until the bill was repaid. Rebecca asked Julie if she could handle seventy-five cents or a dollar a week.

Julie was caught completely off guard. She started to make excuses and her mother said, "Honey, let's just figure out how to replace the items." Julie replied, "Okay, how about a dollar each week?"

Parents often take extreme measures like spanking, grounding, and other punitive solutions so their children don't grow up to be thieves. Judging and punishing kids only makes the situation worse. Any parental intervention that is punitive and deals only with the behavior and not the underlying problem makes the situation worse.

Suggestions

1. If something has been stolen, focus on a plan for replacing the item or money rather than on pointing fingers or calling names. Tell your child that the stolen article must be replaced and you need her help in figuring out a plan for replacing it. If necessary, advance her the money to replace it. Work out a payment plan she can handle and deduct it from her allowance each week. Keep a payment record so she can see how she is doing.

2. Give children a chance to replace a stolen item and save face. Say, "I'm not concerned with who took the item, just that it be re-

Julie's mother continued, "Someone said they saw you sharing what they thought were the missing items with your friends."

Julie began to defend herself. In the past, Rebecca would tell her daughter she was lying and an ugly scene would follow. This time, Rebecca said instead, "Julie, I'm sure your friends like you for who you are, not for what you give them. If you would like to entertain your friends, why don't you invite them over to make cookies and play?"

Julie said, "Yeah, maybe," but she gave her mother a big hug as she left the room.

Julie stopped stealing when she learned she would be held accountable and have to pay for what she stole. Her mother closed the escape route of defensiveness and power struggles when she showed unconditional love and stopped labeling and shaming Julie while dealing directly with the problem. She had also dealt with underlying issues such as improving their relationship, boosting Julie's self-esteem, and the importance of focusing on solutions instead of blame.

turned. I trust that sometime during the next hour the item will be put back where it belongs with no questions asked."

3. When you know your child has stolen something, don't try to trap her by asking, "Did you steal this?" Tell her, "Honey, I know you stole this item. I did that once when I was little. I felt scared and guilty. How did you feel when you did this?" Continue with more "what" and "how" questions in a nonthreatening tone: "Have you ever thought about how the store owner might feel when things are stolen? How many items do you think store owners have to sell before they make enough money to pay their employees and rent and still have enough left over for their needs? What could you do to help?" Many children have not thought about these questions, and you can help them become concerned for other people.

4. Support your child in returning stolen goods to the store. Instead of being punitive, show compassion. Tell your child, "I

know this can be scary and embarrassing, but that is what we have to experience sometimes to correct a mistake. Store owners usually appreciate it very much when children are willing to admit they made a mistake and try to make it right."

5. If toys appear that you know belong to a friend of your child's, simply say, "I'm sure Billy must be missing this. Let's call him so he knows it's safe and take it back as soon as we have time."

6. If you suspect your child is stealing to support a drug habit, get professional help. This is too hard to deal with alone.

Planning Ahead to Prevent Future Problems

1. Many children steal because they believe they are unloved and don't belong. They think they have the right to hurt others, since no one cares about them and it hurts. It is called a "revenge cycle." Therefore, it is important to find ways to let children know they are loved. Separate the deed from the doer and show love while working out a plan to fix the problem.

2. Often children steal because it is the only way they have to get what they want. Make sure your children have allowances that are realistic to cover their expenses while still fitting into the family budget (see also *Materialism*).

3. Sometimes stealing occurs because money is laying out and is too tempting. Keep your money and valuables out of sight. If you suspect one of your children is stealing from another, help the victim get a locked box for items to protect.

4. Children may steal from a sibling because they are jealous. Ask your children whether perhaps they think you favor one sibling over another. Listen to their responses for clues as to whether you are on target. Tell them that feeling jealous is natural and that you love them very much. Discuss what you find special about each one and be sure it is positive and not critical.

5. During another family meeting, help children explore the consequences of stealing before it happens. (If stealing has already occurred, be sure this conversation is friendly and generic instead of focused on an individual.) Do this by asking "what," "why," and "how" questions: "Why do you think someone might steal? What are the consequences of stealing? What do we need to do in our family so we can all feel trust and safety?"

6. Convey a message of unconditional love that does not include rescuing. In other

words, let your children know what you will do instead of trying to control what they will do. To a teenager who was stealing hubcaps and car parts to support his pot habit, one parent said, "If you go to jail, I will love you and I will bring you cookies, but I will not bail you out." To a ten-year-old who broke a toy he "borrowed" from a friend, a parent said, "I will help you figure out how to solve the problem, but I will not solve it for you."

Life Skills Children Can Learn

Children can learn that they can save face and take care of the problem without losing the love and respect of their parents. Their financial needs are important and their parents can help them figure out ways to get what they want without stealing. They realize that they are not bad; they have just made a mistake that can be corrected.

Parenting Pointers

1. Teens may steal for the thrill and for peer acceptance. It helps for them to get caught and be allowed to make restitution. Don't rescue them or bail them out when this happens. Otherwise, they may think they are invincible and that no one can stop them.

2. Dealing with a child's hurt feelings and the pain of feeling that she doesn't belong will stop stealing quicker than punitive measures.

Stepfamilies

"I have two children and have recently married a woman with three children. Our children don't seem to be adjusting too well. Two of her children seem to resent me most of the time, and my son seems to resent her most of the time. It is causing a lot of strain on our relationship. We don't know what to do."

Understanding Your Child, Yourself, and the Situation

Blending families is a process that takes time. Children get used to certain roles in their original family, and it can be very disruptive for them to change their perceptions of how they belong in a new family constellation (see also *Birth Order* and *Sibling Rivalry*). Some new stepparents feel they need to let the children know they are the parent. Others think that any problems should be handled by the birth parent. Any of these scenarios creates division rather than respectful partnerships. It helps to have a united front to deal with the divorced parent who may be having a difficult time accepting the new situation his or her children are in and could be undermining any possible adjustments from afar.

Booster Thoughts

When Jose and Marie married, they each brought three children to their newly blended family. The six children ranged in age from six to fourteen. Obviously, there were many adjustments to be made.

Marie worked outside the home. She really enjoyed her new family and was anxious to get home to them after work—except for one problem. The first thing she would notice was the mess. The children would come home from school and leave their books, sweaters, and shoes all over the house. To this they would add cookie crumbs, empty milk glasses, and toys.

Marie would start nagging and cajoling. "Why can't you pick up your things? You know it upsets me. I enjoy being with you, but I get so angry when I see all this mess that I forget about joy." The children would pick up their things, but by then Marie was upset and displeased with them and with herself.

Marie finally put the problem on the agenda for their weekly, Monday night family meeting. She admitted that it was her problem. It obviously didn't bother the children to have the house cluttered, but she asked that they help with her problem.

The children came up with a plan for a "safe-deposit box." This was a big cardboard box, which they would put in the garage. Anything that was left in the com-

Then there are the day-to-day logistics that can be overwhelming, like where children will sleep, how to deal with children who come every other week, weekends only, just in the summer, and so on. Blending families creates an extremely complex system of new relationships and issues.[50]

Suggestions

1. Allow time for the process to unfold. Expect some anger, jealousy, rivalry, and grieving, but know that it will not last forever if handled sensitively. Just knowing that adjustment to change takes time can

50. See also Jane Nelsen, Cheryl Erwin, and H. Stephen Glenn, *Positive Discipline for Blended Families* (Rocklin, CA: Prima Publishing, 1997).

mon rooms, such as the living room, family room, and kitchen, could be picked up by anyone who saw it and put in the safe-deposit box. It would have to stay there for a week before the owner could claim it.

The plan worked beautifully. The clutter problem was taken care of and the safe-deposit box was jammed with things.

However, it caused some other problems, which tested the plan. If they hadn't stuck to the rules, the whole thing would have been ineffective. For instance, twelve-year-old Carlos lost his school shoes. He looked everywhere and then remembered the safe-deposit box. Sure enough, that is where they were.

Carlos wore his smelly old tennis shoes to school, but the next day he lost those. He didn't have any other shoes, but the children insisted he couldn't take his shoes out for a week.

Carlos turned to his mother, who wisely said, "I'm sorry. I don't know what you are going to do, but I have to stick by the rules, too." His helpful siblings finally came up with the solution of his bedroom slippers. Carlos didn't have a better idea, so he wore his slippers to school for three days. After that week, he never left his shoes out again.

This story illustrates the importance of building family togetherness by getting the kids involved in problem solving.

ease the frustration. In some cases, the adjustment happens in weeks or months, while in others it may take years.

2. Allow your children to express their feelings without criticism or judgment. Show understanding instead of telling them they shouldn't feel what they do. Be a good listener, but don't try to fix things for your children by running interference between your children and their new stepparent. Set up times to discuss serious issues when everyone is present. Let your children know that you will help bring up the discussion if they feel too intimidated to do so but that not discussing problems with the people involved isn't an option.

3. Schedule regular family meetings in which everyone can brainstorm to solve problems and create new routines. (Some children resent the word "family," so you may wish to call these meetings or planning sessions.) Acknowledge that things

were different in the original families and express your need for their help in creating new guidelines that work for this family.

4. When the kids spend time with their other parent, allow time for them to adjust when they move from family to family. You might take them out for hamburgers or let them spend time with their friends or in their room.

5. Scheduling is more complicated as children move back and forth between their families. Have different job charts for different groups of kids (see *Chores, Age-Appropriate*). Read Chapter 9 in *Chores Without Wars* for many practical, workable suggestions.[51]

Planning Ahead to Prevent Future Problems

1. Honor the need of your children to love their original parents. Do not say bad things about their other parents. Don't make them feel they have to choose. Realize that the difficulties their parents are having adjusting are theirs to work out. Don't let that stop you from maintaining a relationship with your child or maintaining agreed-upon routines (see also *Divorce*).

2. It is important for married couples to work on agreeing that they have equal responsibility to love and follow through with all children. Some couples prefer to allow the birth parent to handle discipline with his or her children while the stepparent works on being a friend. Others feel that the person who is having the problem is the one who should deal with it. Many blended families find that the family meeting is the best place for everyone to be heard.

3. Children will pick up your attitude. A healthy attitude is one of "I know this is hard. I understand why you feel hurt and angry. This new relationship is important to me, and I know that, with time, we can create a healthy, loving family."

4. Early in the blending process, the original parent may need to take the primary role in discipline if the children resist the stepparent's discipline. The children may be looking for ways to express their frustrations—withholding cooperation and provoking conflict are great ways to get even. After allowing for a period of adjustment, move toward discipline that involves everyone concerned. When discipline is nonpunitive and children are included in the problem-solving process, they are less likely to feel resentful.

5. It is a mistake for either parent to let his or her children come first. This is not healthy for the relationship or for the kids. Children need to know that their parents

---

51. Lynn Lott and Riki Intner, *Chores Without Wars* (Rocklin, CA: Prima Publishing, 1997).

and stepparents value their relationship and are loyal to each other. Children need to know that they are loved but that they can't manipulate their parents against each other.

Life Skills Children Can Learn

Children can learn that it is okay and normal for them to experience hurt and anger when their lives are disrupted. They can deal with that hurt and anger in productive ways that help them learn important life skills.

Parenting Pointers

1. When stepparents use discipline that is nonpunitive, it is not threatening to the original parent (unless that parent is being overprotective).

2. Time, if filled with love, understanding, and positive problem solving, can heal wounds.

3. If you as the birth parent are feeling embarrassed by how your children are treating the person you love, have faith in your new spouse and your children to work out difficulties without you interfering or protecting your mate.

Suicide

"My teenager has been threatening to commit suicide. I'm so scared. I can't think of anything worse than losing a child to suicide."

Understanding Your Child, Yourself, and the Situation

Suicide is cause for concern more with adolescents than with younger children. Adolescent hormones create wide mood swings. Suicide is a real danger if the downswings are accompanied by a lack of confidence to live up to adult expectations, a lack of skills to solve problems that seem insurmountable, a lack of unconditional love, or involvement with drugs. Children, especially teenagers, need courage, confidence, and skills to deal with the ups and downs of life.

Suggestions

1. Know the warning signs of suicide:

- Verbal threats to commit suicide.
- Extended periods of depression, loss of appetite, sleeping more than usual, poor hygiene, spending a lot of time alone, substance abuse, or general despair.
- Acting out extreme behaviors, such as stealing, setting fires, becoming physically violent, giving up on school, throwing up, abusing chemicals, or leaving drug paraphernalia around the house.

- Signs of suicide attempts, cutting or mutilating one's body, getting pregnant, or staying loaded all the time.
- Getting one's life in order and giving away possessions.

2. Many teens will show some of these signs as part of the turmoil of adolescence. Seek professional help if you suspect at all that the signs are serious.

3. When talking to children about suicide, it's important to use the words "suicide" and "death" and not shy away from them for fear of introducing an idea you think hasn't already occurred to them.

Booster Thoughts

The following shows the wrong way to react when children express their feelings. We include it because, unfortunately, it is all too typical of parental responses. It shows a lack of compassion, a judgmental attitude, and an unwillingness to listen.

Cliff: No one cares if I live or die.

Dad: You always feel so sorry for yourself.

Cliff: Well, you and Mom split up and you expect me to live with that disgusting person who calls himself my stepfather.

Dad: How dare you use such language like that around me! Your stepfather is doing the best he can.

Cliff: Oh, yeah? Then why does he scream and yell at me all the time?

Dad: Cliff, I know your stepfather, and I know that just isn't true. Why do you tell such lies?

Cliff: Nobody believes me. I hate you all and I wish I were dead! A lot you guys would care!

Dad: Cliff, there you go exaggerating again. You know you don't mean what you say. Now settle down and think about how you can get along with your stepfather.

Cliff didn't kill himself, but he did run away at the age of fourteen and no one knows where or how he is.[52]

---

52. From Jane Nelsen and Lynn Lott, *Positive Discipline for Teenagers* (Rocklin, CA: Prima Publishing, 1994), 318–319.

4. If you suspect your child is thinking about suicide, ask if she has a plan or if she has already tried. Finding out her plan shows how far along she is in her thinking. If she actually has a plan, get professional help immediately.

5. Ask the child how killing himself would change things. His answer may tell you what is bothering him.

6. During some quality time with your child, ask her to share with you how things are going in each of the four areas of life: school, family, friends, and love relationships. If things are not going well in any of these areas, your child may need professional help.

Planning Ahead to Prevent Future Problems

1. Teach over and over again that making a mistake is an invitation to try again and not a cause for suicide.

2. Before suicide is even an issue, tell kids that some people make a mistake when they choose suicide because it is a permanent solution to a temporary problem.

3. Take children seriously. Encourage them to share their feelings with you or with someone else with whom they feel comfortable.

4. Tell your teenagers about the times you felt discouraged and that those times passed. One mother who suspected her daughter was thinking of suicide told her, "Honey, I remember a few times when I felt like committing suicide. I felt so bad I couldn't imagine things getting any better. But they did. I hate to think of how much I would have missed if I had killed myself. For one thing, I would have missed you."

Life Skills Children Can Learn

Children can learn courage, confidence, and the skills to deal with the ups and downs of life.

Summer Vacation

"It looks like summer vacation will never end. The kids are driving me crazy. They're bored and demanding, and I wish school would start tomorrow. They've only been out of school one week. Help!"

Understanding Your Child, Yourself, and the Situation

Often parents think it is their job to entertain their children and make sure they have fun during the summer break (see also *Boredom*). Parents alternate between trying to take care of all the kids' needs and shooing them out of their way. Many parents work all day and leave the kids home by themselves with a list of rules and chores, hoping for the best. Children need help from their parents to make summer vacations an enjoyable, productive time, but entertaining them is not the way to help.

Most kids, when asked how they would like to spend their summer vacation, say, "Doing nothing, sleeping in, watching TV, and playing with my friends." Most parents, when asked what is their biggest concern about summer vacation, say, "My kids will sleep late, watch endless television, and do nothing." Resolving these separate realities can be a challenge, but what works best is joint planning to come up with a vacation both parent and child can live with.

Suggestions

1. Set up and maintain a routine, even if it's different from the rest of the year. Make sure the kids are involved in planning it.

2. Spend some time each day alone with each child doing something that you both enjoy. If you work close enough to home, try lunch dates with your children. Otherwise, get the kids involved in helping with dinner, so you will have energy for some fun time after dinner.

3. Set up a chore time during which everyone works together, instead of leaving lists of assignments to do while you are gone. Don't worry about messes the rest of the day. A good time for chores is before breakfast or before dinner—usually everyone is around at those times.

4. Check your local resources for lessons, special programs, or summer activities. Be sure to involve the kids in deciding what they would like to sign up for.

5. Remember how nice it feels to have a day or more just to do nothing? Don't be alarmed when the kids spend their days that way.

6. Limit television viewing (with input from the kids) and turn it off when it's not television time. Do not let the television baby-sit your kids.

7. Do not underestimate the importance of downtime for kids to wind down from the busy school year, think, or simply rest.

Planning Ahead to Prevent Future Problems

1. Brainstorm with the kids a list of ideas for those times when they feel bored. Then when the kids say, "I'm bored, what can I do?" say, "Why don't you check your list for an idea?"

2. Kids need to be with their friends during the summer. If you don't trust them having friends over when you aren't home, you need to arrange for someone to stay at the

Booster Thoughts

Twelve-year-old Trina decided that summer vacation was a perfect time to play all the computer games she never had time to play during the school year and to catch up on the new programs in the family computer. Since both of her parents worked, she pictured spending every day at the computer with no interruptions. When her parents discovered this was how she was spending her time, they became alarmed and told her she had to limit her computer use and plan a more well-rounded schedule. Trina looked at them with alarm, told them what they wanted to hear, and continued with her plan.

It didn't take long before her father caught on to what she was doing, as he often came home for lunch and always found her at the computer. He became angry that she was defying him and dismantled the computer so Trina couldn't use it. He told Trina she would have to figure something else out. Trina switched from the computer to the TV, and in no time, her mother realized what she was doing and told her father, who decided to "cut the cable" so Trina could have a better, more enriching summer. Trina's mother told her she had to have a plan away from the house every day.

Trina was upset, sullen, depressed, and moody. On her own, she was unable to improve the situation. Finally her parents decided to enroll her in a sports camp, and even though Trina objected and balked, to their amazement, she actually enjoyed the camp and seemed to be in better spirits. Based on this experience, her parents decided that Trina needed a bit more direction than they had been providing. Even though she was a very mature twelve-year-old, she was unable to create a summer plan that was good for her without their help.

house some of the time. Sometimes you can work a trade with another family so the kids have a place to play where a grown-up is around.

3. If you have to leave the kids with a sitter, tell the sitter about the routines instead of expecting the sitter to work things out with the kids. Don't expect older kids to baby-sit

younger ones without pay or having a choice in the matter. Be frank with the kids about your need to work and ask them to look out for each other.

4. Even though it may be difficult, it is important to spend some time with the kids when you get home from work and before doing chores—just to let them know you are glad to see them and enjoy hearing how their day has been. Make clear to them that this is not complaint time but sharing time.

5. Plan some special outings and traditions that are "for summer only" for you and the kids.

Life Skills Children Can Learn

Children can learn that they can entertain themselves or just feel bored. They can learn that just because they're on vacation doesn't mean they can forget all their responsibilities around the house.

Parenting Pointers

1. With so many parents working, summer vacation is not what it used to be. Many children need a break from school but don't have opportunities to use this time productively. Planning ahead for productive use of time—including rest time—is important.

2. Some children become depressed during summer vacation for lack of things to do. Others handle their boredom by getting involved in unhealthy activities, such as joining a gang. Children need a productive focus to avoid these pitfalls.

Swearing/ Foul Language

"I have two sons, aged six and three years old. My younger son has begun to call people names like 'You poopy diaper' and 'You dodo head.' He also yells that he doesn't like me or whoever is trying to discipline him. Both kids have attended the same child care since they were infants, but I never had this problem with the older one.

"We try giving him a hug and explaining that that is not nice and our family does not talk that way. He usually pulls away and continues yelling that he doesn't like us. We've also tried following up with a short time-out period, but it hasn't helped. Help, please!"

Understanding Your Child, Yourself, and the Situation

Whether dealing with children who swear to copy their little playmates and startle the adults around them, or with children who use foul language to test their power and/or to seek belonging and significance among their peers, responding calmly, instead of reacting with horror, could confine this phase to a brief interlude.

Swearing and the use of foul language have become very commonplace in so many arenas of life (the media and with adults) that it is very important to teach children the difference between respectful and disrespectful behavior.

Suggestions

1. Swearwords usually get an impressive response. Rather than expressing dismay or anger, simply state that such language is inappropriate because it is disrespectful. Sometimes it helps to designate a place in the house or outside where a child may run through his list of swearwords and then return to the common rooms when he's finished.

2. Be kind and firm with preschool children. Say, "We do not use those words in our home." Walk the child who has cursed to another room, and invite her to return when she will use acceptable words. Ignoring inappropriate language fails to give young children guidelines for their behavior.

3. Another possibility is to do the unexpected: When very young children use garbled swearwords or bathroom language ("poo-poo head"), enter into a silly word game: "Pow pow, put put, pum pum." They will quickly forget about the original inappropriate words and have fun alliterating sounds or making up nonsensical words.

4. Use your sense of humor. If you really know that your child doesn't understand the words as much as the reaction, give him a different reaction. When your child calls you "dodo head," say, "You Mickey Mouse" or some other nonsensical phrase that is not disrespectful. He will probably try harder to get the old reaction and will escalate his name calling. Just keep coming back with, "you petunia," and so on. Eventually, he will give up. You might both end up giggling.

5. When children swear, let them know how this affects you: "I feel uncomfortable when you swear, and I would appreciate it if you would choose another word to describe how you feel."

6. With small children, diffuse the situation with humor. Become a tickle monster and say, "Here comes the tickle monster to tickle little boys until they say nice things." Some people may think this rewards the "misbehavior." This may not be so, if the purpose was to shock you. If it doesn't help stop the behavior, try another suggestion.

7. When swearing comes from anger or upset, validate their feelings. "I can see that you are very angry. This must be very hard

for you." Or, "Sounds like you are really angry. You sound very upset. It is frustrating when we don't get what we want." Wait until later to discuss more appropriate ways of expressing feelings if you or your child need time to cool off. Otherwise, say, "It's fine to feel angry, but please express it by saying 'I'm angry' instead of swearing."

8. Practice mutual respect: "I respect you, and I want to hear what you have to say. I respect myself, and I want to hear what you have to say without the swearing."

9. Decide what you will do. When your child swears, you could decide to leave the room without saying a word. Actions usually speak louder than words. Later, during a family meeting or a calm time, you might discuss the issue further (see "Planning Ahead to Prevent Future Problems," item 2).

Planning Ahead to Prevent Future Problems

1. Encourage your children to share the impact that swearing has on them personally. Hearing other family members' responses has a much stronger effect on children who habitually swear than does listening to the usual lecture from parents. (However, don't be surprised if some children say that swearing doesn't bother them.)

2. Use a family meeting as a forum to discuss swearing in an open and nonjudgmental way. Help your children discern inappropriate language and its consequences by asking such questions as "How does your grandmother feel about swearing?" "What happens when you swear at school?" Then let the children decide on solutions and rules that are respectful to all concerned.

Booster Thoughts

Mrs. Stone became very concerned when her teenager started to swear at home. She decided to count the number of times he used improper language around her. She then told him how many times he used certain words and told him she would continue to count them. She shared, "I have found that he is more conscious of his use of swearwords and they have decreased in the past week. I think that it was a matter of unawareness rather than disrespect here at our home."

3. Children may swear to gain status with their peers or for its shock value with adults. Often parents focus on the behavior and forget about the belief behind it. Be aware of the four mistaken goals of misbehavior (see Part 1). Children may not resort to swearing if they have positive ways to get attention, to have power, to deal with hurt feelings, and to get help when they feel like giving up.

4. Be aware of your own use of language around children. They are very sensitive to double standards.

5. Acknowledge that the use of certain swearwords is a way to express strong feelings. During a family meeting, brainstorm for acceptable sounds or words that express intensity of feeling.

6. Sometimes children use words without understanding their meaning. Ask your child if he knows what the word means. Give the meaning and ask if that is what the child really intends to convey. Teach your children that the use of certain words borders on sexual harassment and racial defamation. Engage them in a discussion about why this is unacceptable.

7. If family members want to help each other cut down on swearing, make a deal that each time a person uses a swear word he has to put a quarter in a jar. When the jar is full, go out for ice cream together.

Life Skills Children Can Learn

Children can learn awareness of the effects their behavior has on others. They can learn acceptable and respectful ways to express themselves.

Parenting Pointers

1. It is important to teach children that there is a difference between what they feel and what they do. Help them find acceptable ways to express their feelings instead of telling them they shouldn't feel that way.

2. Be aware of the impact of television and movies. Monitor the exposure your children have to the media (especially when they are young) and engage them in discussions about the difference between respectful and disrespectful behavior that is portrayed in the media (especially as they get older).

3. Don't expect anything to work after just one try. Modeling respect is the best way to teach it—over and over and over. Remember that children learn more from your model than from your words. Consider that these suggestions model respect instead of retaliation.

4. Preschoolers do not have effective communication skills and problem-solving skills. When they feel frustrated, they often revert to "misbehavior." See this as an opportunity to teach them appropriate behavior—and be patient while they learn. It takes time and maturity—and the opportunity to practice skills.

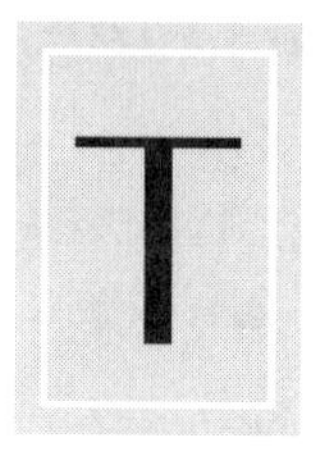

Talk, Refuses to

"My eleven-year-old child won't talk to me. I try to show him I'm interested in him when he comes home from school by asking him questions about his day. I usually get one-word responses: 'Fine.' 'Nothing.' 'Yeah.' 'Nah.' 'Chill.' If I'm lucky, I get three words: 'I don't know.' He used to talk to me. Now I think he hates me."

Understanding Your Child, Yourself, and the Situation

You have a normal preadolescent child. He doesn't hate you, but he hates the *inquisition.* This is what questioning seems like to kids this age. Some of their reasons include protecting their suddenly precious privacy; fear of your disapproval; inner turmoil as they try to sort out what they think, feel, and want; and shifting their loyalty from family to friends. Sometimes younger children don't listen because they have learned that parents don't mean what they say until they yell. Others don't listen because parents are too controlling, and not listening is a passive way to have some power. Some kids may be introverts and will never be big talkers. Accepting kids unconditionally is crucial at this uncertain time of their lives.

Suggestions

1. With teens and preteens, don't take it personally. Know that it is normal and that if you learn good listening skills, it may pass.

2. If you are yelling, stop. Speak with dignity and respect. Don't say it unless you mean it, and if you mean it, follow through.

3. Another possibility is to quit talking and try sign language or notes.

4. Just hang out and be around while your child is home. Pretty soon, you'll probably get some conversation if you can refrain from asking any questions.

Planning Ahead to Prevent Future Problems

1. Sometime during each evening, invite your child to sit with you on the couch "because I need some time just to be with you." Don't ask questions. Allow your child to feel your unconditional love and acceptance.

2. Have regular family meetings where kids have an opportunity to learn communication and problem-solving skills based on mutual respect.

3. Learning good listening skills starts with getting into the child's world. When your

child does talk, try to understand what he is saying instead of trying to mold his thinking with disapproving looks or lectures.

4. Become a closet listener. This means being around without letting anyone know you are listening. Just hang out where your kids are and keep your mouth shut. One mother sits on the edge of the tub in the morning while her daughter is getting ready for school. She doesn't ask any questions. Before long, her daughter is babbling about her life. A father puts his paper down when his son comes into the room and says, "Hi." He keeps his paper down and resists asking questions. Sometimes his son plops down on the couch and they enjoy silent companionship. Sometimes his son starts talking about his day. Another possibility is to be there with cookies after school and don't ask questions. Driving the car pool is another great opportunity to just be available to listen.

5. Many children stop talking because parents respond too quickly with lectures. Learn to listen with your lips closed. Limit your responses to "Uh-huh. Hmm." You'll be surprised how your children sometimes go on and on when they feel listened to.

6. Be curious. When you do open your lips, ask only the kinds of questions that invite more talking: "I'm not sure I understand what you mean." "Could you tell me more?" "What example could you give me of that?" "When was the last time that happened?" An attitude of true curiosity is essential.

7. To encourage even more sharing, ask, "What else is there that you can think of?" When you think your child has said everything there is to say, this question will often get to a deeper issue that she may not have been aware of until invited to explore it. (This is a great way to improve communication between spouses, too.)

Booster Thoughts

Sam resisted participating in "talks" with his mother, a marriage, family, and child counselor who specialized in adolescent counseling. His mom complained, "Sam, other teenagers enjoy talking with me and are willing to pay for the privilege."

Sam pointed out, "If you would take me to your office and talk with me the way you talk with them, I would probably enjoy it too."

All Mom could say was, "Touché!"

Life Skills Children Can Learn

Children can learn that they are loved unconditionally. When they feel like talking, they are listened to, taken seriously, and validated for their thoughts, feelings, and ideas. They have a safe place to grow, change, and explore who they are.

Parenting Pointers

1. It is essential to the development of healthy self-esteem that children have their thoughts, feelings, and ideas listened to and taken seriously—even when their parents don't agree with them.

2. Children will listen to you after they feel listened to.

Tattling

"What can be done about children who tattle? It seems like I spend half my day getting involved in settling problems tattlers bring me."

Understanding Your Child, Yourself, and the Situation

Children tattle because they lack the skills to solve their own problems or because they feel discouraged and seek undue attention by trying to prove how "good" they are. Often adults then jump in and try to fix the situation because they think that the children are incapable of figuring out what to do. Instead of getting irritated about tattling, see it as an opportunity to teach your child important life skills.

Suggestions

1. Listen respectfully, with your mouth closed, without fixing the problem. To avoid fixing does not mean abandonment. When adults just listen, some children think of a solution on their own.

2. Use reflective listening to let the tattler know you understand her feelings: "I'll bet you're really angry with _____." You don't have to do anything else to fix the situation.

3. You might ask the tattling child, "Why are you telling me?" or "How is that a problem for you?" Then quietly watch the response. This offers some children an opportunity to think about their reason and to realize they don't have a good one or that it isn't their problem.

4. Take this opportunity to teach your child problem-solving skills. You might ask, "What ideas do you have to solve that problem?" or "Would you like to put the problem on the family-meeting agenda so the whole family can brainstorm for a solution?"

5. Sometimes it is enough to show faith in the child. Say, "I'm sure you can work it

out." Then walk away to demonstrate your faith.

6. Assemble the children who are involved in the problem, including the tattler. Tell them, "I can see there is a problem, and I have faith in you kids to work it out. Here's a place you can talk." You can sit quietly and listen to them discuss solutions, or you can walk away and ask them to find you and tell you how they worked it out.

7. If the kids are arguing, let them know that until they find a solution to their problem, they can't continue doing whatever the argument is about, such as watching television.

Planning Ahead to Prevent Future Problems

1. Change your thinking about tattling. As your children get older, you may wish they would tell you more about what is going on in their lives. Now is the time to let them know you are interested in their concerns and will help them learn skills instead of putting them down or turning them away.

Booster Thoughts

A young mother was taking a parenting class and decided that when kids tattled, she would let them know that "I have faith in you to solve the problem." A few weeks later, she invited her nieces and nephew over to play with her kids. One of the nieces averaged six tattles an hour. Mom decided to try out her new skills and said to her niece, "I'm sure you kids can work it out." Her niece looked at her like she was the meanest, most disgusting person in the world and stomped off to tell the other kids, "Auntie says you have to stop being mean to me." The other kids laughed and continued teasing her. She left the room and played by herself for about ten minutes.

An hour later, the woman overheard this conversation:

"I'm going to tell Auntie on you."

"I wouldn't bother. She'll just say, 'You kids can work it out,' so we may as well work it out."

"Okay. Let's take turns picking out a toy."

"Okay. I like that idea."

2. If you have a kid who is a constant tattler, you might tell her that you love her and have faith that she can solve the problem. Take time to discuss with her what she can do when kids aren't behaving the way she thinks they should.

3. Don't put older kids in charge of their younger siblings. The responsibility may be too great and they may deal with problems by tattling.

4. Place an agenda on the refrigerator so children have a place to write their concerns. Then have regular family meetings so your children can practice looking for solutions instead of blame.

Life Skills Children Can Learn

Children can learn that they can talk to their parents about anything because they won't experience disappointment, punishment, or put-downs. They learn that they can work out problems or leave the scene if they don't like the way someone else is behaving. It's okay to be upset, and the family meeting is a good place to talk about the things that upset them.

Parenting Pointers

1. If you want to encourage a discouraged child, you need to find ways to give recognition without reinforcing the misbehavior. "I love you and have faith in you to solve your problems" is a good message.

2. Most kids can work out problems themselves more quickly and creatively than they can if a well-meaning adult gets involved. Step back and give kids a chance to see what they can do on their own before getting involved.

Television and Video Games

"My children would play video games or watch television all day if I let them. They get angry when I tell them it's time to turn the equipment off."

Understanding Your Child, Yourself, and the Situation

Television and video games aren't the bad guys, but they can become a real problem if parents don't help their children use discretion when using them. Television and video games can be entertaining and informative and can help children develop many transferable skills. It is easy for television viewing and playing video games to get out of hand if they are used as babysitters or background noise. Watching television is a passive activity and can become addictive if limits aren't set and other, more active interests developed.

Suggestions

1. You may not want your children to see certain shows on television, so it is up to you to create guidelines. As your children get older, they need to be part of this planning process.

2. Give young children limited choices, such as watching one show or watching for two hours a day. You might say, "You can watch TV before dinner or after dinner" or "If you watch TV in the morning, you can't watch before bed."

3. Instead of censoring a show you don't like, sit with your children and watch it with them. Talk to the kids about what they think about what they see.

4. Don't overreact to a television show after watching one scene. Talk with your children about why they like a particular show.

5. Discuss commercials with your children and explain advertising to them.

6. Television viewing may run its course. Just because your children enjoy watching at one time in their lives doesn't mean this is a lifetime pattern.

7. Many families have discovered the satisfaction of life without TV after the initial shock of removing it from their homes. Families who decide to "cut the cable" seldom add TV back into their lives.

Planning Ahead to Prevent Future Problems

1. If you watch television excessively, it may be hard to convince your children that too much television isn't good for them. On the other hand, if you keep the television in a room with a door, it is okay for other family members to watch and to ask the children to stay out of the television room, except during the times you have previously agreed on.

2. Use the family meeting to discuss television viewing. Look at the newspaper or *TV Guide* to help your children plan the shows they wish to watch during the week. Have them circle the shows and leave the guide on the television. If it looks like the kids are watching indiscriminately, ask them to show you the guide to see if this is a show they circled.

3. If you think your children are watching too much violence on television, it is okay to tell them why it is not a good idea. Help them find more active ways to let out their aggression.

Booster Thoughts

For the first time in history, a generation of young Americans is receiving its impressions about life passively from the media rather than from hands-on involvement with relevant activities. Generally, this perception of "reality" is deficient in teaching the skills of patience, personal initiative, hard work, and deferred gratification. On the contrary, results are achieved within a half hour by heroes who are pseudopsychopathic rebels and achieve their objectives by breaking bones. On television, our youth sees self-medication, drinking, casual sexuality, acts of violence, and miraculous solutions to problems.

It is important to focus on the actual content of shows children watch on television, sometimes for hours at a time. Essentially, there are five premises portrayed over and over.

The first premise is that drinking or substance abuse is the primary activity in productive social relationships. *The Breakfast Club,* an immensely popular movie several years ago, gave the clear impression that even the most intelligent young people could not have a good time until someone brought out marijuana and alcohol.

The second premise is that self-medication is the primary means of eradicating pain, discomfort, and boredom.

4. Help your children make a list of activities they enjoy so that when they are bored they can find something else to do instead of flipping on the television (see also *Boredom*).

5. Talk with your kids about the addictive qualities of television and video games, so they know why you are concerned and want to limit their use.

6. Let the children know they need to set up a system for sharing video games or picking television channels. If they fight over this, either turn off the equipment and tell them they can try again later or you take over the choosing until they have come up with a workable system for sharing.

7. Try establishing a day of the week or a month when no one in the family watches

The third premise is that casual sexuality is the accepted norm. Time and again, this premise is demonstrated in the ease with which people flow in and out of relationships and beds.

The fourth premise conveyed by television is that acts of violence and lawlessness are acceptable solutions to problems. Many television "heroes" would think nothing of breaking, entering, and taking the property of someone else in order to achieve some goal of their own.

The fifth premise is acted out primarily in commercials. It says that patience, deferred gratification, personal initiative, and hard work are unacceptable activities to be avoided through drinking, self-medication, or the use of some product or service. For example, a commercial for a familiar coffee suggests that any stressful, real-life issue or situation, such as the lack of intimacy and warmth in a marriage, can be cured immediately by the coffee in question.[53]

53. From H. Stephen Glenn and Jane Nelsen, *Raising Self-Reliant Children in a Self-Indulgent World* (Rocklin, CA: Prima Publishing, 1988), 42–43.

television and see what the family can learn from the experience.

Life Skills Children Can Learn

Children can learn how to plan ahead and think through using television and video games instead of falling into habits of indiscriminate viewing. Children can develop nonabusive habits that can help them when they are dealing with other potential substances of abuse.

Parenting Pointers

1. Turn the television off during meals and talk with your children instead.

2. Don't expect children to follow agreements concerning television viewing and game playing when you aren't at home to monitor them. If you think they are badly abusing their agreements, disconnect the television until they are ready to follow their commitments.

Temper Tantrums

(See also *Angry Child* and *Upset Child*)

"What can a parent do when a child throws herself on the floor kicking and screaming—especially if it happens in a public place?"

Understanding Your Child, Yourself, and the Situation

Temper tantrums can be infuriating and embarrassing. Sometimes, children have tantrums because they are tired and parents are dragging them to places they don't have the resources and skills to handle. Other times, it helps to remember that your child's behavior may have a purpose. Children may throw temper tantrums to get an adult's attention, to get their own way, to hurt back if they feel hurt, or to get others to leave them alone. Temper tantrums are an emotional display. The child may feel angry or frustrated or vindictive—or even playful. We are most effective when we deal with the tantrum and then later deal with the feeling behind the tantrum.

Suggestions

1. One way to deal with a temper tantrum is to simply ignore it. Stand quietly and wait until it's over.

2. Another possibility is to shut your mouth and act. One way to do this is to kindly and firmly pick up the child or take the child by the hand and leave the public place. If you take the child's hand and she pulls in the other direction, do not resist. While still keeping your mouth shut, let yourself be pulled in her direction until she stops pulling. Then start walking (still holding her hand, kindly and firmly) away from the public place. Keep repeating this every time your child resists. It looks like a seesaw, with you leaning in the child's direction until she stops resisting, then pulling in your direction until she resists, then back in her direction until she stops resisting. When you don't engage in the power struggle, your child will usually stop resisting after three to five times of this seesaw.

3. With some children, it helps to hold them and comfort them when they have a

tantrum. Say, "It's okay to be upset. It happens to all of us. I'm here and I love you."

4. It's okay to say no to your child, and it's okay for her to be angry. You don't have to fix it. It is healthy for children to learn that they can deal with their emotions. They will do so more quickly if parents don't feed the emotional fires with arguments and lectures.

5. Once the tantrum is over, say nothing about it. If your child is using a tantrum for emotional blackmail, she will soon give up if you don't buy into it.

6. Follow through by deciding what you will do instead of what you will try to make your child do. This is effective only after preplanning has taken place (see "Planning Ahead to Prevent Future Problems," item 5 below).

Planning Ahead to Prevent Future Problems

1. Ask your child at a calmer time if she would like to learn some other ways to handle frustration. Teach her to tell you in words how she feels instead of using an emotional display.

2. Pay attention to ways you may be setting your child up to have a tantrum. Most kids don't start off with a tantrum. You may be arguing, demanding, controlling, and fighting with your child until she throws a tantrum in exasperation.

3. Ask your child what she would like you to do when she is having a tantrum. Do this at a time when you can discuss it calmly. Give choices, like "Would you like a hug, would you like me to just wait until you're over it, or would you like to go to your comfort place (positive time-out) until you feel better?" Children are more receptive to an intervention that they have chosen in advance.

4. Role-play before going to a public place. (Three- to six-year-olds will understand it better as the game "Let's Pretend.") Describe the behavior that is expected and let your children pretend you are in the public place and that they are doing what is expected. Let them have fun role-playing a temper tantrum while you role-play what you will do. It is also fun to reverse roles. You play the child who is having the tantrum and let your child play what the parent will do.

5. Set up a time for training shortly after you have played "Let's Pretend." Plan to go somewhere in public where you are willing to follow through immediately with the agreed-upon suggestion. If the tantrum starts, follow through immediately without anger.

6. Decide what you will do and inform your child in advance. For example, you may decide that you will take the child to the car and patiently read a book until she has settled down and tells you that she is ready to try again. Or you may decide that

you will go home immediately. Whatever you decide, be sure to follow through with dignity and respect. In other words, keep your mouth shut and act. The only thing you could say that would be effective is, "You can try again when you are ready" (if you are in the car) or "You can try again tomorrow or next week" (if you have returned home). It might be better to wait until everyone is calm to make either comment.

7. Put the problem of tantrums on the family-meeting agenda and let your children brainstorm for solutions about what to do. After you have a list of suggestions, let the child who typically has tantrums choose the suggestion she feels will help her the most.

Life Skills Children Can Learn

Children can learn that tantrums and emotional blackmail won't get them what they want and that there are more appropriate ways to express their feelings. They can learn that it is okay to have their feelings and that you love and accept them even if they are having a fit.

Booster Thoughts

A skilled tantrum manager once compared the stages of emotional outbursts to other climactic experiences:

- Foreplay or budding
- Climax or peaking
- Postcoital depression or afterglow

If we join the experience during foreplay, we often help heighten it. If we join during climax, no one is in control of where things are going. If we wait for postcoital depression, it is unlikely that energy is left for a repeat performance.

When someone is yelling at you, listen quietly and show your interest nonverbally. When the explosive peak is past, say, "Is there anything else I need to know to understand your position?" or "Okay, what do we need to do about this?"[54]

---

54. From H. Stephen Glenn, *How to Disarm the Male Chauvinist Pig* (Bloomington, IN: Indiana University, 1969), handbook.

Parenting Pointers

1. The more you involve your children in decisions that affect them, the less they feel the need to use tantrums to have a say.

2. Some kids (and some adults, too) like to bluster before they accept the inevitable. It's their style and doesn't hurt anyone. Once the blustering (or tantrum) is done, often they will cheerfully do what needs to be done. Keep your sail out of their wind while they bluster, and it won't rock your boat.

Toilet Training

"I hear so many conflicting ideas about toilet training. What is the Positive Discipline way?"

Understanding Your Child, Yourself, and the Situation

Toilet training has become an issue that is blown out of proportion in our society. It can be the origin of feelings of guilt and shame, power struggles, revenge cycles, bids for undue attention, and competition between parents. If we didn't worry about it, our children would still become toilet trained in due time just because they would soon want to copy what everyone else does.

Suggestions

1. Wait until after your child is two and a half years old before you even start toilet training—unless he begs to start sooner.

2. When introducing your child to toilet training, get a small potty chair that he can manage by himself. At first, let him sit on it for as long or short a period of time as he wants without having to do anything.

3. During warm weather, take your child and the potty chair out in the backyard. Let him play naked while you sit and read a book or simply watch. As soon as he starts to urinate, put him on the potty chair. Say, "Way to go. That is where you are supposed to urinate." You may have to do this often before you child learns the socially appropriate place to urinate and defecate.

4. Lighten up and make toilet training fun. One parent emptied the toilet bowl and painted a target in the bowl. His son could hardly wait to try to hit the bull's eye.

5. When you introduce training pants, do not humiliate or shame your child when he has an accident. Don't put him back in diapers. Simply help him clean up. Say, "It's okay. You can keep trying. You will soon learn to use the potty chair."

6. Avoid rewards and praise, like stars on a chart or candy treats. Instead, use encouraging statements, such as the ones above. Rewards can become more important to your child than learning socially appropriate behavior. It is okay for others to make deals with your children. (See the "Booster Thoughts" below.) When parents make deals, it can sound too much like a bribe or an invitation for a power struggle.

Planning Ahead to Prevent Future Problems

1. Keep using diapers (without even talking about toilet training) until your child asks to stop. You might be surprised how soon this will happen if your child is exposed to other children his age who are not wearing diapers.

Booster Thoughts

Lavonne was a precocious two-year-old who often visited her grandparents. Grandma was of the school that children should be toilet trained before they are two. Lavonne's mom thought that if children aren't using the toilet by the time they are three, it's time to worry. Instead of arguing with her daughter, Grandma went straight to Lavonne and told her, "If you use the toilet, Grandma will take you shopping and buy you beautiful ruffled panties to wear." Lavonne's mom knew this was going on and chose to ignore it.

When Lavonne was two and a half, her parents told her they would be going on a long trip and that she wouldn't see her grandparents for quite some time. Several days before departure, the family was visiting Grandma to say good-bye. Lavonne motioned for Grandma to follow her into the bathroom.

"Look, Grandma," she said, "now I go in the toilet. Let's go shopping."

Grandma took Lavonne to the nearby mall immediately and bought her six pairs of ruffled pants. Lavonne's mom took a three-month supply of diapers on the trip and threw them all away after several weeks when she realized Lavonne had trained herself to cash in on the shopping spree and was done with diapers forever.

2. If your child is still not toilet trained by the time she is three years old, be sure to get a doctor's evaluation to see if there is a physical problem.

3. If there is not a physical problem, you may be involved in a power struggle. Guess who will win? One thing you can't control is a child's elimination functions. It takes two to engage in a power struggle. Stop. Allow your child to experience the consequences of his choice with dignity and respect. Teach your child to change his own clothes during a calm time. When the pants get wet or soiled, kindly and firmly send your child to the bedroom to find new clothes. Then lead your child to the bathroom and ask if he would like to change alone or with you there to keep him company (do not do it for him).

4. If he refuses to use the toilet (which is unlikely if you have truly dropped the power struggle), ask "what" and "how" questions. "How does it feel to have soiled pants? What ideas do you have to solve the problem? Where are the places you can play when you have soiled pants?"

5. During a calm time (when your child is dry), brainstorm with her places she can play if she doesn't want to change her pants. Outside or in the bathroom (have some games in a drawer) might be appropriate.

6. Give a limited choice: "You can change your clothes or you can play in the places we agreed while you are wet or soiled."

7. Teach your child (age four and older) how to put soap in the washing machine and push the buttons to wash his own clothes.

8. Find a preschool where the staff is willing to handle toilet training. This can take a short time when the facility has small toilets that children can use themselves and children have many opportunities to watch each other use the toilet successfully. Many preschools also have frequent toilet routines that help children learn quickly.

Life Skills Children Can Learn

Children can discover that they can learn normal life processes in due time without guilt and shame. Mistakes are nothing more than opportunities to learn.

Parenting Pointers

1. Children face expectations they may not feel they can live up to. This is often the reason behind their misbehavior. It is frustrating to feel powerless. Children may try to prove they have power in useless ways.

2. It hurts when parents don't give unconditional love. Children may want to hurt back without realizing that is their hidden motivation. One way to hurt parents is to refuse to do what is important to them.

3. Take comfort in knowing that your child will probably be toilet trained by the time she goes to college—and even much sooner, when power struggles are eliminated. Relax and enjoy your child.

Touching Things

"I've told my seven-month-old child a hundred times to leave the TV dials alone, but he just won't listen. Slapping his hand doesn't work. What should I do?"

Understanding Your Child, Yourself, and the Situation

It is normal for children to want to touch things as they explore their world. It is a shame to punish children for doing what is normal. This does not mean they should be allowed to touch anything they want. It does mean we need to find other ways, instead of punishment, to teach children not to touch things.

It is a mistake to think that toddlers know they should not touch things after we have told them "a hundred times." They may know touching things creates a response (often negative) from adults, but they don't really understand why. Toddlers cannot understand the kind of abstract reasoning that states that "physical objects, convenience, and what others think are more important than you are."

Suggestions

1. If you mean it, say it once; if you say it, act. "Stop playing with the TV dials now." Then remove your child if he doesn't stop, or put your child in a playpen or another room that has been childproofed.

Booster Thoughts

"We childproofed our home when Brett was a baby. I packed up my crystal collection and put it away for a while. As he got older, I would think about putting it out again, but there was always some reason not to—clumsy walking at two, rough-and-tumble play at four, then the baseballs, footballs, and basketballs. When he went away to college, I put a few pieces out on the bookcase. My husband broke one while rushing to get the dictionary during a heated Scrabble game. I broke another while dusting. Now we have grandchildren. I think a better term for it would be 'people proofing.' If you want to enjoy your fragile valuables, put them in a glass-front case—even if the kids are grown and gone."[55]

55. From Barbara R. and David F. Bjorklund, *Parents Book of Discipline* (New York: Ballantine Books, 1990), 33.

2. Establish eye contact with your child as you talk. It is ineffective to yell at him from another room. Let him know he can try again later. (For small children, thirty seconds later might be enough.)

3. Give a choice: "Do you want to stop playing with the TV dials, or do you want to be in your playpen?" If the child keeps playing with the TV, he has chosen to be in his playpen, so act.

4. Use distraction. Kindly and firmly remove children from what they can't do and show them what they can do instead. For instance, say, "The TV dials are not a toy, but you can play with the dials on your busy box toy."

5. Stand up before you speak so your child knows you are ready for action and not just making noise. The action should be kind and firm—perhaps to remove the child or to show the child another activity.

Planning Ahead to Prevent Future Problems

1. Childproofing a house can cut down on nagging and increase optimal brain development. Put valuables out of reach, put covers over electrical outlets, and stabilize items your child can damage or get hurt on.

2. Set up a special play area where it's safe and okay for your child to play, such as a playpen or a kitchen cupboard filled with interesting things your little one can pull out and leave all over the floor. Long periods of confinement to a playpen or highchair is not healthy for toddlers. Put baby gates in front of areas you don't want children to enter.

Life Skills Children Can Learn

Children can learn that some things are out of bounds and they are treated with respect as they learn what they are. They can't manipulate their parents, because their parents mean what they say and follow through with kind and firm action. Their parents respect their needs with childproofing to make exploration safe, and parents require that children respect their needs by not touching certain things.

Parenting Pointers

1. Many parents feel their children should learn not to touch things, and they refuse to make changes in the decor as children are added to the family. This tells children indirectly that their needs aren't important and that they are in the way.

2. When children know adults mean what they say, they usually listen and do what needs to be done.

Toys, Friends Won't Help Pick Up

(See also *Toys, Won't Pick Up*)

"What should I do when my child has friends who come to the house, get every toy out on the floor, and then leave the room in shambles?"

Understanding Your Child, Yourself, and the Situation

Not cleaning up immediately after playing is normal. Ask any parent on the block. See it as an opportunity to teach the children responsibility and problem-solving skills.

Suggestions

1. For children aged two to six, say, "The mess in your room needs to be cleaned up before you can have another friend over. Would you like to clean it up yourself, or would you like my help?"

2. For children aged seven to twelve, say, "The mess in your room needs to be cleaned up. Would you like to clean it up yourself, or do you want to invite your friend to help you?"

3. If some of your child's belongings disappear after a friend has been playing at your house, help your child call the friend's house and ask if he or she accidentally picked them up. Let the family know

Booster Thoughts

One mother tells about her experience: "In our family, the kids learned early that if I said something, I meant it, so they didn't bother testing me. When their friends came to play and refused to help with cleanup, I could hear the kids saying from the next room, 'You may as well start cleaning. She's the kind of mother who means it when she says it's time to clean up. She'll just come in and wait until we're done before she lets us leave the room.'

"Occasionally, one of their friends would insist on testing the limits. Then my kids would come in and ask me if I would help them get their friend moving. I would sit in the center of the room and pick up one toy at a time, handing it to the recalcitrant friend. I'd say, 'Who wants to put this one away? Thanks so much for putting it away. How about this toy? Who wants to do this one?' I wouldn't leave until the last toy was cleaned up."

you will be happy to stop by to get the "lost" toy.

Planning Ahead to Prevent Future Problems

1. During a family meeting, ask your kids to brainstorm with you to see how many ideas you can all come up with in advance to deal with this situation.

2. For ages two to six, put each toy or set of toys (especially those with small pieces) in separate plastic drawstring bags. Teach your child that she and her friends can have one or two bags at a time. The toy they are playing with must be picked up and put back in the bag before they can have another one.

3. Tell your child and his friend what is expected in advance and give them a choice: "You can agree to leave the room as clean as it is now when you're through playing, or you can choose to stay out of the room."

4. If they agree to clean up their mess, help them come up with a plan to accomplish it: "How much time do you think you will need to clean up? Do you want to set a timer, or would you like me to tell you when it is time to clean up?" Before your child's friend leaves, check the room and wait in the doorway while the kids clean up if it isn't satisfactory.

Life Skills Children Can Learn

Children can learn that shared privileges mean shared responsibility. They can learn to plan ahead with their parents' help to make sure their friends cooperate.

Parenting Pointers

1. Look for solutions instead of blame.

2. Your children may be quite responsible about cleanup, but their friends may not have to do it at home. Help your children involve their friends in the process instead of assuming it is up to your children to work it out alone.

Toys, Won't Pick Up

(See also *Toys, Friends Won't Help Pick Up*)

"It is a constant battle to get my child to pick up his toys. Any suggestions?"

Understanding Your Child, Yourself, and the Situation

Responsibility is not instinctive in young children. It must be taught. It doesn't help when parents become angry or frustrated over a behavior that is normal for that age.

It doesn't help to punish or to be permissive and do for children what they can learn to do for themselves. It does help when parents take time for training to teach the skills children need to learn.

Suggestions

1. Do not clean up the mess yourself.

2. Do not verbally abuse your child by yelling, threatening, or putting him down.

3. When children are preschool age, clean up with them.

4. As your child gets older, take him to the scene of the mess and ask, "What do you need to do to take care of this problem?" After a while, all you'll have to do is point with a knowing grin on your face.

5. Say, "As soon as you pick up your toys, we will go to the park." This is not meant as a bribe or a reward; it is to teach the child a sense of order and first things first—that when the work is done quickly, there is time for something fun. (Don't offer this choice unless it is okay with you not to go to the park if the toys aren't picked up.)

6. Honor your child's system for cleanup. Some children like to put the puzzle pieces in with the Legos and the toy figures in with the baseball cards. Do not insist that the toys are organized according to your standards.

Planning Ahead to Prevent Future Problems

1. Tell your children what you will do instead of what you are going to make them do: "When you don't pick up your toys, I will. When I pick them up, you will lose the privilege of having them for one week." (With younger children, one or two days may be long enough.) If they don't miss their toys, you might consider donating some of them to Goodwill, the Salvation Army, or a local child care center.

2. Follow through on what you have decided to do in a firm and friendly manner without lectures. When your children know you will follow through and they will lose the toys you pick up for a week, they will move quickly when you ask, "Do you want to pick up your toys, or do you want me to?"

3. As the children get older, plan regular times to go through their toys with them and let them help you pick out some toys that they no longer play with and are willing to donate to a charity.

4. If your child wants a new toy, let him save his money to pay even a small portion

of the purchase price. If he has put forth some effort, he is more likely to take care of his investment.

5. Create a space in the house other than your child's bedroom where she can play with her toys. If her toys are left lying around the house, you can expect her to return them to the toy area or the bedroom. Children do not always want to be alone in the bedroom when they play with their toys.

6. During a family meeting, invite your children to help plan solutions to the problem.

Life Skills Children Can Learn

Children can learn that taking care of their possessions is part of having them.

Parenting Pointers

1. Your attitude and the way you do things are more important than what you do. A firm and friendly attitude invites cooperation. A disrespectful attitude invites resistance or unhealthy compliance.

2. If your child doesn't miss the toys you pick up, it could be that the problem is yours. Perhaps you have purchased too many toys so your child won't be deprived. Stop buying so many toys.

Booster Thoughts

When Courtney, age six, went to spend a week with his grandparents, his mother decided this would be a good time to repaint his room and clean out the toy shelves. She purchased new furniture, cleaned out all the toys he no longer played with, removed three rocks from his collection of rocks from the backyard, painted, and reorganized. She was so pleased and thought Courtney would be too.

When Courtney came home, he went in his room and came out crying. "Mom, I won't have anything to play with now. You threw all my toys away! (He still had over fifty toys.) And Mom, what did you do with those rocks from the backyard? I can't find them anywhere."

So often when we think we are doing our children a favor, we may be frustrating them because we neglect to get their input.

Traveling with Kids

"We want to take our children on vacations with us, but they are very difficult to deal with. Are there some ways to make vacations with children more fun and manageable?"

Understanding Your Child, Yourself, and the Situation

Vacations are times for creating family memories. They can be a nightmare or a lot of fun, depending on the parents' attitude and the amount of advance planning. Children don't stop being children just because they are on vacation. Their needs must be considered to have a successful vacation. Adults often expect their children to magically act like grown-ups while on vacation and are disappointed when the kids still behave like kids. Many adults have a picture of what a vacation should be, and they may be both surprised and disappointed to find that other family members have a very different picture. It is important to match pictures of their expectations ahead of time to improve the experience.

Suggestions

1. When you take children on a vacation, there are still chores to be done and plans to be made. The more you involve the kids in the planning, the more it will be a vacation for everyone. Use the family meeting to discuss vacation plans, such as packing their clothes, packing the car, chores, and what each family member wants to do on the trip.

2. Let young children help pack their suitcases or even pack them without your help if they are able. You may wish to make a checklist with them or tell them about the type of clothing that will be suitable for the activities you plan to do and the weather conditions.

3. Car trips can be more enjoyable if you rotate the seating arrangements. Leave plenty of extra time for frequent stops to run and play at a rest area or to pull over and wait quietly for children to settle down if they are fighting or getting too rowdy.

4. Don't push it until everyone is tired and cranky. Stop early and enjoy some space from each other and time to unwind.

5. Wrap several inexpensive items, such as a coloring book and crayons, a card game, a pack of gum, stickers, and small puzzles. Tell the kids they can open a new surprise every hour. Prepare a surprise snack.

6. At the end of the trip, ask each family member what was most special for him or her. Let everyone help put photos in a trip album.

7. Arrange for the kids to spend some special time with their relatives without you being around. This may include putting your child on a plane alone to visit Grandma and Grandpa or having the rela-

Booster Thoughts

One family traveled around the country in a van for seven months when the children were four and two years old. It was a very special time once the parents learned to drive short distances and stop for the kids to play or explore. It also helped to create a routine the kids could count on. That included finding a camping spot by 4 P.M., doing something physical before going into a restaurant, having a quiet time each day, taking turns to sit with the kids, and staying extra days if another family with children was camping nearby.

The kids read books from local libraries, played with a piece of rope and sticks for hours, and made forts out of picnic tables. The family was on a limited budget, so they found fun things to do that didn't cost money, such as the going to the beach or playground, hiking, playing games around the fire, cooking together, coloring, and fishing.

Traveling with kids can be a great experience once their needs are considered.

tives looking after the kids while you have an afternoon to yourself.

Planning Ahead to Prevent Future Problems

1. Let the kids help pack a special bag to take on trips with toys they can play with on a plane or in the car. Include snacks if appropriate. You may wish to include cameras or diaries for the kids.

2. Don't just talk about taking vacations. It's discouraging to kids to just hear promises. A vacation can be a day trip to an interesting nearby attraction, an overnight to a city close by, a family camping trip, or another activity that is not as overwhelming as a week or two away from home. Sometimes just spending the night in a motel with a pool in the city you live in can be a real treat for the kids.

3. If you are flying with an infant, reserve an aisle seat and notify the airline of your need for extra help. Check as much baggage as possible, as it is a handful just to carry your child and his toys and diaper bag.

Life Skills Children Can Learn

Children can learn how special it is to take a trip with their family. They see other parts of the country or reconnect with relatives who help them feel special.

Parenting Pointers

1. It's okay to take some vacations without your children.

2. If you hate to camp, send your kids to camp or let them go camping with a neighbor while you stay at home.

3. It is not necessary to spend a lot of money to have a good time on a vacation, but it is important to make the trip special by doing things that are different from what you do at home.

Upset Child

"How can I get my child to stop getting upset at the least little thing?"

Understanding Your Child, Yourself, and the Situation

Feelings give us valuable information about who we are and what is important to us. Children need to learn that it is okay to feel whatever they feel. Acting on the feelings is a different matter, however. Feeling angry doesn't mean it is okay to hit someone. Once children have their feelings validated and have calmed down, they are usually open to appropriate solutions.

Suggestions

1. Take your child on your lap (or sit down next to her if she is over seven years of age) and ask, "Would you like to tell me about it?" Then be quiet and listen.

2. When your child has stopped talking, stifle the temptation to lecture, explain, or try to fix things for him. Ask, "Is there anything else?" This question often encourages the child to go to deeper feelings.

3. After a long enough silence that you are sure your child is through talking and feels calmer, ask, "Would you like to brainstorm with me on some solutions?" Many times there is no need to work on solutions. Your child simply needs comfort and to be listened to and taken seriously.

4. When your child feels too upset or hostile to sit on your lap or to talk, say, "You have a right to your feelings. Let me know if you want to talk about it." Then leave

Booster Thoughts

Steve Glenn was doing some research in K-Mart one day when he found a seminar in "How *Not* to Deal with Kids and Feelings" just getting under way. A thirteen-year-old, who had obviously started puberty because his feet belonged to Michael Jordan but the rest of him was in various stages of struggling to catch up, was having a negative emotional experience of some kind. His father stepped in to "help" him by saying, "Why are you angry? There's no reason for you to be upset! Why do you want to carry on like that?"

At that moment, Steve wanted to drop to his knees, replace the boy, and give the father an honest answer to his questions: "I'm angry because a frontal system passing through has upset the pressure gradient in ways that produce subtle changes in my limbic system; I ate an overabundance of highly processed starches, sugars, fats, and carbohydrates that they loaded me up with at lunchtime because they were cheap; I'm dealing with the overwhelming frustration of trying to contain those ambient calories without moving or wriggling while sitting through four hours of required classes with only four minutes in between to get to the bathroom, my locker, and the next class; and I finally came out of school with all that energy roaring through me and they put me on a bus and told me, 'Sit down, shut up, roll up the windows, or I'll tell your parents.' After I stepped off the bus with all of that still roaring through me, I had caffeine and sugar in a Pepsi and theobromine in a brownie, which went up through the inherent instability of my hypothalamus from three generations of alcoholics—which we haven't even discussed yet. That surged down and hit a massive dose of testosterone that is roaring through me getting me ready for puberty and was interrupted by a constant wall of frustration and hostility from trying to anticipate adult expectations all day. It was more than I could handle!"

Since this was too much for a thirteen-year-old to articulate (or even be aware of), what this one said was, "Because!"

The father yelled, "What do you mean, 'Because'?"

(continues)

(continued)

The boy finally said, "I don't know," and was quiet.

This taught the boy that the last thing his father wanted was a thoughtful exploration of his feelings and ways to deal with them effectively. What he really wanted was to make the boy feel dumb, bad, and inadequate for having the problem. Just remember that feelings are often very complex and not clearly understood. Many things can and do affect our feelings, even when we're not aware of them.

the room if she is being verbally abusive to you, or suggest, "You might find it helpful to go to your room or somewhere else until you feel like being around people."

Planning Ahead to Prevent Future Problems

1. Start early to teach your child that his feelings are okay by not correcting him. When he says, "I'm hungry," don't say, "No, you aren't. You just ate twenty minutes ago." Say, "I'm sorry you are hungry. I just cleaned up from lunch and I'm not willing to fix any more food right now. You can either wait until dinner, or you can choose something from the healthy snack shelf." This is respectful of the child's feelings and needs and also your own.

2. Teach children to use emotional honesty to express their feelings: "I feel _____ because _____ and I wish _____." ("I feel angry when my brother hits me because it hurts, and I wish he would stop.") Using emotional honesty does not mean others will feel the same or give us what we want, but we can respect our own feelings and desires. Emotional honesty teaches children to express their feelings and to accept that their feelings are okay.

3. Encourage children to put things they are upset about on the family-meeting agenda so the whole family can help with solutions.

Life Skills Children Can Learn

Children can learn that their feelings are important and others will listen to them and help them share their feelings. Family members can help them solve their problems. Their feelings are separate from their actions. They can experience their feelings quietly when they don't feel like sharing. Feelings are not right or wrong. They are just feelings and can give people valuable information.

Parenting Pointers

1. It is usually impossible to solve a problem at the time of conflict or upset.

2. Teach children the value of taking time out to cool off and calm down before deciding what to do. Taking time out to calm down and feel better doesn't mean it is not okay to feel what they feel.

Whining

"My child whines, and it is driving me crazy. Punishment and bribery haven't worked. Does it sound like I'm whining? I'll do worse than whine if I don't get some help!"

Understanding Your Child, Yourself, and the Situation

Children do what works. If your child is whining, he or she is getting a response from you. Oddly enough, children seem to prefer punishment and anger to no response at all. Whining is usually based on the goal of seeking undue attention. This child believes, "I belong only if you pay constant attention to me—one way or the other." For some children, it is the only method they know to get their needs met. Other children go through a whiny time and it then disappears as quickly as it started. Some of the suggestions here may seem contradictory, depending on whether they address the belief or the behavior. Choose the approach that feels best to you.

Suggestions

1. Every time your child whines, take him on your lap and say, "I bet you need a big hug." Do not say anything about the whining or what the child is whining about—just hug until you both feel better.

2. Let your child know that you love him but you can't stand whining. Tell him that if he whines you'll leave the room. You'll be happy when he stops, so you can spend time with him. Then, every time your child whines, leave the room. If your child follows, go to the bathroom, lock the door, and turn up the radio. It is more effective if

you don't say a word when you follow through on what you said you would do. Kind and firm actions speak louder than words.

3. Address the problem your child is whining about, by saying, "Let's put that on the family-meeting agenda and work on a solution at our next meeting."

Planning Ahead to Prevent Future Problems

1. Plan for regular, scheduled special time with your child to help her feel special, important, and that she belongs.

2. During a happy time, work out a signal with your child about what you will do when you hear whining. Perhaps you will put your fingers in your ears and smile. Another possibility is to pat your hand over your heart as a reminder that "I love you."

3. Tell your child what you are going to do: "When you whine, I will leave the room. Please let me know when you are willing to talk in a respectful voice so I will enjoy listening to you." Still another possibility is to explain, "It's not that I don't hear you. I just don't want to have a discussion with you until you use your regular voice. I don't answer whiny voices."

4. Have regular family meetings.

Life Skills Children Can Learn

Children can learn that their parents love them but will not fall for their manipula-

Booster Thoughts

Mrs. Jones had a little girl, Stacy, who whined incessantly and demanded almost constant attention. Mrs. Jones scolded Stacy and pushed her away, telling her she could entertain herself.

One day, a friend of Mrs. Jones talked her into having her fortune told at a county fair. The fortune-teller implied that Mrs. Jones would not live to see the flowers bloom next spring. Even though Mrs. Jones didn't believe in fortune-tellers, she was plagued with the possibility that she might not live to watch her little girl grow up. Suddenly, she could not get enough of Stacy. She wanted to spend time with her, hold her, read to her, play with her. Stacy loved all the attention—for a while. Then she began to feel smothered. Instead of demanding constant attention, she started pushing her mother away and demanding more independence.

tive tactics. Children feel better about themselves when they learn effective skills to deal with their needs and wants.

Parenting Pointers

1. Some fascinating studies have been done with children of deaf parents. The researchers found that the children would make facial expressions that looked like they were crying, but they weren't making any sounds. The children had learned from experience that their deaf parents didn't respond to sounds but did respond to their facial expressions. Whatever works!

2. A misbehaving child is a discouraged child. A cooperative child is an encouraged child. Whining could be a sign of discouragement that will stop when the child feels enough belonging and significance.

Working Outside the Home

"I have a friend who works outside the home because she has to. I work outside the home because I want to. We are both worried that our children may be harmed emotionally because they have working mothers. Is this possible?"

Understanding Your Child, Yourself, and the Situation

With the increased number of single-parent families and with many families' need for more income, working outside the home has become an issue for both mothers and fathers. It is not what you do but how you handle it that makes a difference. Some children may experience difficulty because both parents do not work. These parents may neglect their children because they are overwhelmed, depressed, or too busy socially. They may go to the other extreme and stunt the growth of their children by being overprotective. Working parents may also be overwhelmed, depressed, too busy, or overprotective. Children can thrive whether their parents stay home or work outside the home, if the parents use the respectful parenting methods advocated in this book. Working outside the home can give children a chance to feel needed and to develop useful skills while helping at home.

Suggestions

1. Do not convey the attitude that your children are deprived. Instead, convey the attitude that "This is how it is in our family, and we can make the most of it by creating a loving atmosphere of sharing and contribution."

2. Involve children in planning how they can contribute, help create routines, and

Booster Thoughts

This story continues one mother's experience with working and guilt, begun in the "Booster Thought" in the *Guilt* entry.

"When my children became teenagers, my guilt button about working reappeared. This time, I decided I would stop working for a while so I could be home during their teen years. I announced my decision at a family meeting. I mentioned that this would mean tightening our belts a little—a small reduction in allowances, fewer pizza nights, a budget vacation.

"I was surprised at the kids' reaction: 'No way. We don't want you to stop working. We are proud of you and all you do. What a drag it would be to have a stay-at-home mom sticking her nose in our business and nagging us all the time.' (I don't know where they got that idea.)

"I didn't miss out on this great opportunity. I said, 'Well then, if you want to enjoy the opportunities of having a working mother, you will need to take more responsibilities around the house to help me out. I know you have been doing chores, but I would like help with the bigger jobs, like scrubbing floors and deep cleaning.'

divide up chores (see "Routines" in Part 1, *Chores, Age-Appropriate,* and *Chores, Getting Cooperation*).

3. Give up your guilt (see *Guilt*).

Planning Ahead to Prevent Future Problems

1. Make special time a priority. During every family meeting, take time to plan and schedule family fun times. Also list the children's events, such as soccer games, dance recitals, plays, and school open houses, and make your attendance a priority. Spend individual special time with each child on a regular basis.

2. If needed, get therapy or take self-help classes to deal with your guilt, depression, feeling of being overwhelmed, or need to buy your children's love because you are spending less time with them.

3. Have faith that your children will benefit from their circumstances when they are treated with dignity and respect and you treat yourself with dignity and respect.

"They said, 'No problem.'

"We then created the following plan. Every day, I would put two big chores (in addition to their routine chores) on the kitchen whiteboard for each of my two teenagers. They agreed to look at the board and do their chores before they went to bed at night. I wanted them done right after school but agreed to their plan for before bedtime. They even agreed that if they didn't get their chores done before bedtime, I could circle their name the next day and they would do all four chores right after school.

"This plan worked beautifully for about six months. Then they started complaining that the other person was getting the easy jobs. I had tried to rotate duties fairly, but my efforts were not appreciated. We discussed their complaints at a family meeting. They came up with a brilliant plan: Put four jobs a day on the whiteboard, and the first person to show up and start working got to choose. The first week, they were setting their alarms to get first choice. That wore off quickly as they decided they would rather sleep in and take whatever was left."

Life Skills Children Can Learn

Children can learn that they are capable and responsible. They can pitch in and help their families in any circumstances.

Parenting Pointers

1. Too many parents have the mistaken belief that being good parents means they should always be present and take care of their children's every need. This actually robs their children of the opportunity to learn self-reliance and cooperation.

2. Children will buy into your attitude. If you feel they are deprived, they will feel deprived. If you have faith in them and teach them problem-solving skills, they will have faith in themselves and use those skills.

Zits (Acne)

"My children are starting to get zits. How can I help them? I told them that at a certain age people's bodies start getting pimples. This is the time they have to be concerned about a good diet, not eating chocolate, and getting enough sleep. I didn't get to finish the lecture before they walked away."

Understanding Your Child, Yourself, and the Situation

Most parents worry that their children might be unhappy and unpopular if they have bad skin. They want to help their children by fixing the situation. One of the most popular ways parents have of "helping" their children is to give them a lecture. Kids have lecture antennas: as soon as parents start lecturing, they immediately tune them out.

Suggestions

1. Lectures can be changed to sharing valuable information by asking for permission first. Say, "I have some information on pimples. Would you like to hear it?" If your child says yes, she will be willing to listen. If she says no, there is no point in sharing.

2. Ask your child, "Do you want my help, or would you like to make an appointment with a dermatologist or someone who does facials?"

3. If your child says he would like your help, offer one suggestion at a time. Keep it simple. For instance, "Let's go to the drugstore and see if there are some special soaps you can use." Then let him pick out a bar of soap and read the instructions himself.

4. Ask your child if she has asked her friends what they do for this problem. Inquire whether she is the only one in her class with acne. This helps her see that it is normal at this age to have skin problems and that she isn't a freak.

5. Instead of telling kids what not to do, tell them what will work. For instance, mention that hot packs work better than squeezing.

6. If the problem becomes severe, take your child to a dermatologist. Medications can help correct this problem.

Planning Ahead to Prevent Future Problems

1. Let your kids know that they may not be able to stop zits completely but there are some things they can do to control the extent of the problem, such as eating a healthy diet and drinking eight glasses of water a day. Then it's their choice whether they follow your recommendations.

2. Set up a skin care routine and have facials together.

Life Skills Children Can Learn

Children can learn that they can't stop normal development from happening but they can control how severe the problem gets.

Parenting Pointers

1. If the problem is beyond your ability to help, it's okay to take your child for professional help, but only if he or she is willing.

2. Unless acne is severe, most kids will pass through this phase undamaged both physically and emotionally. Reassure the kids that acne is not forever and that there are times it's really bad and times that it gets better.

Booster Thoughts

Nancy was hysterical about a zit she discovered while getting ready for the prom. Her mother invited Nancy to stand in front of the full-length mirror. She stripped off all her clothes to display cellulite and sagging flesh and asked Nancy, "Want to trade—my sags for your zit?"

Nancy burst out laughing, covered her pimple with makeup, and went to the prom.

SELECTED BIBLIOGRAPHY

Bjorklund, Barbara R., and David F. Bjorklund. *Parents' Book of Discipline.* New York: Ballantine Books, 1990.

Clifton, Donald O., and Paula Nelson. *Soar with Your Strengths.* New York: Dell Publishing, 1992.

Dreikurs, Rudolf, with Vicki Soltz. *Children: The Challenge.* New York: Plume Books, 1990.

Ferber, Richard, M.D. *Solve Your Child's Sleep Problems.* New York: Simon and Schuster, 1986.

Gibran, Kahlil. *The Prophet.* New York: Alfred A. Knopf, 1963.

Glenn, H. Stephen. *Bridging Troubled Waters* (audiocassette). Orem, UT: Empowering People Books, Tapes, and Videos, 1989.

Glenn, H. Stephen. *Developing Capable People: Session 1* (audiocassette). Orem, UT: Empowering People Books, Tapes, and Videos, 1989.

Glenn, H. Stephen. *Developing Healthy Self-Esteem* (videocassette). Orem, UT: Empowering People Books, Tapes, and Videos, 1989.

Glenn, H. Stephen. *The Greatest Human Need* (videocassette). Orem, UT: Empowering People Books, Tapes, and Videos, 1989.

Glenn, H. Stephen, and Jane Nelsen. *Raising Self-Reliant Children in a Self-Indulgent World.* Rocklin, CA: Prima Publishing, 1989.

Kvols-Riedler, Bill, and Kathy Kvols-Riedler. *Redirecting Children's Misbehavior.* Boulder, CO: R.D.I.C. Publications, 1979.

Ilg, Frances L., and Louise Bates Ames. *The Gesell Institute's Child Behavior from Birth to Ten.* New York: Harper & Row, 1955.

Kline, Kris, and Stephen Pew. *For the Sake of the Children.* Rocklin, CA: Prima Publishing, 1992.

Lott, Lynn, and Jane Nelsen. *Teaching Parenting the Positive Discipline Way.* Orem, UT: Empowering People Books, Tapes, and Videos, 1998.

Lott, Lynn, and Riki Intner. *Chores Without Wars.* Rocklin, CA: Prima Publishing, 1998.

Nelsen, Jane. *Positive Discipline.* New York: Ballantine, 1996.

Nelsen, Jane. *Positive Discipline Workbook.* Orem, UT: Empowering People Books, Tapes, and Videos, 1998.

Nelsen, Jane. *Understanding: Eliminating Stress and Finding Serenity in Life and Relationships.* Rocklin, CA: Prima Publishing, 1997.

Nelsen, Jane; Cheryl Erwin; and Carol Delzer. *Positive Discipline for Single Parents.* Rocklin, CA: Prima Publishing, 1994.

Nelsen, Jane; Cheryl Erwin; and H. Stephen Glenn. *Positive Discipline for Blended Families.* Rocklin, CA: Prima Publishing, 1997.

Nelsen, Jane; Cheryl Erwin; and Roslyn Duffy. *Positive Discipline for Preschoolers.* Rocklin, CA: Prima Publishing, 1998.

Nelsen, Jane; Cheryl Erwin; and Roslyn Duffy. *Positive Discipline: The First Three Years.* Rocklin, CA: Prima Publishing, 1998.

Nelsen, Jane, and Lynn Lott. *Positive Discipline in the Classroom Teacher's Guide.* Orem, UT: Empowering People Books, Tapes, and Videos, 1997.

Nelsen, Jane, and Lynn Lott. *Positive Discipline for Teenagers.* Rocklin, CA: Prima Publishing, 1994.

Nelsen, Jane; Lynn Lott; and H. Stephen Glenn. *Positive Discipline in the Classroom, Revised Edition.* Rocklin, CA: Prima Publishing, 1997.

Nelsen, Jane; Riki Intner; and Lynn Lott. *Positive Discipline for Parenting in Recovery.* Rocklin, CA: Prima Publishing, 1996.

Nelsen, Jane; Roslyn Duffy; Linda Escobar; Kate Ortolano; and Debbie Owen-Sohocki. *Positive Discipline: A Teacher's A–Z Guide.* Rocklin, CA: Prima Publishing, 1996.

Redlich, Fritz, and June Bingham. *The Inside Story: Psychiatry and Everyday Life.* New York: Alfred A. Knopf, 1953.

Taylor, John F. *Helping Your Hyperactive or Attention Deficit Child.* Rocklin, CA: Prima Publishing, 1990.

Wallerstein, Judith S., and Joan Berlin Kelly. *Surviving the Breakup: How Children and Parents Cope with Divorce.* New York: Basic Books, 1980.

INDEX

A

B

G

H

I

N

O

P

Even More Bestselling

Build a Positive Foundation for Your Child's Development

Positive Discipline for Preschoolers, Revised 2nd Edition offers exactly what parents of preschoolers are looking for—loving, affirming tools for communication and discipline designed to specifically address the most important years of a child's life. Since a child's principal beliefs and feelings of self-worth are established between the ages of one and six, this insightful book addresses critical areas of development and interaction between parent and preschooler. Topics include:

- **Mastering preschooler challenges—sleeping, eating, and potty training**
- **Encouraging positive behavior**
- **Developing logical consequences that are respectful and reasonable**
- **And much, much more!**

ISBN 0-7615-1515-1 / Paperback / 368 pages
U.S. $16.95 / Can. $25.95

Positive Discipline Books

Make a Difference During Your Child's Most Important Years

As a caring parent you want to start your child out in life on the proper foundation. But where do you go for the answers to such questions as: How do I communicate with an infant who doesn't understand words? How can I effectively teach boundaries to my toddler? Should I ever spank my child?

In *Positive Discipline: The First Three Years,* you'll learn how to use kind but firm support to raise a child who is both capable and confident. Inside you'll find practical solutions and solid advice on how to:

- **Encourage independence while providing appropriate boundaries**
- **Identify your child's temperament**
- **Use non-punitive methods to instill positive behavior**
- **And more!**

ISBN 0-7615-1505-4 / Paperback / 304 pages
U.S. $16.95 / Can. $25.95

Even More Bestselling

For Teachers and Parents

Positive Discipline in the Classroom, Revised 3rd Edition addresses the popular concept of class meetings, where students and teachers discuss moral, ethical, and behavioral issues and work together to solve problems. Students learn a number of social skills through the class-meeting process, such as how to listen, take turns, hear different points of view, negotiate, and communicate. This book covers:

- **Building blocks for successful class meetings**
- **Effective problem-solving skills**
- **Classroom management skills**
- **And so much more!**

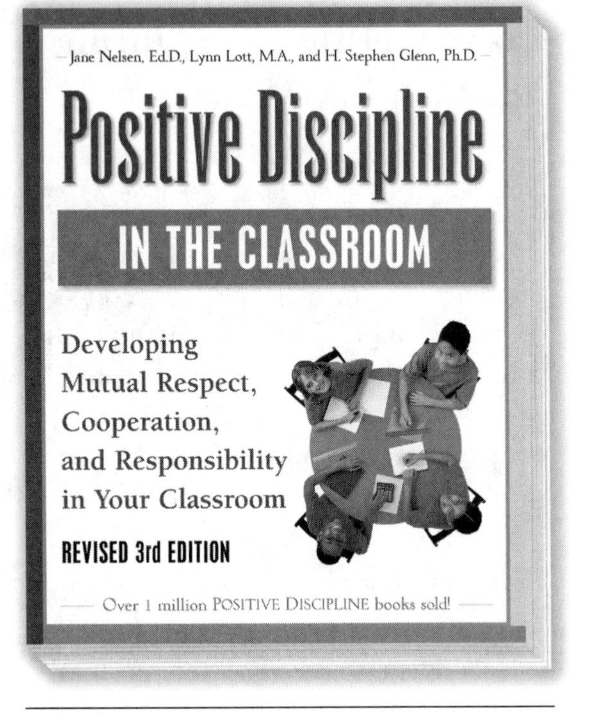

ISBN 0-7615-2421-5 / Paperback / 272 pages
U.S. $16.95 / Can. $25.95

Positive Discipline Books

Positive Discipline Makes a Difference

Finally, a win-win discipline guide to the vast array of problems and challenges teachers face today—from everyday issues such as gum chewing, name calling, and note passing to more serious concerns such as bullying, hyperactivity, gangs, and violence. This book will show you:

- **Methods for solving classroom problems**
- **Exercises for empowering students with problem-solving skills**
- **Suggestions for establishing a respectful, nurturing learning environment**
- **And more!**

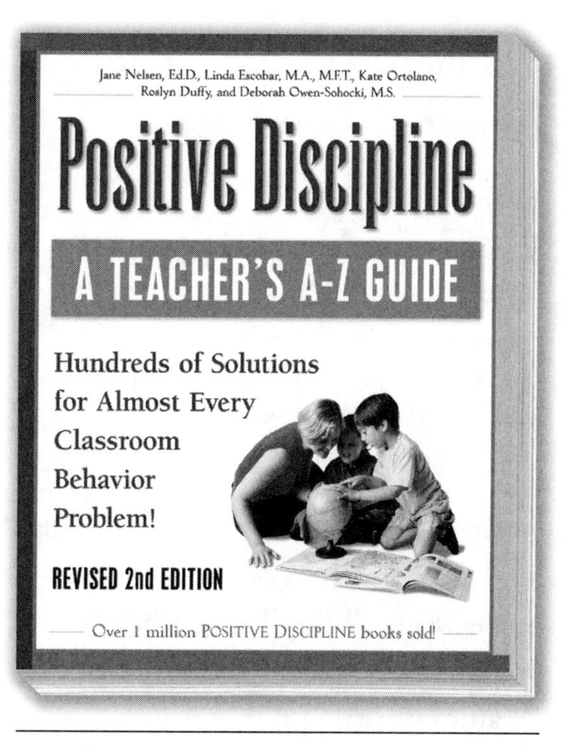

ISBN 0-7615-2245-X / Paperback / 336 pages
U.S. $16.95 / Can. $25.95

Even More Bestselling

A Blueprint for Bringing Together Two Families

Living in a stepfamily is challenging. But a household where yours and mine must become ours *can* become a harmonious family unit. *Positive Discipline for Your Stepfamily* helps you understand the process of stepfamily living and empowers you to make the right decisions. Inside, you will discover how to:

- **Resolve responsibility and role issues**
- **Build effective communication between all family members**
- **Develop respect and affection among rival children**
- **And much more!**

ISBN 0-7615-2012-0 / Paperback / 256 pages
U.S. $16.95 / Can. $25.95

Positive Discipline Books

Raise Your Teenager with Positive Discipline

Everyone knows adolescence opens up vast new interests, problems, and potential in children. *Positive Discipline for Teenagers* shows you how to turn off the cycle of guilt and blame and begin working toward greater understanding and communication with your teenage child. Inside, you'll learn:

- **How to win cooperation without threatening**
- **How to see the world through a teen's eyes**
- **How you and your teen can grow and change together**
- **And more!**

ISBN 0-7615-2181-X / Paperback / 368 pages
U.S. $16.95 / Can. $25.95

FOR MORE INFORMATION

The authors offer lectures, workshops, and seminars for parents, parent educators, therapists, psychologists, social workers, nurses, counselors, school administrators, and teachers.

Workshops include:

Teaching Parenting the Positive Discipline Way
(a two-day workshop)
Positive Discipline in the Classroom
(a two-day workshop or a one-day inservice)

Workshops, seminars, and facilitator trainings are scheduled throughout the United States each year. Dates and locations are available by contacting:

Jane Nelsen
Positive Discipline Associates
969 W. Harmony Rose Circle
So. Jordan, UT 84095
www.positivediscipline.com

Lynn Lott
Lynn Lott Enterprises
120 Commodore Drive
Richmond, CA 94804

H. Stephen Glenn
Capabilities, Inc.
11230 Gold Express Drive, Suite 310–373
Gold River, CA 95670

The authors are also available for lectures, teacher inservice training, and conference keynote presentations. For more information or to schedule Jane Nelsen call 1-800-456-7770; for Lynn Lott call 707-526-3141, ext. 3#; for H. Stephen Glenn call 1-800-222-1494.

ORDER FORM

To: Empowering People, P.O. Box 1926, Orem, UT 84059-1926
Phone: 1-800-456-7770 (credit card orders only)
Fax: 801-762-0022
Web Site: www.positivediscipline.com for discount prices

BOOKS	Price	Quantity	Amount
Positive Discipline for Your Stepfamily, by Nelsen, Erwin, & Glenn	$16.95	______	______
Positive Discipline for Single Parents, by Nelsen, Erwin, & Delzer	$16.95	______	______
Positive Discipline in the Classroom, by Nelsen, Lott, & Glenn	$16.95	______	______
Positive Discipline: A Teacher's A–Z Guide, by Nelsen, Duffy, Escobar, Ortolano, & Owen-Sohocki	$16.95	______	______
Positive Discipline for Preschoolers, by Nelsen, Erwin, & Duffy	$16.95	______	______
Positive Discipline: The First Three Years, by Nelsen, Erwin, & Duffy	$16.95	______	______
Positive Discipline, by Nelsen	$12.00	______	______
Positive Discipline A–Z, by Nelsen, Lott, & Glenn	$16.95	______	______
Positive Discipline for Teenagers, by Nelsen & Lott	$16.95	______	______
Positive Discipline for Parenting in Recovery, by Nelsen, Intner, & Lott	$12.95	______	______
Raising Self-Reliant Children in a Self-Indulgent World, by Glenn & Nelsen	$15.95	______	______
Positive Time-Out: And 50 Other Ways to Avoid Power Struggles, Nelsen	$12.95	______	______
From Here to Serenity, by Nelsen	$14.00	______	______
Positive Discipline in the Christian Home, by Nelsen, Erwin, Brock & Hughes	$16.95	______	______
Positive Discipline for Childcare Providers, by Nelsen & Erwin	$16.95	______	______
MANUALS			
Teaching Parenting the Positive Discipline Way, by Lott & Nelsen	$49.95	______	______
Positive Discipline in the Classroom, by Nelsen & Lott	$49.95	______	______
TAPES AND VIDEOS			
Positive Discipline audiotape	$10.00	______	______
Positive Discipline videotape	$49.95	______	______
Building Healthy Self-Esteem Through Positive Discipline audiotape	$10.00	______	______
	SUBTOTAL		______
	Sales tax: UT add 6.25%; CA add 7.25%		______
	Shipping & handling: $3.00 plus $0.50 each item		______
(Prices subject to change without notice.)	**TOTAL**		______

METHOD OF PAYMENT (check one):

______ Check made payable to Empowering People Books, Tapes, & Videos

______ MasterCard, Visa, Discover Card, American Express

Card # ____ Expiration _____/_____

Ship to ____

Address ____

City/State/Zip ____

Daytime phone (_______)____

ABOUT THE AUTHORS

Jane Nelsen is a popular lecturer and coauthor of the entire POSITIVE DISCIPLINE series. She has appeared on *Oprah* and *Sally Jesse Raphael* and was the featured parent expert on the "National Parent Quiz" hosted by Ben Vereen. Jane is the mother of seven children and the grandmother of sixteen.

Lynn Lott is a sought-after therapist, motivational speaker, frequent TV talk-show guest, and prolific writer. Lynn has coauthored many books, including *Chores Without Wars* and *Positive Discipline in the Classroom.* Lynn has appeared on *The Joan Rivers Show, The Today Show, The Home Show,* and *Phil Donahue.* She is the mother of two children and two stepsons, and divides her time between Pt. Richmond and Truckee, California.

H. Stephen Glenn is the creator of Developing Capable People, a course that teaches skills for living and building strong relationships in homes, schools, and organizations. He has coauthored many books, including *Raising Self-Reliant Children in a Self-Indulgent World* and *7 Strategies for Developing Capable Students.* Steve is the father of four children, stepfather of three, grandfather of ten, and has been a foster father of several young people.